Rethinking the Knowledge Controversy in Organization Studies

A Generative Uncertainty Perspective

ORGANIZATION AND MANAGEMENT SERIES

Series Editors

Arthur P. Brief

University of Utah

Kimberly D. Elsbach

University of California, Davis

Michael Frese

National University of Singapore–NUS Business School

Ashforth (Au.): *Role Transitions in Organizational Life: An Identity-Based Perspective*

Bartel/Blader/Wrzesniewski (Eds.): *Identity and the Modern Organization*

Bartunek (Au.): *Organizational and Educational Change: The Life and Role of a Change Agent Group*

Beach (Ed.): *Image Theory: Theoretical and Empirical Foundations*

Brett/Drasgow (Eds.): *The Psychology of Work: Theoretically Based Empirical Research*

Brockner (Au.): *A Contemporary Look at Organizational Justice: Multiplying Insult Times Injury*

Chhokar/Brodbeck/House (Eds.): *Culture and Leadership Across the World: The GLOBE Book of In-Depth Studies of 25 Societies*

Darley/Messick/Tyler (Eds.): *Social Influences on Ethical Behavior in Organizations*

DeCremer/van Dick/Murnighan (Eds.): *Social Psychology and Organizations*

Denison (Ed.): *Managing Organizational Change in Transition Economies*

Dutton/Ragins (Eds.): *Exploring Positive Relationships at Work: Building a Theoretical and Research Foundation*

Earley/Gibson (Aus.): *Multinational Work Teams: A New Perspective*

Elsbach (Au.): *Organizational Perception Management*

Garud/Karnoe (Eds.): *Path Dependence and Creation*

Harris (Ed.): *Handbook of Research in International Human Resource Management*

Jacoby (Au.): *Employing Bureaucracy: Managers, Unions, and the Transformation of Work in the Twentieth Century, Revised Edition*

Kossek/Lambert (Eds.): *Work and Life Integration: Organizational, Cultural, and Individual Perspectives*

Kramer/Tenbrunsel/Bazerman (Eds.): *Social Decision Making: Social Dilemmas, Social Values, and Ethical Judgments*

Lampel/Shamsie/Lant (Eds.): *The Business of Culture: Strategic Perspectives on Entertainment and Media*

Lant/Shapira (Eds.): *Organizational Cognition: Computation and Interpretation*

Lord/Brown (Aus.): *Leadership Processes and Follower Self-Identity*

Margolis/Walsh (Aus.): *People and Profits? The Search Between a Company's Social and Financial Performance*

Messick/Kramer (Eds.): *The Psychology of Leadership: Some New Approaches*

Miceli/Dworkin/Near (Aus.): *Whistle-Blowing in Organizations*

Nord/Connell (Aus.): *Rethinking the Knowledge Controversy in Organization Studies: A Generative Uncertainty Perspective*

Pearce (Au.): *Organization and Management in the Embrace of the Government*

Peterson/Mannix (Eds.): *Leading and Managing People in the Dynamic Organization*

Rafaeli/Pratt (Eds.): *Artifacts and Organizations: Beyond Mere Symbolism*

Riggio/Murphy/Pirozzolo (Eds.): *Multiple Intelligences and Leadership*

Roberts/Dutton (Eds.): *Exploring Positive Identities and Organizations: Building a Theoretical and Research Foundation*

Schneider/Smith (Eds.): *Personality and Organizations*

Smith (Ed.): *The People Make the Place: Dynamic Linkages Between Individuals and Organizations*

Thompson/Choi (Eds.): *Creativity and Innovation in Organizational Teams*

Thompson/Levine/Messick (Eds.): *Shared Cognition in Organizations: The Management of Knowledge*

Rethinking the Knowledge Controversy in Organization Studies

A Generative Uncertainty Perspective

Walter R. Nord
University of South Florida
Tampa, Florida, USA

Ann F. Connell
University of South Florida
Tampa, Florida, USA

Routledge
Taylor & Francis Group
New York London

Routledge
Taylor & Francis Group
270 Madison Avenue
New York, NY 10016

Routledge
Taylor & Francis Group
27 Church Road
Hove, East Sussex BN3 2FA

Routledge is an imprint of Taylor & Francis Group, an Informa business

Printed in the United States of America on acid-free paper
10 9 8 7 6 5 4 3 2 1

International Standard Book Number: 978-0-415-87512-7 (Hardback)

Visit the Taylor & Francis Web site at
http://www.taylorandfrancis.com

and the Psychology Press Web site at
http://www.psypress.com

Contents

Series Foreword

Walt Nord and Ann Connell have done all of us who study management and organizations a favor. They have written a book that demands readers to reflect on how they know they know. That is, they pose the big question: What counts as knowledge? Walt and Ann's pursuit of answers to the question is guided by values they openly profess—an appreciation for knowledge that focuses on context, a relish for the freedom to adopt any idea that makes sense, and combine it with other favored ideas, and striving for precision and intellectual integrity. Essentially, their book suggests how we as organizational scholars can cope with the uncertainty inherent in the construction of knowledge. Read on, think, and enjoy.

Arthur P. Brief
Seagrove Beach, Florida

Preface

This book is rooted in our experiences as late 20th- and early 21st-century North American social scientists. While we were psychology doctoral students we were socialized to be scientists. In many respects, this meant aiming to do research that was objective and value-free, as our teachers seemed to believe physical scientists had done to achieve their widely heralded success. Questions about the philosophical explanation for why these methods worked were not raised. In this context, it was easy to assume that physical scientists' findings reflected a true picture of some independent external reality.

For a long time after we graduated, the social science literature offered little reason to question that assumption. Most influential members of the disciplines that related to the study of organizations did their research as if, to use Kaplan's (1964) term, their "logic in use" was the reconstructed logic attributed to the physical sciences.

However, all this began to change in the last part of the 20th century. Some social science scholars questioned the validity of the traditional image of science as a path (let alone *the* path) to truth. With these challenges we and a number of our colleagues became aware of our field's philosophical void. This awareness produced heated debates about what social scientists were and should be doing. The debates often resulted in dysfunctional arguments. Some scholars, such as Gibson Burrell (1996), questioned whether communication among holders of the diverse perspectives was possible. Others, such as Pfeffer (1993), urged the field's leaders to exercise strong control to reestablish order.

In the introduction we show that organization studies was not the only field experiencing conflicts about the nature of knowledge. Some natural scientists, such as Fox-Keller (1985), called for their colleagues to create new ways to think and communicate in order to deal with new developments.

The present book is intended to provide students of organization studies with a new way of thinking to improve communication about issues that currently divide their field.

As we see it, a key matter that underpins the controversy in organization studies relates to the matter of how much humans can know about the world. At the risk of oversimplification, much of the controversy appears to be between scholars holding one of two opposing views. One group advances the somewhat bold view that science permits humans to gain knowledge about some reality that is highly certain. The other group, frequently called postmodernists, sometimes waves an antiscience banner and maintains that much of what members of the first group call scientific knowledge may not be knowledge at all.

Our studies of the history of the controversy revealed that a key to approaching the dispute was recognizing and understanding how each side dealt with questions that the ancient Greek skeptics raised millennia ago. On one hand, those waving an antiscience banner espoused a position that was consistent with that of many of the skeptics: Specifically, humans cannot know much, if anything, about any external reality that might exist. In contrast, those advancing the traditional science idea appeared to assume that modern science after Newton made it possible to know an independent external reality with some certainty and ignore the skeptics' questions.

We began by being agnostic about the nature and accessibility of such an independent reality. As our work continued, our interest in the history of this question in Western philosophy grew.

While initially the controversy appeared to result from the emergence of postmodernism in the 20th century, attention to the history of skepticism revealed that the issues attributed to postmodernism might be something like what Cummings (1996) called a "resurfacing of premodern wisdom."

What appeared to have happened is that often the fundamental concern of the Greek skeptics was overshadowed in Western thought by perspectives that appeared to offer certainty. Actually, waves of uncertainty about human knowledge surfaced episodically in the West, beginning at least with the Greek skeptics.

With this insight, the current controversy in organization studies seemed very different. The controversy that appears to result from the postmodernist challenge to traditional science had a long history.

Study of this history led us to a way of thinking that we call generative uncertainty. We believe this perspective can help our organization studies colleagues (and other social scientists) deal with the controversy.

REFERENCES

Burrell, G. (1996). Normal science, paradigms, metaphors, discourses and genealogies of analysis. In S. R. Clegg, C. Hardy, & W. R. Nord (Eds.), *Handbook of organization studies* (pp. 642–658). London, UK: Sage Publications.

Cummings, S. (1996). Back to the oracle: Post-modern organization theory as a resurfacing of pre-modern wisdom. *Organization, 3*(2), 249–266.

Fox-Keller, E. (1985). *Reflections on gender and science*. New Haven, CT: Yale University Press.

Kaplan, A. (1964). *The conduct of inquiry: Methodology for behavioral science*. Scranton, PA: Chandler Publishing Company.

Pfeffer, J. (1993). Barriers to the advance of organizational science: Paradigm development as a dependent variable. *Academy of Management Review, 18*(4), 599–620.

Acknowledgments

We are very grateful for the help from numerous people in making this book what it is. So many people helped us we fear we probably omitted some in these acknowledgments. If so, we sincerely apologize. That said, we turn to some people who contributed so much that we could not possibly publish the book without expressing our enormous gratitude to them.

Michele Walpole stayed with us through what must have seemed to be endless revisions. She continued to retype and edit numerous drafts, and as she did this she helped us greatly improve the manuscript. Through it all, her standards for us remained high, and the quality of her own work never varied from excellent. She constantly went beyond what we could reasonably expect to try to help us make our arguments clear and our references accurate. We gratefully acknowledge her great work. Also, at various points in this project, Connie Toole, Norma Walker, Wendy Jennings, and Ellen Padilla provided helpful typing assistance.

In addition, a number of other friends and colleagues offered extremely insightful and constructive comments on earlier drafts.

Philosopher and friend Dr. Kristin Schraeder-Frechette pointed out errors we made and scholars we overlooked. We think the final product is much better as a result, and we are deeply indebted to her.

Organization scholar and friend Dr. Samuel Culbert read a number of chapters carefully and commented extensively. As we responded to his insights, we think we improved the work significantly. Thank you, Sam.

Other friends and colleagues, Dr. Stacey Kessler and Dr. Patricia Latshaw, studied and gave us helpful feedback, especially on early drafts. Dr. Fred Stier and Dr. Jane Jorgensen helped in a similar way with later drafts.

In addition, no one could ask for a better editor than Anne Duffy. Despite the time it took us beyond the initial deadline for submission of our manuscript, Anne was always encouraging and supportive. She provided just the right amount of guidance to get us where we needed to be without even a hint of dysfunctional pressure. Likewise, the editors of the series, Dr. Art Brief and Dr. Jim Walsh, were patient and helpful. We are especially grateful to Art for helpful feedback on early drafts of some of our chapters on the history of organization studies. Also, when we needed it, our editors made it possible for us to benefit from the insights of three anonymous reviewers. We thank the reviewers for the helpful combination of encouragement and criticism they provided.

Finally, when we thought we were done, we were fortunate that two highly valued colleagues and very good friends, Bill Starbuck and Craig Pinder, guided us to some significant improvements. Bill directed us to ways to improve the front end. Craig's insightful critique led us to make some major improvements and gave us the term *generative uncertainty* that became part of the book's title.

Finally, we are very grateful to a number of people who contributed to our work in a less hands-on way. The reference staff at the University of South Florida (USF) Library was dedicated and extremely helpful. Similarly, members of the interlibrary loan department always found the resources we needed in a prompt and friendly manner. In particular, Sandra Law provided consistently outstanding service.

We are grateful to Dr. Alan Balfour, chair of the Department of Management of the College of Business at USF. Contrary to the fashion in many contemporary universities that emphasizes research activity that yields quick publication, Alan recognized that work of the sort we saw as important took time. He was patient and supported our work. Among other things, he saw to it that Connell (who was not employed by the university) had office space. Constance Toole, the department's office manager at the time, facilitated this arrangement and we gratefully acknowledge her help. Also, Dr. Ken VanVoorhis made it possible for us to purchase some Naturally Speaking® software that proved to be a big timesaver.

Other colleagues were also extremely supportive in a variety of ways. Dr. Steve Turner was always willing to answer our questions. Frequently, he pointed us to ideas that, without his wisdom, we would never have been aware. Also, Dr. John Jermier frequently lent us books and journals from his personal library and stimulated us to reflect more deeply on our ideas than we would have without his insights. Two members of the USF Department of Physics most graciously helped us with the chapter on physics. Dr. Robert Flynn provided valuable initial guidance, and Dr. Dennis Killinger was always willing to answer our questions about the practices of physicists and commented extensively on a near-final draft of the chapter. Also, Elizabeth Victor and Emre Kestin helped us to improve Chapter 9, "Letting Go of Misguided Attempts to Emulate Physics."

Also, the University of South Florida provided sabbatical time for Nord to complete this work.

Finally, thanks to Tara Nieuwesteeg, the project editor of this book, for her gracious and confident help.

Introduction

Recently, the field of organization studies has been plagued by intense, disruptive controversy about what counts as knowledge. We call this the knowledge controversy. This controversy distracted organization scholars from giving appropriate attention to the research of many of their colleagues. We believe the situation requires rethinking some central tenets of our field.

The following quotation from Evelyn Fox-Keller (1985) reveals the presence of similar concerns in other fields:

> Discourse about science continues for the most part on two non-communicating levels: one an increasingly radical critique that fails to account for the effectiveness of science, and the other a justification that draws confidence from that effectiveness to maintain a traditional, and essentially unchanged, philosophy of science. What is needed is a way of *thinking* and *talking* about science that can make sense of these two very different perspectives—that can credit the realities they each reflect and yet account for their differences in perception. (p. 6)

The typical reader of a book on organization studies may be surprised to learn that the above observations by Fox-Keller were not about the current turmoil in organization studies; rather, she wrote from the standpoint of her own field, mathematical biophysics. The intellectual strife so rampant in organization studies also plagues numerous other fields of inquiry; in fact, as Fox-Keller indicated, it occurs throughout science and the philosophy of science.

In this book, we attempt to respond to her call for a way of thinking and talking about knowledge that makes sense of the two perspectives she described, applying our approach specifically to organization studies.

We offer generative uncertainty as the primary vehicle for this rethinking. Although we owe this specific term to Craig Pinder, we arrived at the concept through two interrelated phases of inquiry. First, some years ago we (Connell & Nord, 1996) advanced an agnostic perspective for study of organizations. We advocated abandoning dogmatic assertions about the nature of reality and about the existence of universal rules of reason. Since then, we also have seen the merits of remaining agnostic about the existence and nature of universal, correct human values, and correct methodology for inquiry. Our agnosticism is an admission of uncertainty. We prefer admitting uncertainty to making unwarranted assumptions.

In our view, at the root of the knowledge controversy is conflict about the possibility of knowledge that is certain. Concern about this possibility was present for millennia throughout Western intellectual history. It did not, as many participants in the recent knowledge controversy appear to believe, originate with the so-called postmodernism of the late 1900s. In fact, questioning the possibility of knowledge that is certain goes back to before the time of Socrates.

The second phase of our work that led us to generative uncertainty emerged as we studied the history of skepticism in Western thought. A major insight was the recognition that in developing modern science, some leading members of the Royal Society of London did not reject skepticism. They relied on "mitigated" skepticism. They apparently believed that skepticism could not be refuted, but that that condition did not need to inhibit scientific inquiry. We propose that to deal with the knowledge controversy, organization scholars might follow a similar path, what we call generative uncertainty. This means accepting uncertainty about some fundamental questions that humans may not be capable of answering for sure, while simultaneously using regularities of observed phenomena (such as the Sun's motion) to build useful patterns.

Recognizing that some leading members of the Royal Society did not reject skepticism is important for rethinking the knowledge controversy. It is commonly held that modern science grew from the work of Isaac Newton and other early members of the Royal Society of London. Disagreements about the ability of this science to provide knowledge that is certain figured prominently in the organization studies controversy. We fear that misunderstanding of the positions some of these early scientists held about the certainty issue fueled and misguided the controversy.[1] Generative uncertainty helps set things on a better course by drawing attention to the fact that many early modern scientists, reflecting the influence of ancient Greek skepticism as it came to them through English theologians, such as Wilkins and Glanvill, acknowledged a high degree of *un*certainty.

Some of these theologians were early members of the Royal Society. Their theology treated uncertainty in ways that strongly influenced the philosophy of Newton, Boyle, and other prominent members of the society (Van Leeuwen, 1963). We discuss their ideas in "In the Shadow of Certainty" (Chapter 3). For now, we quote Van Leeuwen (1963) concerning Newton's views on certainty:

> Newton's views on the certainty of scientific knowledge … seem … to be similar to those of Wilkins, Glanvill, and Boyle. Although he does

> not develop extensively the skeptical arguments they do, he nonetheless agrees with them that the real structure of nature is unknown and thus far beyond the reach of science. What the scientist regards as true may in fact turn out to be false since his conclusions are based merely on human principles. (p. 120)

At the same time as these early scientists professed a sort of skepticism, they accepted "probable truths about appearances" (Popkin, 1979, p. 29) as knowledge.

Some (e.g., Hume, 1748/1961) labeled this view that paired nonrefutable skepticism with the possibility of what we now call scientific knowledge as "mitigated" or "constructive" skepticism. Our "generative uncertainty" shares much with this approach.

For us, practicing generative uncertainty calls for identifying our assumptions as assumptions (not certainties) and attempting to avoid unnecessary assumptions. It entails acknowledging uncertainty about the nature of reality, about universal rules for thinking and for scientific methodology, and about universal human values. It also means that despite these limitations we believe that humans can develop useful patterns about phenomena based on regularities of appearances. This perspective is consistent with valuing what Buddhists refer to as beginner's mind. It is also compatible with the following words of the great early scientist Sir Francis Bacon. In expressing his concern about how established philosophies created idols that interfere with human inquiry, Bacon (1620/1960) wrote:

> So much concerning the several classes of Idols and their equipage; all of which must be renounced and put away with a fixed and solemn determination, and the understanding thoroughly freed and cleansed; the entrance into the kingdom of man, founded on the sciences, being not much other than the entrance into the kingdom of heaven, where into none may enter except as a little child. (p. 66)

To better understand what we mean by generative uncertainty, please consider its components separately. The uncertainty component reflects our belief that we do not currently have answers to a number of fundamental questions. The generative component recognizes that this uncertainty does not doom us to doing without useful information. It acknowledges that we have numerous useful patterns (i.e., configurations) about phenomena or appearances. Furthermore, as we see it, uncertainty provides more fertile ground for developing insights and for learning from others (two important features of inquiry) than does a dogmatic approach.

Please note that we do not offer generative uncertainty as a compromise between two polar positions in the controversy. Rather, we offer it as the position that makes sense to us and one we believe can be valuable in thinking about the controversy.

One contribution generative uncertainty makes to thinking about the knowledge controversy is the bright light it shines on the sometimes unrecognized commonality between so-called postmodernism and modern science. Although some participants in the knowledge controversy, like Kruger (2002), polarize the two, modern science and postmodernism both incorporate a skeptical approach.

We see acceptance of uncertainty in both Newton's reluctance to hypothesize about the cause of gravity and postmodernist Lyotard's (1984) distain for meta-narratives. In these ways, intellectual leaders of both perspectives advised leaving some questions unanswered rather than filling the gaps with unnecessary assumptions.

The absence of certainty leaves room for practicing reflexivity and our conversational approach as opposed to adversarial interchange among scholars.

Because we value reflexivity, we want to tell you some things about ourselves. First, both of us have an iconoclastic bent. We have histories of questioning dogma, authority, and theory. In addition, we both appreciate scholarship that focuses on context. Undoubtedly, these tendencies contributed to our attraction to and comfort with the generative uncertainty we advance in this book.

Second, we value creativity and eclectic, integrative scholarship; we relish freedom to adopt any idea that makes sense to us and combine it with other ideas we favor, without regard for conventional theoretical boundaries. Consequently, developing frameworks and language that foster sharing ideas among different theories, while it would repel some scholars, appeals to us.

Third, we also value both precision and intellectual integrity. Accordingly, acknowledging our own areas of uncertainty is consistent with our values.

In addition to sharing these introductory points about ourselves, we try to practice reflexivity throughout the book. To encourage our own reflexivity and promote conversation, we often use the first and second person in our writing. We believe that the traditional third person style of academic writing implicitly lays claim to an impartial omniscience that interferes with both reflexivity and conversation. As physicist P. W. Bridgman (1959) wrote:

> Attention to … the first person emphasizes the insight that we never get away from ourselves. Not only do I see that I cannot get away from myself, but I see that you cannot get away from yourself. The problem of how to deal with the insight that we never get away from ourselves is perhaps the most important problem before us. (pp. 5–6)

In this book we present a perspective for rethinking and talking within organization studies that promotes reflexivity, holding assumptions lightly, and conversational interchange while at the same time encouraging research and related pattern-making activities.

OVERVIEW OF BOOK

The chapters in Section 1 describe generative uncertainty and some of the ramifications it has for thinking about knowledge in organization studies and related social sciences. In Chapter 1, "Generative Uncertainty," we define the term and call attention to questions that figured prominently in the knowledge controversy for which we profess to not having the answers. These include matters of ontology, universal rules of rationality, universal values, and universal best method of inquiry.

Having summarized the key features of the generative uncertainty perspective, in the next chapter we consider some of the ramifications it has for rethinking some common concepts in the organization studies literature: perception, representation, the self, other minds, agency (free will), communication, and knowledge.

Section 2 explores historical factors pertinent to the organization studies knowledge controversy. This material illustrates a key component of our message—the importance of historical context.

Chapter 3, "In the Shadow of Certainty," demonstrates the long history of uncertainty in Western thought. Many contemporary organization studies scholars mistakenly attribute the origin of recent concerns about uncertainty to so-called postmodernism. On the other hand, study of the history of Western philosophy shows that Western philosophers discussed the matter on and off for well over two millennia before postmodernism. In this chapter we discuss how the issue of uncertainty lurked in the shadows of Western thought as clerics, scholars, and scientists focused their attention on other problems. Today, many social scientists, apparently unaware of skepticism's role in the history of science, seem to expect unwarranted certainty from scientific inquiry.

The chapter attempts to show how episodically the issue of uncertainty was hidden in the shadows. It begins by discussing uncertainty in ancient Greek thought and concludes by considering uncertainty's place in contemporary philosophy. As we will see, ideas from some leading modern philosophers played a major role in the organization studies knowledge controversy.

In Chapter 4, "Neo-Institutional View of Scientism," we show that both social scientists and the general public in North America came to assume that so-called scientific methods provided a privileged path to truth. In this chapter we refer to this view of science as scientism and try to understand how scientism became so central in the social science disciplines that spawned organization studies. We use principles from neo-institutional organizational theory to help us understand scientism's ascendancy. We argue that as social scientists attempted to gain legitimacy, they were rewarded for appearing to use the methods and approaches of the natural sciences, especially physics. As social scientists imitated their image of the 19th-century physicist, they adopted a set of practices without articulating a solid rational/philosophical justification for the approach.

Chapter 5, "Origins of the Knowledge Controversy in the History of Organization Studies," examines the evolution of organization studies from other social sciences. We suggest that organization studies imported scientism from these fields. Scientism became part of its identity. For some time, scientism provided organization scholars with at least a modest operating consensus. However, it did not last.

In Chapter 6, "Key Themes in the Debate About Orthodox Science in the Study of Organizations," we consider how in the late 20th century a series of social and intellectual changes unraveled the prior modest operating consensus and produced the tensions present in the knowledge controversy.

In Chapter 7, "Organization Scholars' Responses to the Breakdown of Orthodoxy," we consider these tensions. Discussions of these tensions led many organization scholars to see their field in radically new ways.

We hope that after Section 2, you will be aware of

1. The record of uncertainty in Western intellectual history
2. The inability of scholars and scientists to refute the uncertainties of ancient Greek skepticism
3. The way the quest for certainty and the political value of claiming certainty helped move unresolved uncertainties into the shadows and keep them there for long periods of time
4. How institutional processes made scientism central in organization studies
5. How keeping uncertainties in the shadow provided fertile soil for scientism and ultimately for the knowledge controversy

If Sections 1 and 2 accomplished their objectives, you might be prepared to agree that some established components of organization studies need to be rethought and others perhaps abandoned.

In Section 3, which consists of only one chapter, "Alternative Approaches for the Knowledge Controversy" (Chapter 8), we consider some of the rethinking organization scholars have already done.

Two things are noteworthy when the alternatives are considered together. First, almost all of them have some very attractive aspects. Second, many of them include some acceptance of uncertainty.

Often, serious rethinking involves adding new ideas and letting go of some old ones. In the remainder of the book, we do both of these. We begin these tasks in Section 4, "Letting Go."

Chapter 9, "Letting Go of Misguided Attempts to Emulate Physics," responds to perhaps the most prominent features of institutionalized scientism—the efforts of American social scientists to try to imitate 18th-century physics. In this chapter we examine two questions related to these attempts: (1) Do physicists tend to espouse commonsense realism? (2) What do physicists actually do?

Our challenges are congruent with the concerns of industrial and organizational (I/O) psychologist John Campbell's (1976) questioning the value of physics as a model for I/O psychology. He suggested that part of the reason psychologists worship at the altar of physics is that, as outsiders, they do not understand how physics operates. In this chapter, we take Campbell's concern seriously and study how physicists do their work.

Chapter 10, "Letting Go of Agonism," considers the history of the argumentative style that seems to dominate modern academic discourse in the West. Once again, we begin with the ancient Greeks. We then summarize concerns of some contemporary scholars about the dysfunctions of this mode of communication and consider some specific examples of how agonism furthered the knowledge controversy.

We urge letting go of the agonistic style. Our major suggestions in this chapter build directly on both the case we made for letting go of agonism and our view of inquiry as a social process.

In sum, Section 4 demonstrates the value of abandoning some elements that have long been part of what social scientists have thought and believed. Letting go of agonism and misguided attempts to emulate physics moves us closer to a beginner's mind.

At this point, having analyzed some of the dysfunctional practices that we believe contributed to the knowledge controversy in organization studies, we are ready to suggest improvements to the ideas we began with in Section 1 for the field to move beyond the controversy. Section 5 consists of one chapter, Chapter 12, "Generative Uncertainty for the Practice of Organization Studies."

We develop ideas from the generative uncertainty perspective to suggest how we in organization studies can better communicate with each other. These improvements are related to the philosophical ideas we discussed earlier. The chapter centers on ways to improve communication among organization scholars. It proceeds from the idea of accepting uncertainty in human communication. We review suggestions by organization scholars and others for improving communication and make our own recommendations derived from generative uncertainty.

Of special note is our assertion that uncertainties about reception of messages are common in both everyday experience and scientific communication. We suggest that people typically rely on supposition of accurate reception (SOAR) to proceed despite these uncertainties.

We conclude with a short chapter, "Generative Uncertainty for the Practice of Organization Studies." This chapter integrates a number of suggestions presented earlier. These include increased attention to context and history, recognition of the importance of preferred patterns in the inquiry process, and merits of accepting generative uncertainty.

ENDNOTE

1. Given the impact of misunderstanding of early scientists' positions on certainty in the organization studies controversy, it is useful to explore the

views of Newton and other early members of the Royal Society about the matter of certainty. As we note in this introduction and in more detail in Chapter 3, many members of the society accepted a mitigated skepticism.

However, it is difficult to know for sure Newton's position on the matter for several reasons. On one hand, Newton explicitly believed that mathematical certainty was possible and strongly argued for its place in natural philosophy (a term that in his day represented what we today call science). However, the idea of mathematical certainty provides less certainty than it at first appears. The ambiguity is revealed by the question Guicciardini (2009) asked: "Which among the available alternative mathematical methods were exact and legitimate and how could they be injected successfully into experimental discourse?" (p. 29). A second source of difficulty in knowing Newton's position is that, as Van Leeuwen (1963) and Janiak (2008) observed, Newton did not systematically explicate his philosophical position as did other greats of his era, such as Descartes. Third, some of his work appeared to contradict a belief in certainty. As Van Leeuwen (1963), for instance, noted when writing about light and gravity, Newton disclaimed knowledge of their real natures. Finally, Newton's thinking about the possibilities of certainty from science changed during his lifetime. After extensive study of Newton's published and unpublished writings, Shapiro (2004) concluded: "After a long and productive career, Newton, I am sure, recognized that the program that he espoused in his youth of establishing a more certain science founded on mathematics was unrealistic and that experiment or rather phenomena, must serve as both the foundation of any new science and a fundamental limiting factor" (p. 216). Thus, the results of scholarly studies of Newton's thoughts about certainty reveal a complex picture that, especially in the context of the mitigated skepticism of his colleagues, makes attributing any simple epistemological certainty to him suspect.

REFERENCES

Bacon, F. (1960). *The new organon and related writings* (F.H. Anderson, Ed.). Indianapolis, IN: Bobbs–Merrill. (Original work published in 1620)

Bridgman, P. W. (1959). *The way things are*. Cambridge, MA: Harvard University Press.

Campbell, J. P. (1976). Motivation theory in industrial and organizational psychology. In M. D. Dunnette (Ed.), *Handbook of industrial and organizational psychology* (pp. 63–130). Chicago, IL: Rand McNally.

Connell, A. F., & Nord, W. R. (1996). The bloodless coup: The infiltration of organization science by uncertainty and values. *Journal of Applied Behavioral Science, 32*(4), 407–427.

Fox-Keller, E. F. (1985). *Reflections on gender and science*. New Haven, CT: Yale University Press.

Guicciardini, N. (2009). *Isaac Newton on mathematical certainty and method*. Cambridge, MA: MIT Press.

Hume, D. (1961). An equiry concerning human understanding. In *The empiricists* (pp. 307–430). Garden City, NY: Dolphin Books. (Original work published in 1748)

Janiak, A. (2008). *Newton as philosopher*. Cambridge, UK: Cambridge University Press.

Kruger, D. J. (2002). The deconstruction of constructivism. *American Psychologist, 57*, 456–457.

Lyotard, J. F. (1984). *The postmodern condition: A report on knowledge* (G. Bennington & B. Massumi, Trans.). Minneapolis, MN: University of Minnesota Press. (Original work published 1979)

Popkin, R. H. (1979). *The history of scepticism from Erasmus to Spinoza*. Berkeley, CA: University of California Press.

Shapiro, A. E. (2004). Newton's "experimental philosophy." *Early Science and Medicine*, *9*(3), 185–217.

Van Leeuwen, H. G. (1963). *The problem of uncertainty in English thought 1630–1690*. The Hague, The Netherlands: Martins Nijhoff.

SECTION

1

Rethinking Organization Studies

CHAPTER

1

Generative Uncertainty

All our knowledge is but the knowledge of schoolchildren. Possibly we shall know a little more than we do now. But the real nature of things, that we shall never know, never.

—Albert Einstein (Calaprice, 2000)

According to Plato (1961/c. 399 B.C.E.), after the oracle at Delphi declared Socrates the wisest man in the world, Socrates went about interviewing men with reputations for wisdom expecting to prove the oracle wrong. However, all the interviews ended in a similar fashion, with Socrates concluding, "Well, I am certainly wiser than this man. It is only too likely that neither of us has any knowledge to boast of, but he thinks that he knows something which he does not know, whereas I am quite conscious of my ignorance" (pp. 7–8). We agree with Socrates about the wisdom of acknowledging ignorance.

In the introduction to this book, we asserted that organization studies was rife with unnecessary and often dysfunctional conflict about knowledge. We promised that in the remainder of the book we would present a perspective, generative uncertainty to help alleviate this conflict.

This chapter begins to deliver on that promise by sharing what we mean by generative uncertainty and why we consider it a useful view. In later chapters we apply the perspective to organization studies.

Our generative uncertainty perspective follows Socrates' principle of recognizing ignorance. To state the principle another way, we try to acknowledge our assumptions *as* assumptions and to question them freely. (Please note: Unless we indicate otherwise, *we* or *us* refers to the authors, Nord and Connell. Likewise, *you* indicates the reader.)

Since this book has implications for the controversy between traditional scientific organization studies and postmodernist organization studies, we want to point out that many, perhaps most, members of both groups, traditional scientists and self-proclaimed postmodernists, are likely to agree with the principle of acknowledging and questioning assumptions. We believe, and will demonstrate as we go along, that much unnecessary controversy between the two groups could be avoided if they both gave more priority to that principle.

DEFINITION OF GENERATIVE UNCERTAINTY

There are two components to generative uncertainty. The uncertainty component emphasizes the value of admitting ignorance when we do not know something. This admission benefits inquiry by making room for creative insight and discovery of new patterns.

The generative component emphasizes that despite ignorance about many matters, people can develop useful patterns and have done so.

WHAT WE DON'T KNOW

There are many things we do not know. But, for present purposes, we will consider only those most relevant to the organization studies knowledge controversy. We personally are agnostic about four main questions related to knowledge in organization studies: (1) What is the fundamental nature of reality? (2) Are there universally correct principles for thinking (with a small *t*)? (3) Are there universal values? (4) Is there one correct method for inquiry? Our uncertainty on these questions leads to a nontraditional approach to a number of other matters, such as representation and communication, which we discuss in the next chapter. Now let us go to our first unanswered question: What is the nature of reality?

Uncertainty About the Nature of Reality

The traditional view of reality, the one that many Westerners find comfortable, is commonsense realism, the idea that there is an external, physical reality, independent of humans, that human perceptions capture this reality as it is. This physical reality may or may not be supplemented by a mental or spiritual component.

This prevalent view presents philosophical difficulties. Both Eastern and Western philosophers for over two millennia posed questions about the existence of an objective, knowable external reality, without arriving at definitive answers. In the East, fourth-century B.C. philosopher Chuang Tzu (1968) wondered how he could know whether he was a man who previously dreamed he was a butterfly, or a butterfly now dreaming he was a man. Western scholars wrestled with the same fundamental question in different ways. For instance, ancient Greeks asked skeptical questions. Later, Descartes asked how he could know his perceptual experiences had not been programmed by an evil genie. Some 20th-century thinkers suggested that a person could exist as a brain in a vat, manipulated by research scientists, and never know it. (Brueckner, 2004.)

Principal Positions on the Nature of Reality

The most prevalent ontological positions for organization studies are idealism, realism, materialism or physicalism, dualism, and social constructionism. (These positions are not mutually exclusive.) Each of these positions has been held by important individual scholars, as well as entire traditions. We will not go into the philosophical arguments surrounding these various positions here, except to say that there are pros and cons for each and none has been either proven or disproven to our satisfaction. We will give simple definitions of these five points of view:

Idealism. By this we mean the belief that ultimate reality is mental or spiritual. A number of major philosophers, including Plato, Berkeley, and Hegel, held idealist positions. Idealist models occur in religious and spiritual, as well as philosophical, traditions. The Hindu idea that everything is part of Vishnu's dream exemplifies idealism in a spiritual tradition, as does the Buddhist belief that perceptions are *maya*, illusion. In the West, *Christian Science* and "A Course in Miracles," a Christian-based course of study, also assert that the perceptual world is an illusion.

Realism. We define realism as belief that there is an external reality that exists independently of humans. Many philosophers and scientists have held some version of this belief.

Materialism or physicalism. The belief that physical matter is the only reality is also well known and common in the West. Realism may overlap with materialism.

Dualism. Dualists believe that reality is made up of two components, the material and the spiritual or mental. Like materialism, dualism is compatible with realism. People sometimes talk as if dualism originated with Descartes, who did bring his unique perspective to the position. However, Descartes was born into a Christian culture that had embraced dualism for centuries before his arrival. Dualism still permeates thinking and language in the West.

Social constructionism. Social constructionism gained prominence in modern social science largely through the work of Berger and Luckmann (1966). These writers pointed out many ways in which human experience is constructed by culture rather than received directly through individual perception. Social constructionists may believe in a material external world (as Berger and Luckmann appear to have done), but they do not quite fit our definition of realists because of their doubts about people's ability to know that world directly.

Our Uncertainty Perspective on the Nature of Reality

Our own position is that (1) we do not now have enough information for an informed decision about the nature of reality, (2) and we can accomplish many important purposes without making a decision about the nature of reality. We remain agnostic on this issue.

We prefer to label assessments about reality as assumptions rather than treat them as certainties. We also prefer to avoid making assumptions when doing so is not essential in pursuing a line of inquiry, such as the present book. Of course, try as we did to avoid them, undoubtedly we made assumptions we are not aware of. On the other hand, we do not claim it will never be possible to find answers about the nature of reality. Nor are we saying that *no one* knows those answers presently. Both of those statements would be inconsistent with our preferred approach because they involve unnecessary assumptions. It's simpler to merely claim "we don't know."

Now that we have professed uncertainty about the nature of reality, you may wonder what we have left. For one thing, we still have our streams of experience, our "personal movies" made up of shifting patterns, some which seem to originate outside the body and to be mediated through the senses and others of which seem to originate within the body.

We experience ourselves as taking actions, observing consequences of those actions, modifying our behavior on the basis of those consequences, and sometimes seeming to behave in accord with our expressed values and sometimes not. However, to be clear, we do not profess solipsism, that is, the belief that our experience comprises the ultimate reality. We do not consider that position of much interest, although in line with generative uncertainty, we do not claim it is impossible.

Patterns of experience occur whether we believe in external reality, in a largely socially constructed world, or in a dualist world. Consequently, uncertainty about the nature of reality need not change moment-to-moment patterns of experience in any major way.

In this context, even though the English language seems to assume an independent, knowable external reality and we profess uncertainty about such a reality, with two slight changes we use ordinary English in this book. However, as we do so, we are assessing that we are talking about some external reality. Rather, we are talking about our own experienced patterns, including you, our reader, as one of those patterns, without asserting that the patterns are representations of internal or external reality. We take these patterns of experience as our starting point.

The only language changes we introduce are

1. Trying to avoid what we call "quicksand" terms, terms that are used in different ways by different factions, thereby decreasing effective communication and often increasing dysfunctional

controversy. Examples are *positivism, truth, incommensurability,* and *objectivity.* We will discuss such terms at more length later.
2. Avoiding terms that entail what we consider unwarranted assumptions. An example is *truth,* which traditionally implies correspondence between experiences and reality.

While uncertainty about the nature of reality does not make a great difference in our choice of words, it does affect our experiences as scholars in significant ways.

Advantages of Accepting Uncertainty About the Nature of Reality

Uncertainty about the nature of reality offers organization studies scholars the following advantages:

1. Since to our knowledge no assumption about the nature of reality has so far proven to be the one correct account, uncertainty offers appropriate intellectual openness. Assumptions tend to become institutionalized and increasingly difficult to question. Uncertainty reduces the likelihood of this pitfall.
2. Uncertainty offers parsimony of assumptions. Why burden inquiry with unnecessary premises?
3. Uncertainty is conducive to open-minded listening and therefore to learning from people who hold a variety of theoretical positions.
4. Uncertainty provides a blank slate, what Buddhists call beginner's mind, making room for creativity and discovery.
5. Firmly held convictions often acquire a shadow side, a set of suppressed observations and ideas that, if entertained, would challenge the convictions. For example, a firmly held belief in empiricism as the path to truth may lead one to overlook the role of interests and values in research, while a firmly held belief that reality is socially constructed may suppress attention to thought processes of individuals. Generative uncertainty leaves room for a wide variety of observations and concepts.

Common Objections to Uncertainty About the Nature of Reality

1. Many people take certainty about the nature of reality for granted as a simple matter of commonsense. Being uncertain about this matter seems absurd to them.
2. Many Westerners believe a sense of certainty is necessary for comfort, motivation to act, morality, or perhaps all three. Even many philosophers hold this assumption, as demonstrated in their references to the *problem of skepticism,* treating the lack of a solid ontological foundation as an obstacle that needs overcoming.

Let us look at the above objections.

Commonsense Objection The commonsense objection is exemplified in Samuel Johnson's oft-cited "refutation" of Bishop Berkeley's (1710/1961) idealism. Johnson's biographer and friend James Boswell (1792), wrote:

> After we came out of the church, we stood talking for some time together of Bishop Berkeley's ingenious sophistry to prove the non-existence of matter, and that every thing in the universe is merely ideal. I observed, that though we are satisfied his doctrine is not true, it is impossible to refute it. I never shall forget the alacrity with which Johnson answered, striking his foot with mighty force against a large stone, till he rebounded from it, "I refute it *thus.*" (p. 397)

However, Johnson's experience of solidity in the stone, and perhaps of pain in the foot, does not necessarily contradict Berkeley's view. For Berkeley, such experiences were mental events, in the same category as visual sensations. All Johnson did in kicking the stone was add another sensation to the visual one. He did not demonstrate that any of his perceptions corresponded to a material reality.

A good friend of ours makes another commonsense argument: He says he knows the external world is real because people will rush to get out of the path of a moving train. This argument does not hold up, either. Even in a dream, people will get off the tracks of trains coming toward them. Whether reality is material or not, people have *experiences* of behavior followed by consequences; they form expectations about possible unpleasant consequences and try to avoid them.

However, we are not making a case for idealism—we remain uncertain. We merely point out that the commonsense arguments against uncertainty do not hold up.

Next is the assumption that certainty is necessary for comfort, action, or morality. We see this as potentially a self-fulfilling prophecy. Even though many people accomplish their purposes in the absence of certainty, if someone thinks he or she needs certainty to achieve comfort, action, or morality, then the absence of certainty may interfere with accomplishment of one's purposes. Let us look at the three purposes individually.

Comfort We strongly agree that the experience of uncertainty about external reality is highly uncomfortable for people who are used to certainty. Descartes (1641/1977), after his famous experience of intentionally entertaining skepticism, wrote:

> Yesterday's meditation has filled my mind with so many doubts that it is no longer in my power to forget them. Nor do I yet see how I will be able to resolve them; I feel as though I were suddenly thrown into deep water, being so disconcerted that I can neither plant my feet on the bottom, nor swim on the surface. (p. 23)

If you are not used to treating external reality as problematic, you are probably already uncomfortable with our uncertainty stance. However, we ask you to stay with us. After a while, one can adapt to uncertainty and feel at ease with it. We encourage you to experiment with uncertainty by taking a brief plunge into that whirlpool now. Ask yourself how you can be sure that you are awake this minute rather than asleep and dreaming. How you can be sure that your brain is not currently sitting in a jar in a research laboratory with your perceptions determined by electrical signals. How you know that people who believe that their perceptions have been programmed by extraterrestrials are wrong and, if they are right, whether your own perceptions may not also originate on another planet.

Dealing with uncomfortable uncertainties is like dealing with the eventuality of death. In the long run, acceptance may provide a better resolution than denial. Acceptance has more intellectual integrity and uses less energy. Consequently, we do not consider avoidance of discomfort a good reason to claim certainty.

Motivation to Act Philosopher David Hume (1748/1989) expressed the belief that certainty was necessary for action. After concluding that he was unable to prove the existence of external reality, he asserted that in order to act people need to believe in it anyway. He wrote:

> [The Pyrrhonian skeptic] must acknowledge, if he will acknowledge anything, that all human life must perish were his principles universally and steadily to prevail. All discourse, all action would immediately cease, and men remain in a total lethargy till the necessities of nature, unsatisfied, put an end to their miserable existence. (p. 168)

History has not supported Hume's supposition. Skeptics throughout history have fed themselves, held jobs, and even written books. We do, however, accept the possibility of self-fulfilling prophecy. Belief in external reality may be necessary for action if one thinks it is.

Morality Next is the claim that belief in external reality is necessary for ethical and moral values. Here, too, the evidence shows otherwise. Buddhism, which teaches the illusory nature of external reality, advocates strict moral principles. The Dalai Lama, a famous Buddhist leader, works actively for peace and writes books preaching compassion and love. Bishop Berkeley's work, *Christian Science,* and "A Course in Miracles" both demonstrate that Christian values can coexist with lack of belief in external physical reality.

In conclusion, even though insistence on certainty is pervasive in our culture, we do not see any intrinsic connection between feeling certain about the nature of reality and the ability to be comfortable, to act, or to behave ethically. Having expressed our uncertainty about the nature of reality, we turn to our second question: Are there universal rules for thinking? This question has been central in the modernist versus postmodernist debate.

Uncertainty About Universal Rules for Thinking

Taking a postmodernist position *against* universal rules of rationality, Gergen and Thatchenkery (1996) stated, "There is little reason to believe that there is a specifically rational process (or logos) lurking beneath what we take to be rational argument; to argue rationally is to 'play by the rules' favored within a particular cultural tradition" (pp. 362–363). Gergen and Thatchenkery advocated substitution of the term *communal rationality* for *rationality.*

We are agnostic about the existence of universal rules for thinking. Disputes about the law of the distributed middle and about the validity of abduction, even among members of the same (Western) culture, provide grounds for questioning the universality of rules for thinking. So too does the phenomenon of different scholars reaching different conclusions from the same evidence. Mitroff and Mason's (1974) conclusion from their investigation of scientists studying moon rocks supports this position. They observed that since all scientific questions have an important element of openness, scientists vary in their interpretations of phenomena.

On the other hand, we are not ready to assume, with Gergen and Thatchenkery, that there is little reason to believe in a "rational process" beneath so-called rational argument. Our understanding that Asian and Western scientists and engineers are often able to work smoothly together leads us to think perhaps human beings may share some cross-cultural thinking processes.

Although we remain agnostic about universal rules for thinking, and we share Gergen and Thatchekery's concerns about the entailments of the term *rationality,* that is, rationality implies universality, we are not ready to abandon the concept of individual thinking. The terms *thought* and *thinking* can express useful patterns without implying universality. Here are two examples of the usefulness of the concept of individual thought:

1. While using a mulcher, Connell found a wing nut in the grass. It resembled nuts she had previously noticed on the mulcher. Connell thought the nut had probably worked itself off a bolt that must then have fallen into the machine. Concerned that the bolt could damage the blades, she unplugged the mulcher and searched until she found a bolt inside of it. We want to call the mental process she went through *thinking,* rather than using Gergen and Thatchenkery's term, *communal rationality.* Although that term does make the reasonable point that culture plays a role in

individual thinking, it seems to assert that *all* thinking is communal, an assumption we do not wish to make.

2. We want to be able to discuss one person's (e.g., Galileo's) disagreement with the thinking of his or her culture. For this purpose also, we find the concept of individual thinking useful.

One final point: There are many disputes about conventions. However, once people agree to a set of conventions, premises often lead to the same conclusions for everyone. We do not want to minimize the usefulness of conventions, merely on the grounds that they differ among cultures. Therefore, we consider cultural norms about thinking potentially useful.

To summarize our position, we question the assumption that there are universal principles of rational thinking. On the other hand, we have noticed some commonalities in thought processes among people of different cultures, so we do not wish to say there are *no* universal principles. We also have a concern that the rejection of individual thinking would leave us without a way to discuss some patterns we find useful. Therefore, for us, both the traditional assumption that there are universal rules and Gergen and Thatchenkery's treatment of all thinking as communal are unnecessarily limiting. This brings us to our third unanswered question.

Our Uncertainty About Universal Values

We are agnostic about the existence of universal principles of morality. An objection to this stance is that people will not act morally without certainty about moral principles. We have already rejected the contention that people need certainty about the external world in order to be moral. Now we will consider whether people need certainty about values in order to be moral.

At least two organization scholars addressed this issue. Tim Newton (1996) wrote, "In terms of political struggle, our values (feminist, socialist, green, etc.) may offer the most appealing basis for making choices for action, but we are adopting an uneasy (and somewhat contradictory) compromise (assuming that we acknowledge that our values are difficult to reliably defend)" (p. 26). Similarly, organization scholar Martin Parker (1995) wrote, "My central point is that some political, theoretical, ethical positions are wrong and others are right. I do not assert this as an epistemological certainty but as a practical necessity and a moral responsibility" (p. 559).

These quotations reflect two concerns:

1. That a person cannot act morally without the belief that his or her values reflect transcendent moral truth. This concern does not fit with our observation that many times people who want to "do the right thing" are uncertain about what that may be. Consequently,

they just follow their best moral intuition. Thus, lack of certainty does not preclude efforts to act morally.

2. Moral values require intellectual justification. In our view, values have *never* been justified intellectually, and we don't see how they could be. Plato valued beauty, goodness, and truth, and Aristotle valued happiness. Christ preached love; Buddha, the end of suffering; Confucius, peace. Among more recent thinkers, Kant valued the desire to do one's duty, Rawls valued justice, and Habermas, emancipation. We do not see how these thinkers could have justified their ultimate values without using other values as the basis. We suggest they began with their core values and built from there.

As an example, let us try to justify love as a value. We could say love is important because it leads to peace. Then peace is the more basic value, and we would need to justify it. Maybe peace is important because it reduces suffering. Then reduction of suffering is the more basic value.

Our point is that justification of any value ultimately depends on some other value. Consequently, as we see it, the situation regarding justification of values has not changed much since Plato and Buddha. However, if some people think that their values need to be justified by reason, and that now the justification is gone, those people may feel they have lost a basis for moral action.

We are, as we said, uncertain about the existence of universal moral values. Please note that this stance does not make us relativists. Neither one of us believes that all values are equally good. We each prefer our own values to other values we know about. Where we may differ from people who profess certainty about values is that we do not claim that there is any way to prove that our own values are best. Further, we haven't seen such proof for any other set of values. Still, however, we try to live by and promote our values. In our framework, we treat moral values as one type of pattern preference. By pattern preference, we mean the phenomenon that people seem to favor some patterns over others. They may express preferences verbally or by other behavior. In this book, we don't explore where preferences originate or try to discover their nature, although we consider those questions valid and interesting. Here we treat preferences simply as one category of patterns of experience. We now turn to our final unanswered question: Is there one universally best methodology for inquiry?

Universally Best Methodology for Inquiry

Although there were debates about the matter for years, the conventional wisdom in organization studies was (implicitly if not explicitly) that the hypothetico-deductive method is the method of choice for scientific inquiry. Kaplan (1964) called this method a product of "reconstructed logic" because it was based on what scientists appeared, after the fact, to have done.

We think privileging of the hypothetico-deductive method overemphasizes the testing portion of inquiry. Although testing is an important component of inquiry, it often leads to overlooking other important components of the inquiry process.

In addition, this emphasis on hypothesis testing often may underplay the influence of background assumptions on the testing process. Helen Longino (1990), whose work on science as social knowledge we consider more fully in later chapters, made this point convincingly.

Our uncertainty about one correct method for inquiry is congruent with our unwillingness to reject induction as called for by Popper (N.D.). Awareness of how difficult it is for humans to gain knowledge that is certain helps to keep us open to learning from diverse approaches to inquiry. For example, with Popper we recognize the conjectural nature of human knowledge. Further, with Hume (1748/1989) and Popper (N.D.) we accept the idea that all human knowledge, including scientific knowledge, "is rationally totally indefensible" (p. 16). However, here we differ from Popper, who believed that although some deductive inferences were logically viable, *no* inductive ones were. Given the uncertainty that is warranted about all human knowledge, we are troubled by this distinction and are willing to accept induction. For example, based on induction we expect that all people will eventually die.

CONCLUSION

A number of difficult issues about the constitution and acquisition of knowledge remain unresolved among Western scholars. These issues contributed to controversy about the nature of knowledge in organization studies.

At present, we advocate accepting uncertainty regarding many of these issues. The admission of ignorance can help one reap the many benefits of "beginner's mind."

This approach, which we call generative uncertainty, avoids taking positions that close off inquiry prematurely and keeps channels clear for open dialogue.

REFERENCES

Berger, P. L., & Luckmann, T. (1966). *The social construction of reality: A treatise in the sociology of knowledge.* New York, NY: Anchor Books.

Berkeley, G. (Bishop). (1710). *Treatise concerning the principles of human knowledge*. Dublin, Ireland: Aaron Rhames.

Berkeley, G. (1961). A treatise concerning the principles of human knowledge. In *The empiricists* (pp. 135–215). Garden City, NY: Dolphin Books. (Original work published in 1710)

Boswell, J. (1792). *The life of Samuel Johnson, LL.D. Comprehending an account of his studies and numerous works* (Vol. 1). Dublin, Ireland: John Chambers.

Brueckner, T. (2004). Brains in a vat. In E. Zalta (Ed.), *Stanford Encyclopedia of Philosophy*. http://plato.stanford.edu/entries/brain-vat

Calaprice, A. (2000). *The expanded quotable Einstein*. Princeton, NJ: Princeton University Press.

Chuang Tzu. (1968). *The complete works of Chuang Tzu* (B. Watson, Trans.). New York, NY: Columbia University Press. (Original work published between 370 and 301 B.C.)

Descartes, R. (1977). *Meditations on first philosophy* (L. J. Lafleur, Tran.). Indianapolis, IN: Bobbs-Merrill Educational Publishing. (Original work published 1641)

Gergen, K. J., & Thatchenkery, T. J. (1996). Organization science as social construction: Postmodern potentials. *Journal of Applied Behavioral Science, 32*, 356–377.

Hume, D. (1989). *An inquiry concerning human understanding*. New York, NY: Macmillan Publishing. (Original work published 1748)

Kaplan, A. (1964). *The conduct of inquiry: Methodology for behavioral science*. Scranton, PA: Chandler Publishing.

Longino, H. F. (1990). *Science as social knowledge: Values and objectivity in scientific inquiry*. Princeton, NJ: Princeton University Press.

Mitroff, I. I., & Mason, R. O. (1974). On evaluating the scientific contribution of the Apollo moon missions via information theory: A study of the scientist-scientist relationship. *Management Science, 20*, 1501–1513.

Newton, T. (1996). Postmodernism in action. *Organization, 3*(1), 7–29.

Parker, M. (1995). Response: Angry young man has egoistic tantrum. *Organization Studies, 16*(4), 575–577.

Plato. (1961). Socrates' defense (apology) (H. Tredennick, Trans.). In Edith Hamilton & Huntington Cairns (Eds.), *The collected dialogues of Plato: Including the letters*. New York, NY: Pantheon Books. (Original work published c. 399 B.C.)

Popper, K. (N.D.). *The problem of induction* (1953, 1974). Retrieved from http://dieoff.org/page126.htm

CHAPTER

2

Ramifications of Generative Uncertainty for Organization Studies

In this chapter we consider some ramifications of the generative uncertainty perspective for several topics pertinent to contemporary organization studies. We call for rethinking perception, representation, the self, other minds, agency (free will), knowledge, and communication. As part of the rethinking, we propose some substitute terms. We begin with perception.

PERCEPTION

No doubt you regard some, if not all, of your own experiences as perceptual (i.e., patterns based on environmental stimuli). However, this practice leaves open at least one important question. How do you know that your experience is a perception rather than a dream, memory, or illusion? To think about this question, imagine that you have the ability to look at reality directly in order to compare it with the patterns you experience. If you could do this, you could distinguish between externally caused patterns and internally caused ones.

We know of no evidence that, to date, any human being has demonstrated the ability to look directly at reality. This suggests to us that people may be limited to matching some patterns of experience against other patterns of experience. This raises the question: What criteria do people use to label some experiences as externally and others as internally generated? Or, to put it another way, if people are not in a position to look reality in the face, what criteria do people use to distinguish between something that comes from the outside and something that comes from the inside? The difficulty of this question is demonstrated by the sophisticated yet contradictory answers given by two realist scholars.

From her realist perspective, sociologist/philosopher Azevedo (1997) proposed one way to make this distinction:

> For any putative entity ... an indicator of its reality is that it is in fact instantiated in a causal explanation, and hence that it has a reasonably precise set of spatiotemporal coordinates. I refer to entities that are instantiated in space-time in this way as *actual* entities ... the existence of structural descriptions or functional explanations in the absence of causal specifications are not sufficient to establish the reality of anything, because they can apply equally to imaginary objects. The ultimate test is whether the entity, property, or process in question is causal, where causality is defined in terms of energy exchange and is located in space-time. (p. 151)

Also, from a realist perspective, Heylighen (1997) treated the distinction between perception and hallucination as a judgment call. He stated:

> Since, as Campbell (1997) reminds us, we have no direct access to the "Ding an Sich", we can only use indirect means to determine whether a belief corresponds to an objective reality. Like the constructivist cyberneticians von Foerster (1981), and Maturana/Varela (1987) note, in the nervous system there is no fundamental distinction between a perception and a hallucination: both are merely patterns of neural activation. However, subjectively most people have no difficulty distinguishing dreams or fantasies from perceptions.
>
> To find out whether a perception is real, you should determine whether it is caused by an external referent, or by an internal mechanism (e.g., imagination, or malfunctioning of the perceptual apparatus). According to attribution theory (Kelley 1967), people attribute causes of perceived effects to those phenomena that *covary* with the effects. External phenomena will covary with their external causes, but not with changes that only affect internal, subjective variables. (p. 64)

Heylighen (1997) listed some factors for determining whether a pattern will be labeled perceptual or attributed to an "internal mechanism." Examples are the degree of invariance across persons, distinctiveness, and controllability (responsiveness to actions performed on it). We do not include Heylighen's entire list with its detailed explanations, but we recommend it for those interested in this topic more deeply.

Although he provided a useful, well-thought-out list of criteria that people use in portraying patterns as perceptual, he was not, in our view, able to demonstrate the validity of these criteria by checking them out against reality. In contrast, using the generative uncertainty approach leaves open the question of an individual's ability to distinguish between external and internal phenomena. It maintains that one can work with so-called perceptual patterns effectively with or without beliefs that they represent external reality.

This is probably a good place to emphasize that generative uncertainty endorses neither solipsism nor idealism and does not rule out realism. Like Socrates, we admit we don't know. Admitting we don't know allows us to avoid complications that unnecessary assumptions might introduce. For example, we do not have to make truth claims about whether specific patterns are internally or externally generated.

A generative uncertainty perspective is compatible with both empiricism and social constructionism. On the one hand, the approach leaves room for discussing "perceptual" patterns in relation to patterns derived from measurement of stimulation (e.g., light frequency), as many empiricists might wish. On the other hand, it allows for treating patterns as products of culture and language, as many social constructionists might wish. These possibilities directly bear on another concept that is central in the debates in organization studies: representation.

REPRESENTATION

A conventional view of representation is the sameness or matching view. This perspective maintains that people are able to portray external reality using indicators such as pictures and words. An alternative view, expressed recently by many postmodernists, is that reality is better understood as a social construction and that the conventional idea of representation is problematic. From our generative uncertainty perspective as well, the conventional view involves so many philosophical problems that using it as a sense-making device in organization studies seems inadvisable. For us, what has traditionally been called representation depends on an impression of sameness or matching. In our view, representation entails matching various patterns of experience with each other.

Impression of Sameness

The process called representation comes down to saying that two patterns are the same on some relevant dimension. Often, the dimension is not specified. For example, a drawing of a bird may be said to represent the bird. However, whether or not the two patterns are the same entails a judgment and at least implicit acceptance of characteristics used in judging.

Physicist Percy Bridgman (1955) asked, "What is the operation by which we judge … sameness?" (p. 64). He stated that use of "same" is very broad, but we can never construct an example in which "the sameness is complete" (p. 65). For example, even the tree outside my window that I saw yesterday is not the same as the one I see today because the sap has been rising from the roots and evaporating. He concluded,

"'Sameness' is a relative concept—relative to our purposes—and usually a very complicated concept" (p. 66).

We may have an experience of matching between a "perceptual" pattern and a word, as when we say, "That is a bird." For most purposes we do not need to decide whether or not the two patterns *really* match—or on what dimension we compared them—we can simply talk about the experience of sameness.

THE SELF

Generative uncertainty is consistent with agnosticism about the existence of the self as a reified entity. The self has become problematic in organization studies theory; see Gergen (1991) and Nord and Fox (1996) for details. However, we find the concept of the person or individual useful if one is aware that it refers to an experienced pattern rather than a reified entity.[1]

OTHER MINDS

There is a long-standing unresolved philosophical issue about whether or not a person can know that other minds exist.

Generative uncertainty leads us to the following position: Even though we have perceptual experiences of other people who seem to speak our language and to report emotions that appear similar to ours, we cannot prove that those perceptions are triggered by actual, conscious, thinking, feeling beings. An android, such as Data on the TV series *Star Trek*, could present itself convincingly as a human being. To converse or transact business with Data, we would *not* need to assume he has a mind. In short, we do not need to prove the existence of other minds in order to conduct inquiry, and we are content to leave the matter open, meanwhile behaving *as if* other minds exist. We are not saying they *do not* exist, only that we cannot demonstrate with finality that they are more than patterns in our experience.

AGENCY (FREE WILL)

Another controversy in organization studies is about agency (i.e., some force or entity internal to individuals that determines their choices). This issue has concerned some postmodernist thinkers who see the belief in agency or free will as an unfortunate contribution of the Enlightenment. To us, this matter seems to be the old theological discussion of free will in new dress. The belief in free will was embedded in Western culture as a tenet of Christianity long before the Enlightenment. Following generative uncertainty, we are agnostic about free will (agency); we see no need to make an assumption one way or the other about its existence.

However, we want to preserve a distinction we consider useful, namely, that between the experience of having a choice and of not having one. This distinction allows us to differentiate between a reflexive blink and a friendly wink, as well as between social and addictive drinking.

To avoid language that introduces built-in assumptions, in line with generative uncertainty we suggest talking of *attribution of choice* versus *attribution of lack of choice*, rather than using the terms *agency* and *free will*.

KNOWLEDGE

Generative uncertainty encourages rethinking of what is meant by *knowledge*. In this section, we summarize a number of ideas that aid in this rethinking.

Recently, the traditional understanding of the possibility of knowledge has been seen as problematic. The traditional philosophical definition of knowledge maintains that saying "A person *knows* that x" (1) entails that x is true, (2) the person believes that x is true and, (3) the grounds of the person's belief are evident or justifiable. By this definition, if it is 5:00 and a person looks at a clock and sees it registers 5:00, and her past experience of the clock has been that it was accurate, and she then believes the time is 5:00, she is said to *know* the time.

However, some philosophers object to this definition. There is the possibility of what Klein (1971) called a felicitous coincidence. It could be that the clock has stopped and always registers 5:00. Under such circumstances, some philosophers would not want to call the woman's belief about the time "knowledge" even though it satisfies the above three criteria.

In addition, specifying what is true, given that we do not know a way to look directly at reality, is problematic. As Haskell (1998) wrote, "What we catch depends as much on the shape, weave, and texture of our conceptual nets as on what the sea contains. No doubt much eludes us, for beneath its tranquil surface the past contains things stranger than any surface-dweller can readily imagine" (p. 3). In this context, Haskell maintained "that what truth requires is not unassailable foundations but self-correcting social processes" (p. 10).

Philosopher of science Helen Longino (1990) made a similar point in *Science as Social Knowledge*. She observed, "Evidential reasoning is always context-dependent" (p. 215). Moreover, "data are evidence for a hypothesis only in light of background assumptions that assert a connection between the sorts of thing or event the data are and the processes or states of affairs described by the hypotheses" (pp. 215–216). For example, according to Longino, research on effects of human sex hormones on fetal development was influenced by assumptions about (1) brain function, (2) the feasibility of applying results of studies of other mammals to humans, and (3) basic characteristics of human masculinity and femininity.

However, Longino did not consider this state of affairs reason for "unbridled relativism" (p. 221). She wrote:

> We are not forced to admit that anything goes. What we experience at a given time and place can be described and measured in conventionally fixed ways. Once we say of a mark on a gauge that it represents 10 units of a measure, we cannot read it as 7 or 13 without the consent of those with whom we need to communicate about the gauge and without changing other descriptions related to those of the gauge. It is neither our desires, nor beliefs, nor values, nor social conventions that make a gauge register a 10 when employed in measurement but processes independent of those cultural phenomena. That we describe what has happened as attaining degree 10 rather than being intense, or having a certain density or color, or any of the other things we might say is *a social* matter: a function of the language and instruments available and the kind of information we deem it important to have. (pp. 221–222)

Nevertheless:

> As long as background beliefs can be articulated and subjected to criticism from the scientific community, they can be defended, modified, or abandoned in response to such criticism. As long as this kind of response is possible, the incorporation of hypotheses into the canon of scientific knowledge can be independent of any individual's subjective preferences. Their incorporation is, instead, a function in part of the assessment of evidential support. And while the evidential relevance to hypotheses of observations and experiments is a function of background assumptions, the adoption of these assumptions is not arbitrary but is (or rather can be) subject to the kinds of controls just discussed. This solution incorporates as elements both the social character of the production of knowledge and the public accessibility of the material with which this knowledge is constructed. (pp. 73–74)

However, Longino made room for what she called objectivity as a social matter. In her view, individuals' objectivity

> consists in their participation in the collective give-and-take of critical discussion and not in some special relation (of detachment, hardheadedness) they may bear to their observations. Thus understood, objectivity is dependent upon the depth and scope of the transformative interrogation that occurs in any given scientific community. This communitywide process ensures (or can ensure) that the hypotheses ultimately accepted as supported by some set of data do not reflect a single individual's idiosyncratic assumptions about the natural world. To say that a theory or hypothesis was accepted on the basis of objective methods does not entitle us to say it is true but rather that it reflects the critically achieved consensus of the scientific community. In the absence of some form of privileged access to transempirical (unobservable) phenomena it's not clear we should hope for anything better. (p. 79)

We see this community-wide process as valuable and we agree people may not be able to do anything better. Longino's approach to science as social knowledge is consistent with our advocacy in later chapters of using the term *preferred pattern* rather than *knowledge*. Both approaches recognize that scholars appear to favor some and to eschew other information without knowing that the patterns they prefer describe an objective reality. When using the term *preferred pattern* in this way, a person or group seems to favor that pattern through verbal or other behavior. Importantly, the above-mentioned idea seems to work well as a substitute for the problematic term *knowledge*. Moreover, it opens up space for considering how values and background assumptions influence pattern choice.

So much for "knowledge."

RETHINKING COMMUNICATION IN THE CONTEXT OF GENERATIVE UNCERTAINTY

Generative uncertainty permits, indeed demands, rethinking communication in organization studies. Why?

The traditional view is essentialist in that it assumes an absolute meaning that someone (e.g., sender) is attempting to convey to someone else (e.g., receiver). In the traditional view, the assumption is that communication is successful when the meaning that the receiver obtained was identical to the one the sender intended.

From our generative uncertainty perspective, this definition of success is problematic because as we noted a few paragraphs ago that what is the "same" is not always obvious and because people do not have access to that one true meaning. In other words, it challenges the assumption that the transmission of absolute meanings is an appropriate criterion for communication.

Practically, the generative uncertainty view, recognizing the difficulties associated with the traditional view, suggests that in practice, people make suppositions to evaluate communication success. Specifically, they make suppositions about what message was sent and what message was received. When they suppose congruence between the two, they judge accurate reception. We call this supposition of accurate reception (SOAR). Informed by generative uncertainty, it appears that such supposition may be the most people can do with respect to judging the successful transmission of meaning.

We suggest that if members of the organization studies community consciously introduce techniques to increase SOAR, they will be taking an important step for dealing with the knowledge controversy.

Numerous scholars have pointed out that one cannot be certain about a speaker's intended message. Nevertheless, human beings constantly form impressions that a message was or was not received accurately.

And nevertheless, people seem to strive unrelentingly for what we call the supposition of accurate reception.

Please note, as we conceive it, achieving SOAR does not require that meaning was actually transmitted. Rather, achieving SOAR is purely a supposition—it is a judgment made by participants or observers of an interchange that communication was successful. Like all judgments, we never know for sure that they accurately reflect what happened. Consistent with generative uncertainty, we do not know for sure what meanings, if any, were transmitted; nevertheless, we still try to communicate.

Sometimes people suppose that a message they sent was received as they intended. At other times they suppose that they understood someone else's message. At other times they suppose that another listener, other than themselves, received a message accurately. SOAR describes all three cases.

So SOAR can refer to anyone's (the speaker's, the listener's, or a third party's) *supposition* that someone recorded a message as a sender intended it. A receiver's experience of SOAR is akin to the term *roger* used in radio communication to mean "I get the message." A sender or observer's experience of SOAR is like that expressed in the slang term *bingo,* often used to mean that someone "got it."

In a group composed of a speaker, a listener, and one or more observers, it often happens that some members of the group think the listener received the message accurately, while others do not. The idea of SOAR allows us to describe such situations without having to assume that anyone ever knows what a speaker intended.

While we do not have a definitive way to resolve differences of opinion about whether or not someone received a message as the sender intended, there are techniques that increase reported experiences of SOAR, such as paraphrasing, providing context, defining terms, and giving examples. We detail these in Chapter 11.

SOAR allows us to talk about communication while avoiding a major hurdle associated with discussions of "intersubjectivity" (i.e., the assumption of shared meanings). SOAR does not require either shared linguistic meanings or shared cultural assumptions. To give an extreme example, if you say something in English to a non-English-speaking person, your words are unlikely to trigger much in the way of shared meanings. All the same, if you *judge,* however erroneously, that the receiver understands your message, your experience qualifies as SOAR.

In addition, our use of SOAR bypasses the *vouloir dire* problem that we can never be certain of what a writer (speaker) meant to say. Even without such certainty, we can still talk about having or not having SOAR with respect to a communication.

In summary, we believe, as we will develop more fully in Chapter 11, the concept of SOAR can be useful in rethinking conflicts among organization scholars. In the spirit of our generative uncertainty, it takes uncertainty into account; at the same time, it acknowledges the importance we place on the *supposition* of accurate reception as a guide or radar in communication attempts.

CONCLUSION

In this chapter we examined some ramifications the generative uncertainty perspective has for several topics pertinent to organization studies: perception, representation, the self, other minds, agency (free will), knowledge, and communication. As we did so, we proposed some revised language to guide rethinking of some problematic issues.

The fundamental purpose of this book is to think of organization studies in the light of generative uncertainty. In this chapter we saw how doing so helps us to see some ideas that are central to the knowledge controversy in new ways.

The ideas we examined in this chapter and the preceding one play an important role in the organization studies knowledge controversy. In many respects, this controversy became intense when some 20th-century scholars, often calling themselves postmodernists, were interpreted as raising a new intellectual point: the idea that human beings cannot attain certain knowledge. However, this point was not really new in the 20th century. It was raised by the ancient Greeks (and also, incidentally, by the ancient Buddhists), a matter we won't go into further here.

In the next chapter, we will consider the interplay of certainty and uncertainty in the West.

ENDNOTE

1. Having stated our agnostic position about the nature of reality, we should add that we are inclined to agree with the logical positivist tenet that we discuss in more detail in Chapter 8, "Alternative Approaches for the Knowledge Controversy," that metaphysical questions about the ultimate nature of reality do not fit comfortably into an inquiry-based field.

REFERENCES

Azevedo, J. (1997). *Mapping reality: An evolutionary realist methodology for the natural and social sciences.* Albany, NY: State University of New York Press.

Bridgman, P. W. (1955). *Reflections of a physicist.* New York, NY: Philosophical Library.

Gergen, K. J. (1991). *The saturated self.* New York, NY: Basic Books.

Haskell, T. L. (1998). *Objectivity is not neutrality: Explanatory schemes in history.* Baltimore, MD: John Hopkins University Press.

Heylighen, F. (1997). Objective, subjective, and intersubjective selectors of knowledge. *Evolution and Cognition*, *3*(1), 63–67.
Klein, P. D. (1971). A proposed definition of propositional knowledge. *Journal of Philosophy*, *LXVIII*, 471–482.
Longino, H. E. (1990). *Science as social knowledge*. Princeton, NJ: Princeton University Press.
Nord, W. R., & Fox, S. (1996). The individual in organizational studies: The great disappearing act? In S. R. Clegg, C. Hardy, & W. R. Nord (Eds.), *Handbook of organization studies* (pp. 148–174). London, UK: Sage Publications.

SECTION

2

Historical Factors

CHAPTER

3

In the Shadow of Certainty

The Interplay of Certainty and Uncertainty in the West

At the root of the knowledge controversy in organization studies was the issue of the possibility that humans could obtain knowledge that was certain. For some time, most North American social scientists did not concern themselves with this matter because they believed implicitly that by using the methods that proved so successful in the natural sciences, they would gain knowledge that was certain. However, in the late 20th century, a movement known as postmodernism called into question the implicit assumption of certainty.

Some scholars on both sides of the resulting debate appeared to assume that the question about certainty was a new one. The incorrect assumption of novelty resulted from a limited historical perspective. The possibility of obtaining knowledge that was certain was debated for over two millennia. We maintain that greater awareness of this history would have made the debate seem less novel and might have led participants on both sides to arrive at a thesis like the one we advance in this book—generative uncertainty. Specifically, scholars would realize that gaining absolutely certain knowledge may be beyond human reach, but that does not, as some self-proclaimed postmodernists seem to have suggested, mean that inquiry of the sort practiced in modern science is fruitless.

Examining the debate in the context of the history of consideration of certainty–uncertainty in Western thought reveals, among other things:

(1) the issue had a long history and was far from new in the late 20th century, and (2) there were many positions on uncertainty. (In describing these positions, we do not mean to advance any of them. Our intent is to introduce them and to demonstrate uncertainty's long history in the West. For our position on uncertainty, please see Chapters 1 and 2.) The acceptance of some degree of uncertainty was something that the postmodernists shared with some founders of modern science.

This chapter reviews this history in order to sharpen contemporary understanding of the certainty–uncertainty issue in Western history. The issue was discussed by the ancient Greeks. (Incidentally, the ancient Buddhists also discussed it—a matter we will not consider here since our focus is on the West.) We view the history of the interplay of certainty and uncertainty in the West chronologically.

A central thesis of the generative uncertainty approach is that students of organizational studies need to find ways to conduct inquiry in the absence of philosophically certain knowledge about some fundamental issues such as (1) the nature of "reality," (2) universal principles of reasoning, (3) rules for correct methodology, and (4) universal values. We suggest that the recent controversies about what constitutes organization studies, such as the hyperbolic rejoinders (see Hofmann, 2002; Friedman, 2002; Holdstock, 2002; and others) in *American Psychologist* (June/July 2002) to Gergen's (2001) attempt to explain how psychology could benefit from understanding postmodernism, owe much of their intensity to the inability of scholars on both sides of various issues to come to terms with uncertainty.

Reed (2006) summarized the matter:

> Contemporary students of organization find themselves at a historical juncture and in a social context where all the old ideological "certainties" and technical "fixes" that once underpinned their "discipline" are fundamentally being called into question. Over the last two decades, a metatheoretical debate over the nature of organization inquiry and intellectual means most appropriate for understanding organizational phenomena has been underway. This has badly shaken, if not totally undermined, philosophical foundations of and substantive rationale for contemporary organization analysis. (p. 20)

(Tangible changes included a break with functionalist-positivist orthodoxy and efforts to reestablish theoretical hegemony of the traditional research paradigm.)

Calás and Smircich (1999) noted that postmodernism and its close companion poststructuralism introduced reflexivity that helped people realize "that there is … no foundation, no grounding and *no stable structure on which meaning can rest*" (p. 653).

Unfortunately, scholars on both sides of the controversy between the postmodernists and traditional normal scientists seemed to view such doubting of previous certainties as a novel event. Given this, many scholars uncomfortable with challenges to the certainties of their traditional approaches lashed out at challengers, as if by discrediting them they could restore the old certainties. They wrote as if the challengers raised a radically new philosophical issue. Likewise, many of the challengers also appeared to believe that they were raising a new issue.

The attribution of novelty by both sides helped to frame the debate as a battle between two recent views—modernism and postmodernism, with modernists defending the certainty they attributed to traditional science and postmodernists attacking it.

Inattention to history played a major role in producing these positions. Even cursory attention to history would have revealed that the debates about certainty were part of Western culture for thousands of years and, furthermore, that the acceptance of uncertainty played a significant role in the development of modern science. As a consequence of the unfortunate framing, contemporary debaters did not address the uncertainty issue as fully as they might have.

Accordingly, we attempt to reframe the knowledge controversy in light of Western philosophy's long-standing concern with uncertainty. With this history in mind, we call on students of organizational studies to expand their understanding of the interplay of certainty and uncertainty in Western culture.

We summarize this history by supporting the following five ideas:

1. Concern that human beings cannot achieve certain knowledge has a long history in Western thought.
2. The issue of certainty played a role in the evolution of Christianity.
3. Uncertainty was an active concern for the leaders in the development of modern science. In fact, the founders of modern science proceeded while acknowledging that the basic position of the skeptics could not be refuted.
4. Following the origins of modern science, the matter of uncertainty was still not resolved. It was dealt with in three major ways:
    a. Some people, primarily philosophers, continued to be troubled about it.
    b. Others, primarily practicing scientists and laypeople, tended to ignore the matter.
    c. Some people lapsed into scientism, making science itself a source of certainty.
5. In the 20th century, some philosophers and practicing scientists gave increased attention to uncertainty. This attention provided the context in which controversies about knowledge flourished.

Together, these five ideas lead us to conclude that the recent development of postmodernism represents just another reemergence of uncertainty in the West.

LONG HISTORY IN WESTERN THOUGHT OF THE IDEA THAT HUMANS CANNOT ACHIEVE CERTAINTY ABOUT KNOWLEDGE

In early-20th-century North America, the best known treatment of the history of certainty was Dewey's *The Quest for Certainty* (1929/1960). Despite being nearly 100 years old, Dewey's analysis still deserves careful attention.

Dewey on the History of Certainty

Dewey asserted that Western thinkers place a premium on gaining certainty—a certainty that would be "absolute and unshakeable" (p. 6). He traced this penchant to the way ideas of the ancient Greeks filtered into contemporary thinking and to the fact that uncertainty introduces perils into human life.

According to Dewey, in the philosophical tradition of his time, this quest for certainty could be fulfilled only in pure knowing. Natural science was accepted as the source of such knowing because it provided a way of making knowledge directly dependent on sensations derived from the real world. This quest for absolute certainty is "thoroughly entangled with fundamental beliefs and ideas in all sorts of fields" (p. 24). In tracing the seeming need for certainty to ancient Greece, he emphasized the major role Euclidean geometry played in advancing this quest. This geometry, he suggested, seemed to offer the possibility of a science that owed nothing to observation and sense beyond mere exemplification in figures or diagrams. It appeared to reveal a world of ideal forms that were connected to each other by eternal or necessary relations that could be discovered only by reason. Philosophers generalized this perspective into a "complete system of immutable and necessary truth" (p. 16).

In this context, the philosophies of Plato and Aristotle appeared to be rational systematizations of Greek religious and artistic beliefs. This systemization provided logic for a physical science that treated immutable rational objects and operated in the context of a fixed reality. The ideals of such a science became permanent fixtures of Western civilization; a whole system of philosophical conclusions was involved. First and foremost was the assumption that "there is a complete correspondence between knowledge in its true meaning and what is real" (p. 21).

This ancient Greek formulation continued to affect thought. Dewey maintained that "the main tradition of western culture has retained intact this framework of ideas. Perfect certainty is what man wants" (p. 21). Knowledge is thought to concern a region of being that is fixed, eternal, and unalterable. This notion is so familiar, Dewey noted, that we "overlook the unexpressed premise upon which it rests, namely that only the completely fixed and unchanging can be real" (p. 21).

Dewey added that the quest for certitude has determined our basic metaphysics and that our quest for absolute certainty underlies our notions about the nature of the mind and of the world. He concluded that the assumption of the correspondence between reality and knowledge was rooted in a branch of ancient Greek thought. We suggest that the privileging of science in American culture and the faith in ideological certainties and technical fixes in organization studies discussed by Reed (noted earlier) owe a great deal to the above conception of knowledge.

Although Dewey analyzed ancient Greek and Roman influences on the need for certainty, *The Quest for Certainty* gave scant attention to the skeptical side of the story. It understated the contributions of the Greek and Roman Pyrrhonists and Academics, the revival of skepticism during the Renaissance, the role of skepticism in the Reformation, and most significantly, the place of skepticism in the founding of modern science.

Now we consider the part of the story that *The Quest for Certainty* underplayed.

Uncertainty in Ancient Greek Thought

Uncertainty was at the center of Ancient Greek skepticism. *Webster's New World Dictionary* places the origin of *skeptic* in the Greek *skeptikos,* meaning "thoughtful inquiry." Long (1999) wrote, "Doubts about human access to knowledge predate much of philosophy in Greece. From the early poet-philosopher Xenophanes to Socrates we can find numerous antecedents of scepticism" (p. 79). Popkin and Stroll (2002) traced philosophical skepticism back to Greek sophists such as Gorgias (483–378 B.C.E.). They reported that Gorgias asserted nothing exists, and even if it did, nobody could know it. Although skepticism had a long history in Greek thought, what became the recognized schools of skepticism began with Pyrrho of Elis (365–275 B.C.E.). There were two major schools of Greek skepticism: the Pyrrhonists and the Academics.

Many historians distinguish between Pyrrhonic and Academic skepticism, but some, such as Schmitt (1972), think that often these distinctions exaggerate the actual differences. On the other hand, Popkin (1979) drew a clear distinction. According to him, Academic skepticism sought to establish "that no knowledge was possible" (p. xiii). In contrast, Pyrrhonian skepticism sought to establish "that there was insufficient and inadequate evidence to determine if any knowledge was possible, and hence that one ought to suspend judgment on all questions concerning knowledge" (p. xiii). Although for present purposes distinguishing the two is not crucial, a few words about each is helpful.

Pyrrhonian Skepticism

Pyrrhonian skepticism bears the name of Pyrrho of Ellis. Pyrrho, it was said, had an extreme mistrust of his senses. Since he left no written record, much of what we now believe about Pyrrhonism comes from a third-century book, *Outlines of Pyrrhonism* by Sextus Empiricus. From Sextus we learn that the Pyrrhonists, after trying to determine what was true or false, concluded that due to differences among humans in what they sensed, judgment should be suspended. Mates (1996) summarized as follows:

> The Pyrrhonist's message, insofar as he has one, is something like this: "At ease! The notion that in order to live well you have to have beliefs about a supposed reality that transcends all appearances is just a mistake. Go by appearances; put aside your worries about whether they correspond to that so-called 'external world', which the philosophers never manage to describe in a consistent or fully intelligible way; suspend judgment about all such matters and you will reach the equanimity that we all desire." (pp. v–vi)

Academic Skepticism

Academic skepticism was the second branch of ancient Greek skepticism derived from Plato's Academy. Academic skepticism incorporated Socrates' profession of not knowing. Kurtz (1992) wrote that Academic skeptics wished to deny the Stoic claim that there were certain perceptions that were self-evidently true. For example, Arcesilaus challenged the notion of sense impressions that could not be mistaken. Further, Academics proposed that any sense impression might be deceiving and believed that we should suspend judgment (i.e., not accept a position as either true or false). Suspending judgment motivated Academics to develop equally weighty arguments on both sides of issues.

Some of the best known ideas of the Academic skeptics came to us through a Roman philosopher, the writer and orator Marcus Tullius Cicero (106–143 B.C.E.). In the *Academica*, Cicero (c. 45 B.C.E./2006), a proponent of Academic skepticism, summarized the major teachings of the Academics (Schmitt, 1972). He challenged the stoic theory that ordinary sensory processes yielded cognitive certainty.

CERTAINTY IN THE EVOLUTION OF CHRISTIANITY

Cicero's ideas were carried into the Middle Ages through the writings of Lactantius and Augustine, who both lived in the 300s. Schmitt (1972) observed that Lactantius approved of Cicero's skepticism. Lactantius (c. 240–c. 320 B.C.E.) commented on the limitations on the knowledge humans could have.

He noted that Lactantius saw skepticism's critique of dogmatic philosophy as opening a door for true knowledge and Christianity. Lactantius was one of the earliest Christian thinkers to advance the fideistic (known primarily by faith) view using Cicero's Academic position in which "the wisdom of the philosophers counts for nothing" (p. 28).

In contrast to Lactantius, Augustine wrote about skepticism in order to refute it. The Roman Catholic bishop and theologian Augustine (known today as St. Augustine), the most influential church leader after Paul and before Thomas Aquinas, played a central role in suppressing doubt.

Augustine and Skepticism

As a young man Augustine apparently advocated skepticism for a brief period (Schmitt, 1972; Augustine, 1995). The situation changed when he converted to Christianity. His career as a Christian revealed one way powerful actors in the West worked to preserve certainty when uncertainty appeared.

Following his conversion to Christianity, Augustine (386/1957), in *Against the Academicians*, revealed deep familiarity with the position of the Academics and also his rejection of it. He wrote, "Although I am now in my thirty-third year, I do not think I ought to despair of ever attaining wisdom … no one doubts that we are incited to learn by the double weight of authority and of reason. Therefore I am sure that I shall never depart from the authority of Christ" (p. 82).

Augustine reasoned his way out of skepticism by using knowledge of his own existence as a basis, much like Descartes would do centuries later. (We do not know whether Descartes reinvented this argument or inherited it from Augustine.)

Schmitt noted:

> In the different uses made of skeptical arguments to be found in Lactantius and Augustine, we see in miniature the general trend, from beginning to end, of Western Christian thought *vis-à-vis* skepticism. A constantly recurring theme of this study will be the way in which an ideologically neutral philosophical doctrine can be used by adherents to the widest variety of differing positions as an adjunct to their own arguments. History shows us that skepticism is not the province of liberal or conservative, of deist or atheist, of scientist or nonscientist, but at different times and places it has been accepted and utilized by adherents to many different creeds and ideologies. (p. 25)

Certainty and Uncertainty in the Early Church

Under the Emperor Constantine, the Catholic Church became a powerful force in the Roman Empire. The teachings of the church were complicated by the fact that the truth was not always readily apparent from scripture. However, seeing the merits of what today we call a tight paradigm, Constantine pressed hard for resolution of doctrinal disputes, and he convened ecumenical councils in which all the bishops were invited to participate in setting church doctrine. Constantine started the process by calling the first meeting of the Council of Nicaea, which authored the Nicene Creed.

A vital doctrinal issue at the council was a claim of the charismatic leader, Arius, that there was a time when the Son of God did not exist. His chief opponent, Athanasius, considered this to be heresy.

According to Karen Armstrong (1993), "When the bishops gathered at Nicaea on May 20, 325, to resolve the crisis, very few would have shared Athanasius's view of Christ. Most held a position midway between Athanasius and Arius. Nevertheless, Athanasius managed to impose his theology on the delegates, and, with the emperor breathing down their necks, only Arius and two of his brave companions refused to sign his creed" (p. 110).

The council declared Arius a heretic, along with anyone else who claimed that there was a time when Christ did not exist, or that Christ was made from nothing, or that Christ was composed of a different substance than the Father. These heretics were anathematized (excommunicated and condemned to hell). Additionally, Arius's books were burned and Constantine exiled him and his supporters.

Augustine played a major role in establishing how the church would deal with heretics. The precedent he set in his struggle against the heresy of Donatism had especially far-reaching effects. Donatists believed that if a priest in a state of mortal sin administered a sacrament, the sacrament was not valid. It is easy to imagine the enormous problems the church would have faced had this belief become official church dogma.

As he struggled to combat Donatism, Augustine became frustrated over a lack of progress in negotiations and went against his earlier insistence that heretics be treated gently. He justified the use of force by reference to Christ's display of temper toward moneychangers in the temple. He furthered his case for coercion by citing the parable in Luke 14:16–24, which told of a man who invited many people to supper, but they all made excuses. Then he had his servant bring in the poor, the maimed, the lame, and the blind, but still there was room. So, he told the servant to "go out into the highways and hedges, and compel them to enter, that my house may be filled."

Nigg (1962) commented:

> It was one of the darkest hours in the whole history of Christian thought when Augustine, that noble God-seeker and fervent mystic, set forth the terrible principle: *cogite intrare*—compel them to enter.... Whatever we may say to excuse Augustine, the sword had been drawn from its sheath. All those instrumental in the ferocious suppression of heretics in the Middle Ages could call upon the authority of St. Augustine—could and did. The violence and cruelty unleased [*sic*] by this one man was beyond measure. (pp. 116–117)

After Augustine, the church maintained its role as the sole arbiter of truth. Sometimes unity was still achieved through force or the threat of it, as it was during the famous events of the Council of Ephesus in 431. According to Nigg, this council involved such inflamed discussion that "the delegates went at one another with clubs until one party held the field and could enforce the decree it desired" (p. 121).

Centuries later, another Catholic theologian, Thomas Aquinas, also played a major role in the handling of uncertainty in the West.

Thomas Aquinas (c. 1225–1274)

Thomas Aquinas was born in southern Italy to Count Landulf of Aquino and Theodora, Countess of Teamo. As a younger son in a noble family and also a man of strong spiritual interests, Thomas[1] was well suited for a career in the church. He was to become arguably the most influential Roman Catholic theologian in history, and in that role influenced the church's treatment of uncertainty.

We discuss his work under the headings of Influences on Thomas Aquinas: view of natural law, certainty and uncertainty, and continuing impact.

Influences on Thomas Aquinas

Thomas was influenced by Augustine and other church fathers. However, Aristotle had perhaps the strongest influence on him. Thomas lived at the time when Aristotle's works had just been translated into Latin. Thomas became a great admirer of Aristotle, going so far as to refer to him as "the philosopher," rather than by name. Thomas integrated Aristotelian philosophy into Roman Catholicism.

Thomas did not agree with Aristotle completely. There were two major differences between them:

1. Aristotle saw happiness in this life as humanity's goal. Thomas also saw happiness as humanity's goal, but happiness in the next life took precedence over happiness in this one.
2. For Aristotle, reason was the path to truth. For Thomas, there were two (completely compatible) paths to truth: faith *and* reason.

Some truths, such as the existence of God, could be known by reason alone. Thomas's proofs for existence of God reflected the influence of Aristotle, who reached his conclusions about God's existence through reason alone. Other truths, such as the trinity and the incarnation, required faith in scripture and the teachings of the church. Essentially, the pope had the final word on the teachings of the church. Church councils, such as the Council of Nicaea, received their authority from the popes that convened them.

Natural Law Thomas's view of natural law was based on the principle stated in his *Summa Theologica* that "the good is what all desire" (Vol. 20, p. 122). The desire for the good included the inclination humans share with all substances to preserve their own being, the inclinations humans share with animals, such as instincts toward sexual intercourse and education of the young, and inclinations proper to humans by dint of possession of reason, such as wanting to know the truth about God and to live in society.

Synderesis (conscience) is "said to be the law of our intellect because it is a habit containing the precepts of the natural law, which are the first principles of human actions" (Vol. 20, p. 221).

Certainty and Uncertainty Thomas accepted a degree of uncertainty. For example, he wrote that the more detail involved in a moral decision, the less the certainty about the right way to behave. In addition, his moral principles made room for individual differences: "Acts of virtue are not common to all, since a thing is virtuous in one and vicious in another" (Vol. 20, p. 223).

On the other hand, faith in scripture and the teachings of the church offered certainty, more so than did reason alone.

Thomas was certain enough about the teachings of the church to support severe penalties for heresy: "The Church does not condemn at once, but after the first and second admonitions … after that, if [the heretic] is yet stubborn, the Church, no longer hoping for his conversion looks to the salvation of others, by excommunicating him and furthermore delivers him to the secular tribunal to be exterminated from the world by death" (Vol. 20, p. 448). Clearly, Thomas went along with the mandate "compel them to enter."

Influence of Thomas Aquinas

The influence of Thomas on Roman Catholicism (and religions that borrowed from it) can hardly be overstated. Numerous popes and ecumenical councils treated his work as their authority. Even as late as 1879, over 600 years after Thomas's death, Pope Leo XIII wrote an encyclical, *Aeternia Patris,* recommending Thomism as a model for Christian philosophy.

Other important developments in the history of uncertainty in the West took place during the Reformation. Ideas of the ancient skeptics played a role. Skepticism was a major element in religious debates of the time.

Eventually, ideas from the religious debates filtered into the founding of modern science. The ways that influential Anglican theologians dealt with skepticism in these debates influenced early members of the Royal Society of London, who paved the way for the development of modern science by Newton and others.

Skepticism in Religious Struggles During the Reformation

Popkin (1979) observed that between 1500 and 1675 skepticism played "a special … role due to the fact that the intellectual crisis brought on by the Reformation coincided … with the rediscovery and revival of the ancient Greek sceptics" (p. xvi).

During the Reformation, Erasmus and Luther debated how to find a criterion of truth for religious knowledge. Luther challenged the authority of the church, maintaining that the church's proponents offered only opinions on matters of scripture. He called for replacing these opinions with instructions from one's own conscience. His position, as recorded in *Documents of the Christian Church,* was

> That which is asserted without the authority of Scripture or of proven revelation may be held as an opinion, but there is not obligation to believe it.... Transubstantiation ... must be considered as an invention of human reason, since it is based neither on Scripture nor sound reasoning. (Bettenson, 1963, p. 27)

In short, Luther advanced a new criterion for religious knowledge: "What conscience is compelled to believe on reading Scripture is true" (Popkin, 1979, p. 3).

In arguing against Luther, Erasmus used skepticism to defend the authority of the church. The essence of his message was consistent with academic skepticism: Human affairs were so obscure that nothing can be known for sure. Erasmus said he preferred to follow the attitude of the skeptics and *suspend judgment.* In *The Praise of Folly,* Erasmus (1668/1958) commented that "Christian religion seems to have a kind of alliance with folly and in no respect to have any accord with wisdom" (p. 141). One result is considerable debate and "noise of words" (p. 147). Under these conditions he preferred to go with the holy men rather than common people. Popkin noted that Erasmus advanced this position in a spirit of anti-intellectualism—matters of theology were sufficiently complex that the average Christian would be best off by accepting the word of the church.

Responding that religious knowledge was too important to be taken on trust, Luther rejected the idea that humans could not penetrate scripture. He also rejected Erasmus's willingness to submit to the decrees of the church, whether or not one understood the reasons for them. Popkin (1979) summarized the conflict as follows: "This exchange between Erasmus and Luther indicates some of the basic structure of the criterion problem. Erasmus was willing to admit that he could not tell with certainty what was true, but he was willing to accept the decisions of the Church" (p. 7).

The views of many theologians conflicted during the Reformation. Reformers tried to show that the church of Rome had no basis for asserting its absolute certitude. Counterreformers charged that the reformers' ways would lead to complete subjectivism about religious truths.

Participants in the debate often used skepticism to challenge opponents' criteria. A key issue in these disputes was the view of some that Protestantism was damned if it did not recognize the infallibility of the Roman Catholic Church on spiritual matters. Luther called attention to the problem of justifying a standard of true knowledge.

It is evident, based on what we said so far, that skepticism and the attention it drew to uncertainty were active concerns in the history of

Western Christianity. Moreover, the emphasis the Roman Church gave to enforcing certainty repressed but did not resolve, concerns about uncertainty. In other words, uncertainty was hidden in the shadow of the certainty of the church.

Efforts to deal with uncertainty in religious debates spilled over into discussions about science.

UNCERTAINTY AND THE ORIGINS OF MODERN SCIENCE

Following the 16th-century revival of interest in Greek skepticism and extending through the 18th century, the issue of uncertainty continued to influence Western thought. Gradually, philosophers on both sides of the English Channel moved toward versions of a generative skepticism. We treat highlights of the discussions on both sides of the channel separately, although they did not occur independently of each other. We begin with France.

Uncertainty in 16th- and 17th-Century France

Many prominent 16th- and 17th-century French intellectuals, including Michel de Montaigne, René Descartes, Marin Merssenne, and Petrus Gassendi, considered doubt about the possibility of certainty.

Michel de Montaigne (1533–1592)

Montaigne (1580/1958) had a Pyrrhonist motto, "*Je ne sait*" ("I don't know"), carved into the wood of his study. He questioned the reliability of the senses. He even questioned the idea that we cannot know. Montaigne (1575–1576) favorably quoted Lucretius, "Whoever thinks that we know nothing does not know Whether we know enough to say that is so" (p. 372). He pointed out that people from different cultures had different mores and all thought theirs were right. He saw attempts to reach consensus about nature as a self-deception. Montaigne (1580/1958) expressed his distrust of human knowledge eloquently when he wrote, "Before the principles which Aristotle introduced were in credit, other principles satisfied human reason, as his satisfy us at this moment" (p. 429).

Political events of the times limited the influence of Montaigne's doctrine of uncertainty. Toulmin (1990) argued that the assassination of France's Henri IV (also known as Henry of Navarre) stimulated a cultural shift in the early 17th century. In this era, European monarchs needed to cope with seemingly irresolvable religious conflicts. Prior to his assassination, Henry followed a policy of toleration, as he tried to stabilize relations between Catholics and Protestants while guaranteeing civil liberties that respected everyone's right to opinions. Henry's assassination in 1610 was immediately seen "as a historical turning point." It "dashed the last hope of escaping irresoluble conflicts" (Toulmin, p. 48). The assassination led people to believe that religious toleration had been tried and had failed.

In the times leading up to Henry's murder, France was plagued by political and religious turmoil. Uncertainty, ambiguity, and pluralism were perceived as sources of social decay. People took the assassination as evidence that uncertainty, ambiguity, and pluralism were problems. This context predisposed people to seek a rational method for determining whether philosophical, scientific, and theological doctrines were right or wrong. It appeared that skepticism, like religious toleration, had been tried and had failed.

René Descartes

The strong desire for certainty in the postassassination environment helped to make the program offered by another French thinker, René Descartes, more attractive than Montaigne's. As Toulmin put it, "The Cartesian program for philosophy swept aside the 'reasonable' uncertainties and hesitations of 16th-century skeptics, in favor of new, mathematical kinds of 'rational certainty and proof'" (p. 75).

Descartes addressed skepticism by beginning with extreme doubt. At the conclusion of his first meditation, Descartes (1641/1960) observed that there was nothing he believed to be true that he could not somehow doubt. Therefore, he decided to take the opposite stance and doubt or suspend judgment about all things, pretending that they were entirely false and imaginary. He attempted to keep doubting everything that he was not certain about until he found something he *was* certain about. Following this course, he arrived at his famous "*Cogito, ergo sum*" ("I think, therefore I am").

Western intellectuals made wide use of Descartes to champion certainty. However, many were not convinced. Popkin (2003) concluded that Descartes never provided an adequate response to skepticism. Even in the 17th century, skeptically oriented scholars challenged Descartes; they reasoned that if a person's position rested on one's subjective assurance that he or she was right, it was still possible for one to be wrong. In short, if the person started with the *cogito*, every step forward could be "reduced to merely the opinion of René Descartes" (p. 170).

Although Descartes did not actually refute skepticism, he profoundly influenced how Westerners viewed reality. He persuaded many to think in terms of an *internal* and an *external* world. Following his approach, appearances became the "inner" and reality the "outer."

Palmer (2004) commented on this separation:

> From that point of view, staying within the appearances was not an option. Scepticism could not be turned into a problem to be overcome;

> it became, in Kant's words "a scandal to philosophy" that the existence of an external world cannot be demonstrated. The real scandal, however, was, perhaps, the ease and speed with which the distinction between an internal and an external world had been absorbed into post-Cartesian philosophy, replacing the distinction between Appearance and Reality with which the Pyrrhonists struggled. (pp. 266–267)

Thus, it is obvious that the uncertainty issue was prominent in the era of Descartes. That fact has important implications for the contemporary debate in organization studies, because many promoters of certainty-related positions point to Descartes as having provided the philosophical basis for the certainty that they assume. But, as Toulmin (1990) implied, it is possible that the acceptance of Descartes' doctrine was at least as much due to society's desire for certainty as it was to convincing philosophical argument.

In contrast to Descartes, Mersenne and Gassendi accepted uncertainty.

Marin Mersenne (1588–1648)

The French theologian-philosopher Marin Mersenne (1625), despite asserting skeptical doubt, insisted on the truth of science. He came to this position through his interpretation of Hobbes's political theory as a cure for destructive Pyrrhonism.

Mersenne came to what Popkin (1979) called generative or mitigated skepticism. Much of Mersenne's early work consisted of polemics against what he saw as enemies of science, including alchemists and Pyrrhonists. Later, however, he helped forge a view that incorporated Pyrrhonist doubt without negating the findings of science. According to Popkin (1979), he did this by interpreting scientific findings as "hypothetical systems about appearances and not true descriptions of reality, as practical guides to actions, and not ultimate information about the true nature of things" (p. 148).

Petrus Gassendi (1592–1665)

Gassendi, too, was a skeptic with scientific interests. His philosophical writings featured a skeptical challenge to the traditional Aristotelian categories of the Middle Ages; as a scientist he was a dedicated astronomer (Brush, 1972). He drew on Sextus Empiricus to advance two themes about uncertainty: (1) a doubt of all claims to knowledge about the real world; and (2) acceptance of the world of experience or appearances as the sole basis for natural knowledge (Popkin, 1979).

Gassendi was a philosopher and an empirical scientist. His writings are especially interesting for present purposes because he both advanced a version of skepticism and did theoretical and empirical scientific work. The way he resolved possible conflict between skepticism and empirical science anticipated the approach of the Royal Society of London. Accordingly, we treat his work in some depth.

To a considerable extent, his philosophical writings were a polemic against Aristotle, whose views constituted the conventional scientific wisdom of the time. In the preface to a collection of his writings Gassendi (1624/1972) wrote:

> Book II is directed against Aristotle's Logic.... Next comes the main point—I argue that learning and human knowledge are weak and uncertain. Then the fundamentals of Pyrrhonism are confirmed, above all the maxim *nihil sciri* [nothing is known] is established. (p. 24)

In support of his acceptance of uncertainty about the ability of humans to know nature, Gassendi (1624/1972) pointed out how different senses provide conflicting information. He wrote:

> Do you not realize ... that even the astutest of men will be so divided by the diversity of his judgments that he will not be able to pronounce what sort of thing anything is according to its nature? ... Whether he wants to or not, he will be constituted of organs of his body that will represent the same object in different ways to him.... What conclusion then will he reach concerning the object that has been represented in more ways than one? Won't he be able, at best, to say that rainwater, for example, is salutary when applied to the eyes, but harmful when applied to the lungs, but that considered by itself it does not seem any more salutary than harmful or harmful than salutary? ... What we call the properties or affects of things do not seem to have been placed there by nature so much as attributed to them from the outside because of their effect upon us. (pp. 92–93)
>
> Further:
>
> Since there are so many different appearances of one and the same thing, and since so many different judgments are passed upon it ... what other conclusion remains except that we cannot know what anything is like according to itself or to its own nature, but only how it appears to some men or to others? It is appropriate in this exercise to review what we demonstrated earlier, first that men do not know the inner nature of things. (pp. 96–97)

However, those views did not force Gassendi (1624/1972) to take an extreme skeptical position. He developed a mitigated skepticism.

While arguing against true knowledge in the Aristotelian sense, Gassendi maintained that people still have knowledge—it was possible to "know" many things in the way the term was ordinarily used. Gassendi wrote: "There are some things capable of being known, though they are still not ones that can be known with an Aristotelian knowledge, but only experientially" (p. 104).

The gist of Gassendi's position was that while absolute truth may be beyond the reach of humans, useful knowledge was still possible and worth pursuing. This would be knowledge provided by experience. It would be knowledge "of appearances; for our intellect knows or learns through its experience of numerous appearances" (p. 104).

Gassendi sought to reduce the influence of Aristotle's dogmatism. He was concerned that the Aristotelians had become more active as disputers than as seekers of truth. In other words, they did not study experience.

This brief review of late-16th- and early-17th-century French scholarship reveals that important French scholars, as they developed a philosophical orientation for a new science, were actively concerned with uncertainty. One important feature of uncertainty was a type of skepticism that was consistent with empirical science.

Uncertainty and Early Modern Science in Britain

At roughly the same time as these developments in France, a philosophical orientation that featured acceptance of skepticism combined with belief that knowledge could be gained from experience grew in Britain and influenced the fathers of modern science. One of the greatest figures in the history of science, Sir Francis Bacon, evidenced a longstanding concern with uncertainty. Like Gassendi, he sought to replace Aristotelian dogmatism with information gained from experience.

Sir Francis Bacon (1561–1621)

Prior to Bacon, Aristotle was the accepted authority on science. Bacon (1620/1960), in his famous *Novum Organon* (*New Instrument*), made it clear that he wished to replace the Aristotelian approach that emphasized logic and that "now serves … to fix and give stability to errors" and "does more harm than good" (p. 41) with an approach that induced axioms from experience.

Bacon (1620/1960) wrote, "It is idle to expect any great advancement in science from the superinducing and engrafting of new things upon old. We must begin anew from the very foundations, unless we would revolve forever in a circle with mean and contemptible progress" (p. 46).

Bacon's new way was his now famous inductive approach that emphasized: (1) systematic investigation; and (2) research as a cooperative process in which humans interpreted nature by what today we call experiments (i.e., putting natural bodies together or pulling them asunder and letting nature work on them). Based on these observations (Bacon, 1620/1960), axioms were formed and, via gradual and unbroken ascent, "the most general axioms" (p. 43) and building axioms from sensory data, and building general axioms from lower-level axioms or propositions (Redman, 1997).

Bacon, according to Popkin (1990), was familiar with Montaigne's *Essais* and offered *Novum Organon* as "a way of avoiding either complete doubt or unjustified dogmatism" (p. 330). Bacon concluded that despite the contributions of the ancient Greeks, especially Aristotle, the degree of certainty that people of his era were attaching to their ideas was dysfunctional, and it was time to pay more attention to some of the ancient Greeks who proposed lesser certainty. In the preface to *Novum Organon*, Bacon (1620/1960) wrote:

> Those who have taken upon them to lay down the law of nature as a thing already searched out and understood ... have therein done philosophy and the sciences great injury. For as they have been successful in inducing belief, so they have been effective in quenching and stopping inquiry; and have done more harm by spoiling and putting an end to other men's efforts than good by their own. Those on the other hand who have taken a contrary course, and asserted that absolutely nothing can be known ... have certainly advanced reasons for it that are not to be despised; but yet they have neither started from true principles nor rested in the just conclusion, zeal and affectation having carried them much too far. The more ancient of the Greeks (whose writings are lost) took up with better judgment a position between these two extremes—between the presumption of pronouncing on everything, and the despair of comprehending anything; and though frequently and bitterly complaining of the difficulty of inquiry and the obscurity of things, and like impatient horses champing at the bit, they did not the less follow up their object and engage with nature, thinking (it seems) that this very question—viz., whether or not anything can be known—was to be settled not by arguing, but by trying. (p. 33)

On one hand, Bacon suggested that his approach could lead to truth. In Aphorism CXXIV of *Novum Organon* he wrote, "I am building in the human understanding a true model of the world, such as it is in fact, not such as a man's own reaction would have it to be; a thing which cannot be done without a very diligent dissection and anatomy of the world" (p. 113). On the other hand, in the same volume, his discussion of idols revealed extensive concern about the difficulties the human mind has in imaging reality. In introducing the idea of idols he argued that humans' understanding was limited by four deeply embedded types of preconception: (1) idols of the tribe (founded in human nature itself and the tribe or race of men); (2) idols of the cave (owing to an individual's peculiar nature); (3) idols of the market (owing to activities of commerce); and (4) idols of the theater (owing to various dogmas of philosophies and perceived rules of demonstrations).

The idols were associated with two sorts of malady. The first was a dogmatic philosophy that stemmed from feelings of shame about doubt and motivated making some tenets into dogma. The second, following Pyrrho, allowed some things to be viewed as probable but despaired of finding the truth. In contrast to these two, Bacon (1620/1960) proposed "the human senses and understanding, weak as they are, are not to be deprived of their authority" (p. 66).

Bacon's influence on science lived on through the Royal Society. A recent publication of the Royal Society (N.D.), *Brief History of the*

Society, noted that the society, founded in 1660, originated in an "invisible college" of natural philosophers who began meeting in the mid-1640s to discuss Bacon's ideas.

Bacon, according to Van Leeuwen (1963), hoped to gain "absolute certainty" (p. 19) through his inductive method. However, his successors appeared less sanguine about the possibilities of absolute certainty. They developed what was "called 'generative skepticism;' they acknowledged that absolute certainty cannot be attained since there is no rational way to overcome the arguments of the skeptics, and proposed instead that one should settle for as much certainty as is possible in spite of such arguments" (p. 12).

Anglican Theologians and Mitigated Skepticism

In addition to Bacon, several Anglican theologians helped shape how founders of the Royal Society dealt with uncertainty. They did so by moving consideration of uncertainty from religious discussions of the Reformation to secular matters. Pioneers in this movement were William Chillingworth and John Tillotson. Two other theologians, John Wilkins and Joseph Glanvill, also played important roles.

William Chillingworth (1602–1644) Many of Chillingworth's ideas about uncertainty evolved from a debate about whether there was any path to salvation outside the Catholic Church. As might be expected, as an Anglican, he argued that the Roman Catholic Church was not the only path. He asserted that while certainty about religious matters was not possible, one can have a modicum of certainty about the doctrines necessary for salvation. Statements, such as tenets of the church, may be true, but a person might not have sufficient evidence to warrant asserting they are true. From here, Chillingworth tried to determine how much certainty was possible (Van Leeuwen, 1963).

He distinguished three degrees of knowing: "1) … absolutely infallible certainty, 2) conditionally infallible certainty, and 3) moral certainty" (Van Leeuwen, p. 22). Absolutely infallible certainty was beyond human reach.

Chillingworth had a long personal intellectual struggle concerning the Roman Catholic Church's claim of infallibility. Eventually he rejected that claim and became an Anglican. In arriving at his rejection of the church's infallibility, he introduced a distinction between metaphysical and moral certainty that came to influence the members of the Royal Society of London as they built the foundation of modern science.

In his unpublished Wharton manuscripts (see Orr, 1967, p. 51), he defined metaphysical certainty as knowing that a thing cannot be otherwise. Humans arrive at it by divine revelation. Moral certainty assures us that a thing is so, but it still leaves some room for doubt. We arrive at it by presumptions and probabilities. Moral certainty allows for the possibility of correction and criticism (Orr, 1967). Without divine revelation, this was as certain as people could be, but for many purposes this probable knowledge was sufficient.

For example, Chillingworth (1727/1952) observed, "A traveler is not always certain of his way" (p. 332) but proceeds without assurance of being on the right path. Similarly, geometricians and carpenters are not infallible, but are sufficiently certain about what they see demonstrated.

As we will see, this approach, which denied the possibility of absolute certainty while simultaneously encouraging people to act, became a significant theme in the minds of members of the Royal Society as they developed the foundation for modern science.

Another Anglican theologian, John Tillotson, expanded Chillingworth's ideas.

John Tillotson (1630–1694) As an Anglican, Tillotson (1728) shared Chillingworth's position that there were paths to salvation outside the Roman Catholic Church. He held that knowledge is comprehension of the nature of a thing. However, some objects may be beyond human comprehension. Consequently, "man's knowledge is limited to apprehension of appearances only" (Van Leeuwen, 1963, p. 34). Without divine aid, infallible certainty is not possible. Tillotson objected to extreme skepticism because of what he saw as its destructive effects on human life (Van Leeuwen, 1963).

Two other Anglican theologians, John Wilkins and Joseph Glanvill, were also instrumental in moving the above approach to certainty from religion into science (Van Leeuwen, 1963).

John Wilkins (1614–1668) Wilkins (1708), the first secretary of the Royal Society, opposed both dogmatism and skepticism. For him, dogmatism entailed overconfidence without adequate consideration of grounds and reasons, while extreme skepticism was absurd and would result in ending religion and life. In this context, he sought to discover what kinds of certainty and evidence there were (Van Leeuwen, 1963). He concluded that with respect to physical matters, the greatest certainty one can have is based on evidence from one's senses. Absolute certain knowledge, however, is available only to God.

Joseph Glanvill (1636–1680) Joseph Glanvill, another early member of the Royal Society, advanced a position similar to Wilkins'. He held that believing that knowledge was absolutely certain was just as detrimental to the advance of science as was extreme Pyrrhonism. Accordingly, he advised treating opinions as hypotheses, viewing them as probably true accounts (Van Leeuwen, 1963, p. 83). In his view, science could be expected to provide only a *probable* account.

These ideas of two early members of the Royal Society illustrate interest in uncertainty and skepticism at the time of the formation of the Royal Society of London.

Glanvill's (1676) theory of science advised considerable caution about conclusions because "some things (real mechanical causes) cannot be known" (Van Leeuwen, 1963, p. 89). On the other hand, often there is enough evidence to justify some belief. "Depending upon the kind and authenticity of the evidence, the degree of belief or certainty is greater or less" (Van Leeuwen, p. 89).

This perspective appeared to guide many members of the Royal Society as they developed the basis for what we now call modern science. At the head of this list was Robert Boyle.

Uncertainty in the Early Royal Society

Robert Boyle (1627–1691) Known today as the father of chemistry, Boyle believed strongly that Christianity was the religion God instituted. Moreover, he also entertained the possibility that what people believed to be scientific truth was false. Further, he did not think it was possible to gain unexceptionable truth about nature. He used scripture to justify this view.

Boyle's acceptance of uncertainty about knowledge of the natural world is best understood by considering how his theological beliefs provided the foundation for his views on natural philosophy (Wojcik, 1997). Wojcik observed that Boyle claimed that "where both theology and natural philosophy are concerned, the proper role of human reason is to ascertain and acknowledge its limits" (p. 101). In this vein, in an essay "A Discourse of Things Above Reason," Boyle (1681/1979) wrote about matters that seemed to him to be above reason. One of them consisted of things

> whose nature is not distinctly and adequately comprehensible by us: to which sort perhaps we may refer all those intellectual beings (if it be granted that there are such) as are by nature of a higher order than human souls, to which sort some of the angels (at least of the good ones) may probably belong; but more than probably we may refer to this head the divine Author of nature and of our souls, *almighty God*.... We may, indeed, know by the consideration of his works, and particularly those parts of them that we ourselves are, both *that he is*, and in a great measure *what he is not*; but to understand thoroughly *what he is* is a task too great for any but his own infinite intellect. And therefore I think we may truly call this immense object, in the newly declared sense, *supra-intellectual*. (p. 211)

Boyle's moderate skepticism called upon people to gain truth by challenging beliefs. He applied the religion-oriented generative skepticism of Wilkins, Glanvill, and Chillingworth to secular matters (Van Leeuwen, 1963). Given that today many people regard Boyle as the pioneer of the experimental method, his place in the history of uncertainty is especially noteworthy. The conclusions of science could never be absolutely certain—only "morally certain."

The Glanvill and Chillingworth approach resembled the approach to uncertainty embedded in the work of Isaac Newton.

Isaac Newton (1642–1727) Newton's position on certainty was consistent with that of other early members of the Royal Society. For example, he disclaimed any understanding of the real nature or cause of gravity (Van Leeuwen, 1963). In his conclusion to the second edition of the *Principia*, Newton (1687/1999) wrote:

> I have not as yet been able to deduce from phenomena the reason for these properties of gravity, and I do not feign hypotheses. For whatever is not deduced from the phenomena must be called a hypothesis; and hypotheses, whether metaphysical or physical, or based on occult qualities, or mechanical, have no place in experimental philosophy. In this experimental philosophy, propositions are deduced from the phenomena and are made general by induction. The impenetrability, mobility, and impetus of bodies, and the laws of motion and the law of gravity have been found by this method. And it is enough that gravity really exists and acts according to the laws that we have set forth and is sufficient to explain all the motions of the heavenly bodies and of our sea. (p. 943)

Newton apparently incorporated ideas of earlier members of the Royal Society such as Wilkins, Glanvill, and Boyle. However, since "he did not formulate his account of certainty with the precision of either Glanvill or Boyle" (Van Leeuwen, 1963, p. 107), his exact views are less clear.

Furthermore, despite the expressed aversion to hypotheses, Newton did make some. For example, Watling (1983) wrote "that same Newton who, true to his notorious words, set down a law of gravitation in his *Principia*, but made no hypotheses as to its origin. In letters, and in other documents published only after his death, he did speculate on the origins of gravitational attraction" (p. 467).

However, it appears that Newton had a major impact in discouraging those who followed him from making hypotheses. Laudan (1981) wrote:

> As numerous authors have shown, the half century following publication of the *Principia* was marked by a growing antipathy to hypotheses and speculations. Induction and analogical reasoning were all the rage and Newton's doctrine of verae causae—adumbrated in dozens of eighteenth-century glosses on his first *regula philosophandi*—was thought to exclude any entity or process not strictly observable.... Speculative systems and hypotheses were otiose; scientific theories had to deal exclusively with entities that could be observed or measured. For half a century, many natural philosophers sought to develop theories satisfying those demanding strictures. (p. 158)[2]

John Locke (1632–1704) The approach to uncertainty of another famous Royal Society member, John Locke (1690/1961), resembled that of earlier members. In *An Essay Concerning Human Understanding,*

Locke stated that the real natures of things are not knowable. He proposed that the strength of belief should be proportional to evidence and that there are levels of probability.

TREATMENT OF UNCERTAINTY FROM THE ORIGINS OF MODERN SCIENCE TO THE PRESENT

After early participants in the Royal Society laid the basis for modern science by adopting a mitigated version of skepticism, matters of uncertainty and skepticism were sometimes dealt with explicitly but often were relegated to the shadows.

Explicit Treatments of Uncertainty and Skepticism in the 18th and 19th Centuries

During this period, serious discussions of skepticism (including its extreme form, Pyrrhonism) continued in Europe. Popkin (2003) wrote, "Pyrrhonism was to remain a specter haunting European philosophy while philosophers struggled to find a way either to overcome complete theoretical doubt, or to discover how to accept it without destroying all human certitude" (p. 173). The *Dictionaire Historique et Critique* by extreme skeptic Pierre Bayle was a very popular work of the eighteenth century (Lennon, 2003). Bayle (1697/1826) wrote:

> There is no great harm in faying, that the Souls of Men are too narrow to difcover any thing in Natural Truths, in the Caufes which produce Heat, Cold, the Flux of the Sea.... It is enough for us to endeavor to find out fome probable Hypothefes, and to make a Collection of Experiments; and I am fure that there are very few good Philofophers in our Age, but are convinced, that Nature is an impenetrable Abyfs, and that its Springs are known to none, but to the Maker and Director of them. So that all thofe Philosophers are in that refpect, *Academicks* and *Pyrrhonifts*. (p. 2619)

Bishop George Berkeley's (1685–1753) writings provided additional evidence of skeptically driven eighteenth-century concerns. For Berkeley, people were mistaken when they believed "that 'behind' the world of sense lies an unsensed material world, of which ideas are copies or resemblances" (Bracken, 1999, p. 446). In Berkeley's (1710/1961) words:

> ... neither our thoughts, nor passions, nor ideas formed by the imagination, exist without the mind, is what everybody will allow. And it seems no less evident that the various sensations or ideas imprinted on the sense, however blended or combined together ... cannot exist otherwise than in a mind perceiving them ... what is said of the absolute existence of unthinking things without any relation to their being perceived, that seems perfectly unintelligible. Their *esse* is *percipi*, nor is it possible they

> should have any existence out of the minds or thinking things which perceive them. (p. 152)

It is this idea that stimulated Samuel Johnson's famous kicking of a stone while saying, "Thus, I refute you Dr. Berkeley," cited so fondly by contemporary challengers of postmodernism, such as Hogan and Sinclair (1996).[3]

Further evidence of skepticism in 18th-century thought can be found in the writings of David Hume.

David Hume (1711–1776) Many consider Hume the culmination of the British empiricist tradition. He did not believe that Pyrrhonism could be refuted by reason, but he advised that this fact did not deter people from acting. In *Enquiry Concerning Human Understanding,* Hume (1748/1961) argued against excessive skepticism because "no durable good can ever result from it" (p. 426). Instead, he turned to mitigated skepticism as a useful antidote to dogmatism. He wrote:

> There is, indeed, a more *mitigated* skepticism or *academical* philosophy, which may be both durable and useful, and which may, in part, be the result of this Pyrrhonism, or *excessive* skepticism, when its undistinguished doubts are, in some measure, corrected by common sense and reflection. (p. 427)

Furthermore, mitigated skepticism could aid people by getting them to recognize their own limitations.

The matter of philosophical uncertainty continued to intrigue British scholars throughout the eighteenth century. Further, following Immanuel Kant's encounter with Hume's ideas and his publication of *Critique of Pure Reason,* the appreciation of Humean skepticism spread in Germany (Beiser, 1999).

Immanuel Kant (1724–1804) In the 1780s and 1790s, Kant's work advanced the cause of skepticism in Germany. Many of Kant's contemporaries viewed him as a Humean skeptic. Central in Kant's treatment of uncertainty was his discussion of the "thing-in-itself."

Kant (1787/1969) distinguished between the thing-in-itself and appearances. He argued that "man is inescapably ignorant, in the sense that he can know only appearances … never things as they are in themselves" (Wilcox, 1982, p. 99).

Friedrich Nietzsche (1844–1900) Kant influenced another German thinker—Friedrich Nietzsche—who also contributed significantly to thinking about uncertainty. One way he did so was by pointing out distortions introduced by what was traditionally called reason. According to Welsch (2008), however, Nietzsche was "not at all critical of reason, but critical of theories of reason. He refutes the well-established logicotheoretical view of reason and replaces it with an instrumental, pragmatic model" (p. 1).

Nietzsche rejected the view that reason "does nothing to things but wants only to organize them" (Welsch, 2008, p. 1). According to Welsch, Nietzsche saw reason as "doing something quite different: it does not simply render things but schematizes them, knocks them into shape, reshapes them as lies.... Nietzsche continually points out the way in which we cover up the singularity and variability of phenomena by means of fictive generality and constancy" (p. 1). Consequently, in *Thus Spake Zarathustra,* Nietzsche (1883–1885/1958) scorned "pure knowers" with their "immaculate perception": "This parable I give you, you delicate hypocrites, you, the 'pure knowers'. *I* call you—lechers!" (p. 111).

Nietzsche (1873/1959) wrote:

> Every word immediately becomes a concept, inasmuch as it is not intended to serve as a reminder of the unique and wholly individualized original experience to which it owes its birth, but must at the same time fit innumerable, more or less similar cases—which means, strictly speaking, never equal—in other words, a lot of unequal cases. Every concept originates through our equating what is unequal. No leaf ever wholly equals another, and the concept "leaf" is formed through an arbitrary abstraction from these individual differences, through forgetting the distinctions; and now it gives rise to the idea that in nature there might be something besides the leaves which would be "leaf"—some kind of original form after which all leaves have been woven, marked, copied, colored, curled, and painted, but by unskilled hands, so that no copy turned out to be a correct, reliable, and faithful image of the original form. (p. 46)

In this section, we discussed issues of certainty that some of the greatest eighteenth- and nineteenth-century scholars were explicitly concerned with. On the other hand, during this period many thinkers left the matter in the shadows.

Uncertainty in the Shadows in the 18th and 19th Centuries

The scientific achievements that followed the founding of the Royal Society and the Newtonian revolution that it spawned were enormous. These achievements changed how most people in the Western world lived and thought. Purrington and Durham (1990) wrote:

> We need but look around us to see the heritage of Newton. The complex web of science and technology which characterizes modern life is thoroughly Newtonian.... To most of us the world is rational, mechanical, predictable. When entirely new phenomena come to light, they are expected to fit easily under the broad reach of the Newtonian paradigm. We speak, of course, of the much-heralded "Newtonian world-view," surely the greatest of Newton's legacies to our time. (p. 1)

The Newtonian view was associated with great advances in engineering and technology. The ability to predict and control that the principles of Newtonian physics offered made it appear that they were a path to certainty. The success of the Newtonian approach in physics led to its adoption as a model for other fields. As Cohen (1980) put it, for more than two centuries the *Principia* "set the standard against which all other science was measured" (p. 16). In physics itself, the success was so great that by the end of the eighteenth century many physicists believed that all the major questions in their field were, or shortly would be, answered. In this context, it was easy to overlook any traces of uncertainty in the philosophy of Newton and his colleagues. Investigators, including social scientists, attempted to follow the Newtonian model, confident that the path would lead to certainty. However, in the 20th century, once again uncertainty emerged from the shadows.

As reemerging concerns about uncertainty helped reshape 20th-century philosophy, these ideas became part of the organization studies controversy about knowledge.

INCREASED ATTENTION TO UNCERTAINTY IN THE 20TH CENTURY

In the 20th century, both physicists and philosophers gave increased attention to uncertainty. Consideration of these two bodies of scholarship helps set the context for understanding the organization studies knowledge controversy.

20th-Century Physics

The prediction that nearly all the major questions in physics would soon be answered proved to be incorrect. In the 20th century, as we will discuss in more detail in Chapter 9, "Letting Go of Misguided Attempts to Emulate Physics," quantum phenomena introduced profound uncertainty. Physicist/philosopher Sir James Jeans (1943/1981) summarized some of the implications:

> Precise knowledge of the outer world becomes impossible for us.... The processes of nature cannot be adequately represented within a framework of space and time.... The division between subject and object is no longer definite or precise; complete precision can only be regained by uniting subject and object into a single whole.... So far as our knowledge is concerned, causality becomes meaningless.... If we still wish to think of the happenings in the phenomenal world as governed by a causal law, we must suppose that these happenings are determined in some substratum of the world which lies beyond the world of phenomena, and so also beyond our access. (p. 145)

Also, as noted, in the 20th century uncertainty became a major issue in philosophy. The writings of Ludwig Wittgenstein in the first half of the century played a major role.

Developments in 20th-Century Philosophy

Ludwig Wittgenstein (1889–1951)

Wittgenstein, widely regarded as one of the greatest philosophers of the 20th century, was a major contributor to the linguistic turn in philosophy. Rorty (1967) described the linguistic turn as a move toward a "view that philosophical problems are problems that may be solved (or dissolved) either by reforming language, or understanding about the language we presently use" (p. 3).

Wittgenstein wrote two major books: *Tractatus Logico-Philosophicus* (1921/1961) and *Philosophical Investigations* (1953/1958). The second book essentially repudiated the first. Hallet (1977) commented that this case, where a thinker at different points in his life produced two highly original systems of thought that greatly influenced philosophy, with the second rejecting the first, was probably unique in the history of philosophy.

In *Tractatus,* Wittgenstein tried to show how propositions can represent real states of affairs in the world. At the time, he was invested in a representational view of language (Phillips, 1977). However, in *Philosophical Investigations* he changed his position. As Phillips (1977) put it:

> Wittgenstein came to question the fundamental assumption of the *Tractatus* that language is a picture of reality, that its function is to represent the world to us.... Wittgenstein rejected his earlier view that language was a logically rigid essence concealed behind everyday discourse, and instead came to accept language as it actually is to be found in social life—serving a variety of human purposes. Rather than asking what the structure of reality was, he argued that one could only analyse the language in which people talked about it. (p. 27)

Language Games In *Philosophical Investigations,* Wittgenstein used the analogy of "language game" to challenge the traditional perspective that "the individual words in the language name objects—sentences are combinations of such names" (Wittgenstein, 1953/1958, p. 2). In that view of language, "every word has a meaning.... It is the object for which the word stands" (p. 2).

In contrast to his earlier view, Wittgenstein (1953/1958) argued that meaning lies in "the way language functions" (p. 3). The language game analogy aided his analysis by directing attention to language operating as a game that, like other games, had rules, players, nonplayers, spectators, referees, and appropriate fields of play (Phillips, 1977). In this view, the meaning of the king in chess is determined by the rules of the game, not by any particular attributes of the piece itself.

After Wittgenstein, the matter of uncertainty reemerged as a challenge to foundationally oriented philosophy. Taylor (1996) labeled this traditional philosophy "epistemology." He used this label to refer to the view that "knowledge is to be seen as correct representation of an independent reality" (p. 466). According to Taylor, Hegel, Heidegger, Merleau-Ponty, and Wittgentstein were the "most important and influential critics of epistemology. These philosophers shared "a common form of argument" (p. 473). Their arguments concerned "the indispensable conditions of there being anything like experience or awareness of the world in the first place" (p. 473). Taylor maintained that the work of these four men showed the epistemological tradition to depend on "an untenable construal of knowledge" (p. 473).

"Plainly, we couldn't have experience of the world at all if we had to start with a swirl of uninterpreted data. Indeed, there wouldn't even be 'data', because even this minimal description depends on our distinguishing what is 'given' by some objective source from what we merely supply ourselves" (p. 476).

For Taylor, the problem with what he called epistemology was that "the crucial move of the epistemological construal, distinguishing states of the subject—our ideas—from features of the external world, can't be effected" (p. 477).

Thinkers who claim philosophy is without a foundation are sometimes called postmodern.[4]

To further consider 20th-century contributions to thinking about uncertainty, we turn to the work of Foucault, Rorty, and Derrida—each of whom was called (in some cases under protest) postmodernist. Their ideas all played a part in the organization studies controversies about knowledge. We encourage you to consider each of the following ideas on its own merits rather than as part of a total package you think of as postmodernism.

Michel Foucault (1926–1984)

For us, Foucault's (1980) major contribution to thinking about uncertainty was his contention that

> each society has its régime of truth, its "general politics" of truth: that is, the types of discourse which it accepts and makes function as true; the mechanisms and instances which enable one to distinguish true and false statements, the means by which each is sanctioned; the techniques and procedures accorded value in the acquisition of truth; the status of those who are charged with saying what counts as true. (p. 131)

In trying to understand the regime of truth of an era, Foucault sought to understand the structure of the underlying system of thought. He treated texts in the manner of an archaeologist. As Gutting (2005) put it:

> Foucault's history ... does not try to *interpret* what we hear and read in order to recover its deeper meaning. It deals with texts but treats them not as documents but, in the manner of an archaeologist, as monuments.... Archaeologists of knowledge, in other words, do not ask what Descartes' *Meditations* mean (that is, what ideas Descartes was trying to express in them). Rather, they use what Descartes—and many other writers ... wrote as clues to the general structure of the system in which they thought and wrote. The interest, to invoke the archaeological analogy once more, is not in the particular object (text) studied but in the overall configuration of the site from which it was excavated. (p. 34)

Foucault saw knowledge and power as closely related. According to Gutting (2005), Foucault "was clearly impressed by and adopted Nietzsche's technique of looking for power behind sciences, religions, and other cognitive authorities that present themselves as grounded in nothing more the force of disinterested evidence and argument" (p. 51).

Foucault was not concerned with generalizations about radical relativism and skepticism. His concern about certainty was primarily with its contribution to oppression. For example, he saw the cognitive authority of some social scientists as leading to inappropriate treatment of groups such as prisoners and people considered to be mentally ill (Gutting, 2005).

To summarize, we think Foucault contributed to thinking about uncertainty through three major insights: (1) the cultural contingency of "truth," (2) the difficulty of seeing truths of one's own culture as contingent rather than absolute, and (3) the connection between truth and power.

Richard Rorty (1931–2007)

Rorty (1979) urged philosophers to let go of the attempt to discover a foundation for their discipline. He maintained that all three of the most important philosophers of the 20th century (Wittgenstein, Heidegger, and Dewey) tried in their early years "to find a new way of making philosophy 'foundational'—a new way of formulating an ultimate context for thought" (p. 5). However:

> Each of the three came to see his earlier effort as self-deceptive, as an attempt to retain a certain conception of philosophy after the notions needed to flesh out that conception (the seventeenth-century notions of knowledge and mind) had been discarded. Each of the three, in his later work, broke free of the Kantian conception of philosophy as foundational, and spent his time warning us against those very temptations to which he himself had once succumbed. (p. 5)

According to Rorty:

> Wittgenstein, Heidegger, and Dewey are in agreement that the notion of knowledge as accurate representation, made possible by special mental processes, and intelligible through a general theory of representation,

> needs to be abandoned. For all three, the notions of "foundations of knowledge" and of philosophy as revolving around the Cartesian attempt to answer the epistemological skeptic are set aside. Further, they set aside the notion of "the mind" common to Descartes, Locke, and Kant—as a special subject of study, located in inner space, containing elements or processes which make knowledge possible.... They set aside epistemology and metaphysics as possible disciplines. (p. 6)

Rorty titled one of his books *Philosophy and the Mirror of Nature* because, for him:

> It is pictures rather than propositions, metaphors rather than statements, which determine most of our philosophical convictions. The picture which holds traditional philosophy captive is that of the mind as a great mirror, containing various representations—some accurate, some not—and capable of being studied by pure, nonempirical methods. Without the notion of the mind as mirror, the notion of knowledge as accuracy of representation would not have suggested itself. (1979, p. 12)

For Rorty, the "so-called ontological categories," the mental and the physical, which we inherited from Descartes,

> are simply the ways of packaging rather heterogenous [*sic*] notions, from rather diverse historical sources, which were convenient for Descartes's [*sic*] own purposes. But his purposes are not ours. Philosophers should not think of his artificial conglomerate as if it were a discovery of something preexistent. (p. 125)

Derrida (1930–2004)

Derrida's introduction of deconstruction was an important contribution to thinking about uncertainty. Ramey (1998) commented that traditionally, philosophers grounded their structures by deriving them from, or reducing them to, basic self-evident principles. Deconstruction, however, challenged this very move by exposing the basis that made that move possible. This practice exposes hidden assumptions that are embedded in a system of thought. Deconstruction, Ramey added, "seeks to make Western philosophy aware of itself as discourse, as textuality, as rhetoric" (p. 4).

In addition, he pointed out that Derrida's view of deconstruction is often misunderstood:

> Deconstruction does not flout the traditional tools and categories of literary criticism; on the contrary, it makes heavy and rigorous use of them. Proponents and opponents alike have construed deconstruction to mean that any interpretation of a work is valid, but this is not Derrida's view. Rather, an interpretation should be a careful reading that accounts for all aspects of a text, whether recognized by the writer or not. (p. 5)

Furthermore, Derrida did not reject the "necessity of rational discourse" (Ramey, p. 2). He carried on a "tradition" found in Hume, Kant,

Nietzsche, and others who recognized the value of rational thought, but were skeptical about philosophy's ability to specify exactly what grounded rational thought, if anything grounded it at all.

We, Nord and Connell, follow that tradition as well. We cannot think of any way to ground reason that does not ultimately use reason to ground itself, a method that does not seem well founded to us. Nevertheless, in spite of that dilemma, we continue to use and value our thought processes.

For Derrida, it was futile to strive for absolute certainty about an author's actual, intended meaning.

Frequently, 20th-century Western scholars were socialized to believe in the certainty of knowledge. Derrida's focus on the uncertainty surrounding an author's intent troubled many of them. For example, E. O. Wilson (1998) wrote:

> Postmodernism is expressed more explicitly still in deconstruction, a technique of literary criticism. Its underlying premise is that each author's meaning is unique to himself; neither his true intention nor anything else connected to objective reality can reliably be determined. That is what Jacques Derrida, the creator of deconstruction, meant.... At least, that is what I think he meant.... Conversely, if that is what he meant, perhaps we are not obliged to consider his arguments further.
>
> This puzzle, which I am inclined to set aside as the "Derrida Paradox" is similar to the Cretan paradox (a cretan says, "all cretans are liars"). It awaits solution, but one should not feel any great sense of urgency in the matter. (p. 58)

Wilson's comments illustrate two points that we tried to make. The first is that there is an implicit assumption in our culture that humans require certainty about knowledge. Because Derrida denied ultimate certainty, Wilson seemed to overlook Derrida's insistence on careful reading and his respect for traditional methods of criticism.

The second point is that there is a tendency in our culture for uncertainty to be hidden in the shadows of some religious or intellectual framework that either provides an apparent certainty about knowledge or is consistent with the view that such certainty is possible. Wilson illustrated this tendency with his implication that an author's true intention *can* "reliably be determined" (p. 10), an implication that is given the lie by the continuing debates among literary scholars about authorial intent.[5] Our concept of SOAR is an attempt to acknowledge ultimate uncertainty about intended meaning while simultaneously getting on with our business of inquiry.

CONCLUSION

In this chapter we showed that, in the West, uncertainty was a major concern for over two millennia. At times, this concern was hidden by various claims to certainty but reemerged episodically from the shadows. The uncertainty introduced by the 20th-century developments in quantum physics and the after philosophy movement, rather than being a historical first, simply marked the most recent reemergence. These 20th-century ideas became central in the organizational studies controversies about knowledge.

Putting uncertainty in its historical context is essential for the rethinking we promote in this book. Among other things, it reveals that many of the founders of modern science believed that scientific discoveries could be based on appearances without assuming people can know the true nature of reality.

We believe that generative uncertainty provides a lens for viewing the content of organization studies as well as the content of other fields of inquiry. The generative component highlights useful cognitive patterns that inquiry produced over centuries. However, at the same time, the uncertainty feature reminds us of an important point: To date, humans do not appear to have a basis for treating these patterns as certain.

ENDNOTES

1. Since *Aquinas* refers to his place of birth rather than his actual name, we follow convention by referring to this theologian as *Thomas*.
2. *Verae causae* means true cause. What exactly Newton meant by the term is not completely clear (http://science.jrank.org/pages/23118/scientific-method.html). Our interpretation is a cause in harmony with other known causes.
3. Please note that when later we quote Hogan and Sinclair about this incident, they referred to the kicking of a lamppost, not a stone.
4. We prefer to avoid the term *postmodern*, when feasible, for four reasons, any one of which would be sufficient by itself to call the term into question:
   a. It gives the mistaken impression that acceptance of uncertainty is a recent development.
   b. It arbitrarily lumps together a number of ideas and encourages their acceptance or rejection as a total package.
   c. It is a highly charged "quicksand" term, meaning different things to different people and as such, often fosters pointless debate rather than fruitful communication.
   d. Two of the most important writers commonly regarded as postmodern, Foucault and Derrida, both rejected that categorization; we like to honor the way people choose to identify themselves.
5. For further study of the "after philosophy movement," we recommend Baynes, Bohman, and McCarthy's (1996) edited volume, *After Philosophy*.

REFERENCES

Armstrong, K. (1993). *A history of God*. New York, NY: Basic Books.

Augustine, Saint, Bishop of Hippo. (1957). *Against the academicians contra academices* (M. P. Garvey, Trans.). Milwaukee, WI: Marquette University Press. (Original work published 386)

Augustine, Saint, Bishop of Hippo. (1995). *Against the academicians the teacher* (P. King, Trans.). Indianapolis, IN: Hackett Publishing. (Original work published 386)

Bacon, F. (1960). *The New Organon and related writings* (F. H. Anderson, Ed.). Indianapolis, IN: Bobbs-Merrill. (Original work published in 1620)

Bayle, P. (1710). *An historical and critical dictionary* (translated into English, with many additions and corrections, made by the author himself, that are not in the French editions; Vol. 4). London, UK: Eighteenth Century Collections. Retrieved from http://galenet.galegroup.com

Baynes, K., Bohman, J., & McCarthy, T. (1996). *After philosophy: End or transformation*. Cambridge, MA: The MIT Press.

Beiser, F. (1999). Early sceptical, religious, and literary responses to Kantian philosophy. In R. H. Popkin (Ed.), *The Columbia history of Western philosophy* (pp. 518–524). New York, NY: Columbia University Press.

Berkeley, G. (1961). A treatise concerning the principles of human knowledge. In *The empiricists* (pp. 135–215). Garden City, NY: Dolphin Books. (Original work published 1710)

Bettenson, H. (Ed.). (1963). *Documents of the Christian church* (2nd ed.). New York, NY: Oxford University Press.

Boyle, R. (1979). A discourse of things above reason, enquiring whether a philosopher should admit there are any such. In M. A. Stewart (Ed.), *Selected philosophical papers of Robert Boyle* (pp. 209–242). New York, NY: Manchester University Press. (Original work published in 1681)

Bracken, H. M. (1999). George Berkeley. In R. H. Popkin (Ed.), *The Columbia history of Western philosophy* (pp. 445–452). New York, NY: Columbia University Press.

Brush, C. B. (Ed.). (1972). *The selected works of Pierre Gassendi*. New York, NY: Johnson Reprint Corporation.

Calás, M. B., & Smircich, L. (1999). Past postmodernism? Reflections and tentative directions. *Academy of Management Review, 24*(4), 649–671.

Chillingworth, W. (1752). *The works of William Chillingworth … containing his book, entitled, The religion of Protestants a safe way to salvation*. Dublin, Ireland: Printed for B. Motte. (Original work published in 1727)

Cicero. (2006). *On academic scepticism* (C. Brittain, Trans.). Indianapolis, IN: Hackett Publishing. (Original work published 45 B.C.)

Cohen, I. B. (1980). *The Newtonian revolution*. Cambridge, UK: Cambridge University Press.

Descartes, R. (1641/1960). *Meditations on first philosophy*. Indianapolis, IN: Bobbs-Merrill.

Dewey, J. (1960). *The quest for certainty*. New York, NY: G.P. Putnam's Sons Capricorn Books. (Original work published 1929)

Erasmus, D. (1958). *The praise of folly* (J. Wilson, Trans.). Ann Arbor, MI: University of Michigan Press. (Original work published 1668)

Foucault, M. (1980). *Power/knowledge: Selected interviews and other wrtings 1972–1977* (C. Gordon, Ed.). New York, NY: Pantheon.

Friedman, H. (2002). Psychological nescience in a postmodern context. *American Psychologist, 57*, 462–463.

Gassendi, P. (1972). *The selected works of Pierre Gassendi* (C. B. Brush, Ed. & Trans.). New York, NY: Johnson Reprint Corporation. (Original works published 1621–1658)

Gergen, K. J. (2001). Psychological science in a postmodern context. *American Psychologist, 56*(10), 803–813.

Glanvill, J. (1676). *Essays on several important subjects in philosophy and religion.* London, UK: J.D. for John Baker at the Three Pidgeons.

Gutting, G. (2005). *Foucault: A very short introduction.* Oxford, UK: Oxford University Press.

Hallet, G. (1977). *A companion to Wittgenstein's "Philosophical Investigations."* Itaca, NY: Cornell University Press.

Hofmann, S. G. (2002). More science, not less. *American Psychologist, 57*, 462.

Hogan, R., & Sinclair, R. (1996). Intellectual, ideological, and political obstacles to the advancement of science. *Journal of Applied Behavioral Science, 32*, 378–389.

Holdstock, T. L. (2002). Postmodern psychology and Africa. *American Psychologist, 57*, 460–461.

Hume, D. (1961). An enquiry concerning human understanding. In *The empiricists* (pp. 307–430). Garden City, NY: Dolphin Books. (Original work published 1748)

Jeans, J. (1981). *Physics and philosophy*. New York, NY: Dover Publications. (Original work published 1943)

Kant, I. (1969). *Critique of pure reason* (J. M. D. Meiklejohn, Trans.). New York, NY: Dutton Publishing. (Original work published 1787)

Kurtz, P. (1992). *The new skepticism: Inquiry and reliable knowledge*. Buffalo, NY: Prometheus Books.

Lennon, T. M. (2003). Pierre Bayle. In E. N. Zalta (Ed.), *Stanford encyclopedia of philosophy*. Stanford, CA: The Metaphysics Research Lab. Retrieved from http://plato.stanford.edu/entries/bayle/

Laudan, L. (1981). The medium and its message: A study of some philosophical controversies about ether. In G. N. Cantor & M. J. S. Hodge (Eds.), *Conceptions of ether studies in the history of ether theories 1740–1900* (pp. 157–185). New York, NY: Cambridge University Press.

Locke, J. (1961). An essay concerning human understanding (abridged). In *The empiricists* (pp. 7–133). Garden City, NY: Dolphin Books. (Original work published 1690)

Long, A. A. (1999). Hellenistic philosophy. In R. H. Popkin (Ed.), *Columbia history of Western philosophy* (pp. 74–91). New York, NY: Columbia University Press.

Mates, B. (1996). *The skeptic way: Sextus Empiricus's outlines of pyrrhonism.* New York, NY: Oxford University Press.

Mersenne, M. (1625). *La Verité des Sciences. Contre les Scetiques ou Pyrrhoniens.* Paris, France: Chez Tovsainct Dv Bray rue Sainct Jacques, aux Epic-Meurs.

Montaigne, M. de (1958). *The complete essays of Montaigne* (D. Frame, Trans.). Stanford, CA: Stanford University Press. (Original work published 1580)
Newton, I. (1999). *The principia: Mathematical principles of natural philosophy* (I. B. Cohen & A. Whitman, Trans.). Berkeley, CA: University of California Press. (Original work published 1687)
Nietzsche, F. W. (1958). *Thus spake Zarathustra* (A. Tille, Trans., M. M. Bozman, Rev.). New York, NY: Dutton. (Original work published 1883–1885)
Nietzsche, F. W. (1959). On truth and lie in an extra-moral sense. In W. Kaufmann (Ed. & Trans.), *The portable Nietzsche* (pp. 42–50). Kingsport, TN: Kingsport Press. (Original work published 1873)
Nigg, W. (1962). *The heretics*. New York, NY: Alfred A. Knopf.
Orr, R. R. (1967). *Reason and authority: The thought of William Chilllingworth*. New York, NY: Oxford University Press.
Palmer, A. (2004). Scepticism and tragedy: Crossing Shakespeare with Descartes. In D. McManus (Ed.), *Wittgenstein and scepticism* (pp. 260–277). London, UK: Routledge.
Phillips, D. L. (1977). *Wittgenstein and scientific knowldege: A sociological perspective*. Totowa, NJ: Rowman and Littlefield.
Popkin, R. H. (1961). *The history of scepticism from Erasmus to Descartes*. New York, NY: Humanities Press.
Popkin, R. H. (1979). *The history of scepticism from Erasmus to Spinoza*. Berkeley, CA: University of California Press.
Popkin, R. H. (1990). Seventeenth-century philosophy. In R. H. Popkin (Ed.), *The Columbia history of Western philosophy* (pp. 329–336). New York, NY: Columbia University Press.
Popkin, R. H. (2003). *The history of scepticism from Savonarola to Bayle*. New York, NY: Oxford University Press.
Popkin, R. H., & Stroll, A. (2002). *Skeptical philosophy for everyone*. New York, NY: Prometheus Books.
Purrington, R. D., & Durham, F. (1990). Newton's legacy. In F. Durham & R. D. Purrington (Eds.), *Some truer method: Reflections on the heritage of Newton* (pp. 1–13). New York, NY: Columbia University Press.
Ramey, B. (1998). *Derrida and deconstruction: An introduction*. Retrieved April 19, 2008, from http://ourworld.compuserve.com/homepages/billramey/derrida.htm
Redman, D. A. (1997). *The rise of political economy as a science: Methodology and the classical economists*. Cambridge, MA: MIT Press.
Reed, M. (2006). Organizational theorizing: A historically contested terrain. In S. R. Clegg, C. Hardy, T. B. Lawrence, & W. R. Nord, *Sage handbook of organization studies* (2nd ed., pp. 20–54). London, UK: Sage Publications.
Rorty, R. (1967). *The linguistic turn*. Chicago, IL: University of Chicago Press.
Rorty, R. (1979). *Philosophy and the mirror of nature*. Princeton, NJ: Princeton University Press.
Royal Society. (N.D.). *Brief history of the society*. Retrieved August 11, 2008, from http://royalsociety.org
Schmitt, C. B. (1972). *Cicero Scepticus: A study of the influence of the academica in the Renaissance*. The Hague: Martinus Nijhoff.

Taylor, C. (1996). Overcoming epistemology. In K. Baynes, J. Bohman, &T. McCarthy (Eds.), *After philosophy: End or transformation?* (pp. 464–488). Cambridge, MA: The MIT Press.

Tillotson, J. (1728). The *works of the Most Reverend Dr. John Tillotson, Late Lord Archbishop of Canterbury: Containing fifty-four sermons and discourses, preached on several occasions, together with the rule of faith* (9th ed.). London, UK: J. Round in Exchange Alley.

Toulmin, S. (1990). *Cosmopolis: The hidden agenda of modernity*. Chicago, IL: University of Chicago Press.

Van Leeuwen, H. G. (1963). *The problem of certainty in English thought 1630–1690*. The Hague, Netherlands: Martinus Nijhoff.

Watling, J. (1983). Review [untitled]. *Mind, New Series, 92*(367), 467–470.

Welsch, W. (2008). Nietzsche on reason—My restored reason. In J. Beaufort & Peter Prechtl (Eds.), *Rationalität Und Prärationalität* (pp. 107–115). Wurzburg, Germany: Königshausen & Neumann. Retrieved August 13, 2008, from http://www2.uni-jena.de/welsch/Papers/nietzscheReas.html

Wilcox, J. T. (1982). *Truth and value in Nietzsche: A study of his metaethics and epistemology*. Washington, DC: University Press of America.

Wilkins, J. (1708). *The mathematical and philosophical works of the Right Reverend John Wilkins, Late Lord Bishop of Chester*. London, UK: For J. Nicholson.

Wilson, E. O. (1998). Back from chaos. *Atlantic Monthly, 281*(3), 41–62.

Wittgenstein, L. (1921/1961). *Tractatus logico-philosophicus* (D. F. Pears & B. F. McGuinness, Trans.). London, UK: Routledge & Kegan Paul.

Wittgenstein, L. (1958). *Philosophical investigations* (3rd ed., G. E. M. Anscombe, Trans.). New York, NY: MacMillan. (Original work published 1953)

Wojcik, J. W. (1997). *Robert Boyle and the limits of reason*. New York: Cambridge University Press.

CHAPTER

4

Neo-Institutional View of Scientism and the Organization Studies Knowledge Controversy

In our culture, information perceived as produced by science is given more credit than information coming from almost any other source. Such privileging of science was central in the organization studies knowledge controversy.

The generative uncertainty perspective encourages study of a number of sociological and social psychological forces that contributed to the privileging of science. Neo-institutional organization theory serves as a useful perspective for treating them. In this chapter, we develop that view and apply it to the hegemony of scientism in our culture.

Anglo-North American social scientists attempted to follow in the footsteps of the natural sciences. As they did, scientism came to dominate North American social science. For many people, for information to be acceptable, it needed to be presented as science. To understand how this scientism became dominant, we draw on neo-institutional theory from contemporary organization theory. This approach reveals how cultural understandings, efforts to gain legitimacy and other resources, and mimetic processes contributed to scientism's dominance in the social sciences.

Please note, while we are critical of scientism, we recognize that many findings of recognized science have enormous benefits. Scientism troubles us because it seems to foster mindless attempts to emulate the natural sciences and to ignore other extra-scientific sources of insight, such as religion or intuition.

MEANING OF SCIENTISM AND ITS ROLE IN ORGANIZATION STUDIES

Scientism, according to Sorrell (1991), refers to "the belief that science, especially natural science, is much the most valuable part of human learning" (p. 1). In North America, scientism entailed strong admiration for the methods of 19th-century physics. It featured such claims as "(1) science is unified; (2) there are no limits to science; (3) science has been enormously successful at prediction, explanation and control; (4) the methods of science confer objectivity on scientific results; and (5) science has been beneficial for human beings" (Sorrell, p. 4).

Evidence of scientism's dominance in the organization literature includes Miner's (2002) observation that organization behavior "uses the scientific method to establish truth" (p. 3). In the same vein, McKelvey (2002) wrote, "The natural sciences are held in high esteem because … their use of external reality serves as the ultimate criterion variable for winnowing out inferior theories and paradigms" (p. 7530). However, it appears that in both the general culture and in social science, scientism frequently functioned more as a background assumption than as an explicit position. The implicit acceptance of scientism has been a dominant part of Anglo-North American culture for over a century.

Why did social scientists stress appearing scientific to the degree they did? Neo-institutional theory helps us to draw together various reasons. Part of the reason for the stress on appearing to be scientific was American culture's European heritage. In addition, the historical record we present in this chapter is consistent with a neo-institutional interpretation of the privileging of science. Specifically, scientism became a part of the social sciences due to influence of norms, the quest for resources, and mimetic isomorphism. Mizrachi and Fein (1999) viewed mimetic isomorphism as a response to uncertainty. "In situations in which a clear course of action is unavailable, organizational leaders may decide that the best response is to mimic a peer that they perceive to be successful" (p. 657). Almost from the beginning, Anglo-North American social scientists perceived it to be advantageous to dress their work in the cloak of science.

We do not mean to imply that social scientists were consciously opportunistic. Though some might have been, others perhaps bought into scientism and expected that some imitation of natural scientists would produce desired results.

It is worth noting that even Miner (2002), who, as we saw earlier, championed science's value for moving organization behavior along the path to truth, noted how institutional forces motivated the turn to science. He observed that in the mid 20th century, following the criticisms from the Gordon and Howell (1959) and Carnegie reports, business schools turned to the social sciences to gain academic respectability. Business schools responded to the reports by turning to basic scientific disciplines such as psychology and sociology. Miner wrote, "The only solution was to import faculty trained in the social science disciplines.... The business schools badly needed this kind of importation" (p. 50).

In the past, for the most part, leading organization scholars seem not to have taken scientism's origins as problematic. Since much of the recent knowledge controversy in organization studies resulted when some organization scholars questioned the hegemonic scientism, understanding its origins is vital for dealing with the controversy.

Long before the mid 20th century, processes featured in what we call the neo-institutional account shaped North American social science. A review of the highlights of neo-institutional organization theory provides a framework to help us understand the path to scientism.

NEO-INSTITUTIONAL ORGANIZATION THEORY

According to Fernandez-Alles and Valle-Cabrera (2006), neo-institutional theory maintains that social units are "rewarded by legitimacy, resources, and survival based on their acceptance of coercive, normative, and mimetic institutional pressures" (p. 503).

A core idea of neo-institutional theory, according to Scott and Meyer (1994), is that "the visible structures and routines that make up organizations are direct reflections and effects of rules and structures built into ... wider environments" (p. 2). At least two sets of interrelated elements in social systems shape these structures and routines. A first set consists of cognitive elements (e.g., widely held beliefs and taken for granted assumptions) that provide a framework for everyday routines. The second set consists of normative elements (e.g., traditional mores and informally sanctioned social obligations, and socialized, codified knowledge and belief systems).

In addition, according to DiMaggio and Powell (1983), institutional theory posits that many structures and routines stem from mimetic or imitative processes; organizations imitate other organizations that are regarded as superior or more successful. Finally, institutional theory overlaps somewhat with "resource dependence" theory. Both theories posit that organizations may use appearances in order to gain resources from their environments. In this chapter, we apply this framework to the enterprise we call organization studies.

The possibility that scientism's hegemony resulted from institutional forces is significant in the context of the current debate about what constitutes knowledge in organization studies. Recognizing this possibility opens the door to the realization that the emphasis on being scientific may stem less from a rationally considered process than we often assume. As Davis, Diekmann, and Tinsley (1994) observed:

> Organizational forms and practices are institutionalized when they are adopted because actors take them for granted, rather than because a rational choice process found them to be the best suited for the technical requirements of the task. (p. 550)

We employ neo-institutional theory to understand how scientism became so influential in Anglo-North American social science.

NEO-INSTITUTIONAL THEORY AND SCIENTISM IN ANGLO-NORTH AMERICAN SOCIAL SCIENCE

Anglo-North American social scientists' emphasis on emulating the natural sciences was part of a complex social process that included many features of neo-institutional organization theory, such as imitation, accessing resources (including funding and social legitimacy), cultural beliefs, and normative pressures.

We consider three questions about the history of scientism stimulated by neo-institutional theory:

1. Did aspects of the larger culture contribute to scientism? If so, how?
2. Was there a relationship between professionalization and the growth of scientism?
3. Did quests for resources (such as social legitimacy) contribute to scientism? If so, how?

Did Aspects of the Larger Culture Contribute to Scientism? If So, How?

Many scholars have observed that widely shared cultural beliefs fostered scientism, including beliefs America inherited from its European intellectual tradition and the belief that social science needed the kind of objectivism often attributed to physics, and commonsense realism.

European Heritage

Bernard and Bernard (1965) observed that when the social sciences began to develop, the United States was still an intellectual colony of the old world. Among the imports from Europe were (1) the quest for certainty, (2) the use of positivism to secularize science, and (3) a liberal democratic tradition from England and France.

Quest for Certainty One European import, what Dewey (1929) called the quest for certainty, was a long-standing ingredient of Western culture (see Chapter 3 on history of certainty/uncertainty).

Positivism American social scientists were also influenced by how Europeans used Auguste Comte's positivism in managing the tension between science and religious beliefs. Following Comte's stress on the basic cleft between theology and science, Europeans transformed science from a handmaiden of religion to a human secular enterprise. Comte and his followers helped to move social scientists in a scientific instead of a theological direction, and to accord science a role in moral and practical affairs.

Liberal Democratic Tradition From Europe Bernard and Bernard (1965) noted the influence a pre-19th-century stream of European thought about improving human welfare had on social science. They concluded that 19th-century social science took its cues primarily from this liberal democratic tradition stressing the individual and the role of reason and natural laws.

Other scholars noted that special American circumstances affected the impact of European ideas in America and contributed to scientism. Ross (1991), for example, pointed out that some European ideas embodied expectations for modernity and for improving society through advancing rational decision making in politics. However, these expectations produced different results in America than they did in Europe. For example, the pre-Civil War national ideology of an American "exceptionalism" (the belief that in contrast to the French Revolution, the American Revolution had been successful) fostered a notion that America occupied a unique place in history. In this view, Europe was different because special events disturbed history. This meant that the laws of nature would determine American, but not European, history. However, when post-Civil War events contradicted this notion, scientism replaced exceptionalism. Ross wrote that the change in thinking represented "a new impulse toward realism" (p. 58). This realism "reinforced the empirical thrust of the commitment to natural knowledge" (p. 59) and motivated social scientists to make greater use of statistics in an effort to discover fundamental laws of nature and history and to try to appear scientific.

In a similar vein, Bannister (1987) postulated that the absence of a sense of institutional destiny in America contributed to a vacuum that science filled. He maintained that in stable societies a sense of institutional destiny "defines rules, mediates meanings, and induces a comfortable feeling that society and shared values are a natural and enduring aspect of the human condition" (p. 232).[1] The lack of a sense of destiny left an opening for the pursuit of what Bannister called objectivism.

Objectivism

Objectivism entailed empiricism, quantification, and value neutrality, all aspects of what is today commonly termed objectivity. (The view that science provides superior knowledge, of course, often came from its claim to being objective.) Bannister wrote that the spirit behind the objectivists' program "had a strong appeal ... because ... whatever its own class or cultural biases, 'science' seemed the only possible standard in an increasingly pluralistic and fragmented America" (p. 238).

Ross (1991) also noted the push for objectivity, although her explanation differed from Bannister's. She stated, "In the American context, social science required the imprint of 'objective' science to build an institutional power base in capitalist society" (p. 404). She observed that by the 1920s, stress on objective quantitative methods had become a central theme of the social sciences. The emphasis given to objective quantitative methods was associated with attachment to commonsense realism.

Commonsense Realism

To 19th-century intellectuals the natural sciences were obvious exemplars for inquiry; research from them enhanced people's ability to manage affairs in the everyday Newtonian world of inclined planes and billiard balls.

Such success fostered a commonsense realism that made it seem unnecessary for students of the natural sciences, such as physics, to worry about philosophical justification for their approach or methods. In reviewing the history of American physics, Keveles (1978) observed that American physicists were more experimental than theoretical. They followed in the tradition of Francis Bacon, who had emphasized empirical knowledge and urged attending to the facts of nature. Interestingly, Keveles commented that perhaps "few American scientists actually read Bacon" (p. 7). We found no evidence to suggest that 19th-century physicists were very philosophically attentive. They appeared to be strong empiricists, highly interested in applications—so much so that in 1883 a leading physicist criticized his discipline for mistaking telegraphs and electric light for science (Keveles, 1978).

In sum, American cultural beliefs of the 1700s and 1800s contributed to an ethos that favored scientism. This ethos influenced the nature of the social sciences that began to develop in the 1800s. We can now turn to our questions about the role of professionalization.

Was There a Relationship Between Professionalization and the Growth of Scientism? If So, What Was It?

Professionalization can be defined as "a process by which an organized occupation, usually but not always by virtue of making a claim to special esoteric competence and to concern for the quality of its work and its benefits to society, obtains the exclusive right to perform a particular kind of work, control training for and access to it, and control the right of determining and evaluating the way the work is performed" (Freidson, 1994, p. 62).

We suggest that what Mizrachi and Fein (1999) termed normative isomorphism (i.e., isomorphism resulting from professionalization) helps to explain how the development of professionalization contributed to scientism. Two processes are involved: (1) members of professions receive similar training, and (2) ideas spread among members of professional associations. As we will see, the latter was especially important in transferring scientism to the social sciences.

There is evidence of a close relationship between professionalization and the growth of scientism in North American social science. Haskell's (2000) monumental study of the American Social Science Association (ASSA) between 1865 and 1909 demonstrated this relationship. Haskell found that in the 19th century investigators of the social world, congruent with neo-institutional ideas about establishing legitimacy by responding to the social conditions of the times, established their authority through professionalization.

Conditions for Professionalization in 19th-Century Social Inquiry

Mid-19th-century men of science, university reformers, and members of the professional class (a group including ministers, lawyers, and physicians) were anxious about authority (Haskell, 2000). Early leaders of ASSA came from these groups. To establish their authority, these leaders sought to build institutional barriers against "the corrosive consequences of unlimited competition in ideas and moral values in an interdependent mass society" (p. 269). One way of doing so was to institutionalize sound opinion, "to insure … that each emerging 'audience' would find its 'proper' guide" (p. 63). ASSA's approach was part of a general social movement to establish authority. "In almost all fields of cultural endeavor, associations that defined standards and goals appeared in the late 19th century" (p. 64). At the time, professionalization was part of a major cultural reform, "a means of establishing authority so securely that the truth and its proponents might win deference even of a mass public" (p. 65).

The quest for authority played a major role in supporting scientism in the 19th century. Haskell (2000) described the process:

> In the field of natural science one sees most clearly the common pattern of professionalizing action that underlies all the diverse manifestations of the movement. In this field there occurred the most successful of all 19th-century professionalizing efforts—efforts to build an institutional framework that would identify individual competence, cultivate it, and confer authority upon individuals who possessed it. Men of science were so successful in this institution-building enterprise that by the end of the century the word "scientific" seemed to epitomize the very essence of well-founded authority. Through either imitation or independent innovation, all who participated in the movement to establish authority worked toward essentially the same institutional apparatus that scientific men began developing in the 1840's.

> The institutional apparatus pioneered by men of science may be designated by the term "community of the competent." The concept was as old as the professions themselves, but it took on a new relevance in the 19th century. In science ... it was applied with most spectacular success. (pp. 65–66)

The practices used to establish a community of the competent in social inquiry shared much with what natural scientists had done to establish their authority earlier in the century. Many of these practices became defining attributes that 20th-century social scientists used to claim they were scientists and thereby legitimize their research. These practices stemmed from a vision of what constituted authoritative opinion in the 19th century (Haskell, 2000).

Envisioning Authoritative Social Inquiry Joseph Henry was a physicist who headed the Smithsonian Institution. In 1846 he explained the need for a community of the competent. Because newspapers of the day reported large amounts of quackery, he argued that a means to discredit charlatans and incompetent practitioners was needed to establish science's authority. Henry advocated developing a "community of the competent." Members of this community would insulate themselves from society and be judged by those who were most competent to judge them. Those most competent would certify and guarantee the soundness of the views of other community members. (It is worth noting that the peer review system serves this function today.)

Later in the century, this approach was developed further by the pragmatic philosopher Charles S. Peirce (1868), who postulated a social basis for achieving certainty. In doing so, Peirce articulated "an elegant epistemological rationale for the whole movement to establish authority" (Haskell, 2000, p. 67).

People began to believe that the judgments of a community of inquiry, as advocated by Peirce, were as close as humans could come to the "truth." Haskell (2000) cited Pierce's assertion that "the opinion which is fated to be ultimately agreed to by all who investigate, is what we mean by the truth and the object represented in this opinion is the real. That is the way I would explain reality" (p. 237). Haskell also observed that the word *scientist* was not coined until the 1840s.

Implementing the Vision of a Community of the Competent An early step in institutionalizing this sort of scientific authority took place in 1840 when geologists formed America's first professional scientific society, the Association of American Geologists.

The Association of American Geologists' meetings attracted such a wide variety of scientists that by its third meeting it became the Association of Geologists and Naturalists. It continued to expand its scope, and by 1847 it became the American Association for the

Advancement of Science (AAAS). Eventually, several of AAAS's founders became leaders in the American Social Science Association (ASSA).

Overlap in leadership between these two organizations provided a channel through which the practices of the earlier natural science-oriented organization flowed into the developing social science-focused organization. Many of those interested in establishing the authority of science played a role in transforming the 19th-century "social thinker" into the "social scientist."

In the meantime, AAAS shaped the character of American science by devising ways to define the boundary between legitimate science and charlatanism. Recruiting the "competent" was one means for doing so. Higher education became the recruiting and training grounds. ASSA served as the institutional focal point of the movement to establish authority in the social sciences. To some degree, the transfer from the natural sciences was played out in the halls of ivy where the rising prestige of science put late 19th-century "defenders of the fixed classical curriculum on the defensive" (Haskell, 2000, p. 73).

A key issue, which affected the efforts of most all the professions at the time to gain authority, centered on establishing "causation." Providing what would be judged as acceptable causal accounts was key for gaining authority. Meanwhile, the criteria for acceptable causal accounts were changing.

Whereas before individual actions and intentions were presumed to be causal, now the causes of behavior were believed to be more complex. This change depended on at least two factors. First, growing acceptance of the ideas of Charles Darwin and Adam Smith shifted attributions of causality from the individual to larger systems; second, people recognized the growing interconnectedness of elements of society. As society was viewed as being more interdependent, acceptance of proximate causes became less tenable. More complex attributions of causality were required. With these changes, what were previously considered to be independent variables came to be viewed as dependent on other variables.

So long as human affairs appeared to be readily explicable there was little need for social science. However, changes in beliefs about causation helped to make room for professional social science. Common sense came to seem inadequate for the task of explanation, and a felt need for professional expertise emerged. At first, the American Social Science Association (ASSA) played a role in meeting this need, but soon it was bypassed by the beginnings of modern social science disciplines.

ASSA was part of the diffuse movement to institutionalize sound opinion that was also found in law, medicine, politics, education, and most fields of cultural endeavor.

Many of the leaders of this movement worked to increase the role of science in higher education. ASSA's leaders worked to establish a community of the competent that resembled that of the natural sciences. In the natural sciences, the community functioned to ensure expert opinion by insulating its members from society. Specifically, judgments by professional peers would guarantee the soundness of the views expressed by the profession's members.

In 1909 ASSA held its last meeting. By then it had served as an effective vehicle for establishing what counted as authoritative opinion. Along the way it operationalized many of the defining characteristics of 20th-century social science.

Operationalizing Components of a Community of the Competent The defining characteristics of being scientific included: (1) being value-free, (2) quantification and use of statistics, (3) peer review and control, and (4) evidence of ties to previous research. Commitments to value-freeness and quantification were evident in ASSA prior to its death. The latter two characteristics became more visible in the publication practices of the 20th-century social sciences.

Value-Freeness A central tenet of much of 20th-century social science was value-freeness. Haskell's (2000) analysis revealed that early on ASSA emphasized this quality. To claim authoritative knowledge, an individual had to be free of idiosyncrasies and maintain a disciplined place in the practitioner community. "No person or point of view could be privileged; all had to submit to the potential tyranny of the competent" (p. 89). The scientific community would employ universalistic criteria in establishing its authority. These criteria would not, in any obvious way, be personal, partisan, or particular.

Quantification and Use of Statistics To ASSA's founders, in the 1860s, gathering even the most basic statistical data about society appeared so difficult that it was easy to believe that "adequate information would, in itself, lead almost automatically to vast social improvement" (Haskell, 2000, p. 102). Ultimately, the commitment to statistics attracted individuals who studied mathematics and the exact sciences, to the social sciences. As they entered the social sciences, quantitative approaches became more central in defining social sciences as scientific.

According to Haskell (2000), establishing authority in the 20th century required additional practices beyond those described above. Among other things, a disciplined community of full-time inquirers was needed. To build such a community, early-20th-century social scientists introduced mechanisms for controlling their members that today many of us take as given. Over time, these practices evolved into the structure of 20th-century social sciences that came to reside in universities.

> Such a community would provide for its perpetuation … by establishing more or less uniform training programs of a highly selective nature. Having no sufficient clientele among private individuals or business corporations, it would have to find a home in government, the church, or

> the university.... It would not leave its members entirely free to select research subjects and methods idiosyncratically, but would forcibly inculcate at the apprenticeship level a division of labor and certain acceptable methodologies. (p. 236)

Peer Reviews The "ruthless policing" of the work of others foreshadowed peer review. As we wrote this book in the early years of the 21st century, we were highly aware of how this practice serves to define the nature of community membership. Admission to and continued participation in social science careers requires publication in peer-reviewed journals (see Starbuck, 2005).

Evidence of Ties to Previous Research Today social scientists take a review of the literature as the starting point for almost all published research. Although we can think of a number of sound intellectual reasons for such a practice, Haskell implied that this norm may well have originated in the quest for a community of the competent.

Returning to our question: Was there a relation between professionalization and the growth of scientism? We believe Haskell's work clearly demonstrates that there was. In the 1800s, natural scientists sought and gained legitimacy through institutional processes. Later in the century, social scientists sought to gain legitimacy by following in these footsteps. This conclusion is consistent with a neo-institutional account of the role of scientism in Anglo-North American social science.

Scientism and professionalization appeared to feed off each other. While Haskell's study provided substantial evidence consistent with a neo-institutional account, please note that his account emphasized somewhat different aspects of institutional theory than the mimetic processes other scholars used to explain scientism. For Haskell more than blind imitation was involved.

We now turn to our third question concerning the neo-institutional account for scientism.

Did Quests for Resources Contribute to Scientism?

Considerable evidence supports the proposition that as American social scientists sought financial support they frequently donned the cloak of science. This garb helped them gain tangible resources and legitimacy.

Gaining Tangible Resources

Early in the 20th century, support from large foundations played a major role in shaping the basic structure of inquiry. Donations from capitalist-funded charitable foundations (including Sage, Carnegie, and Rockefeller) cemented the turn to a scientific, especially quantitative, social science (Ross, 1991).

At least some of the supporters for moving in the "scientific" direction seemed to have had political motives. The Rockefeller Foundation was a major player. Its funding of the Social Science Research Council (SSRC) brought social scientists from various disciplines together in a professional affiliation. Ross (1991) commented that the Rockefellers wanted to combat the opprobrium the Rockefeller fortune was subjected to and, at the same time, avoid radical social change. For these purposes, "the emerging scientific idiom of social science was attractive, promising both distance from political controversy and knowledge that would allow the real control of social change" (p. 400). A major step in the SSRC's championing an emphasis on methods was sponsorship of a volume edited by Stewart Rice (1931/1981), *Methods in Social Science.* Rice asserted that methods in the social sciences had not been sufficiently scientific. At the time, "method" in the social sciences referred to a wide variety of practices.

Rice's volume was conceived as a casebook; it consisted mainly of essays authored by leading social scientists of the time from a variety of fields about work in their specialties. In an appendix, Rice described the book as a product of "an inductive approach to the study of methods in social science" (p. 731).

The book expressed admiration for the methods of the physical sciences and advocated applying them to the social sciences. However, there was vagueness about where the methods of the physical sciences were applicable and where they were not. In addition, defining methods precisely was difficult—"method must be regarded as a term of variable meanings" (p. 7).

Other foundations, such as Carnegie and Russell-Sage, also supported scientism (Ross, 1991). While external funding did not create new procedures, it did "greatly strengthen some things rather than others" (p. 402). Specifically, it supported the scientific orientation of social science and its emphasis on method.

Gaining Legitimacy

Further evidence of how scientism was used to gain resources comes from events in the 1800s and early 1900s showing that social scientists used the appearance of being scientific to gain legitimacy from public and university decision makers. These efforts were of two general types: distancing and attaching.

Distancing used the appearance of being scientific to weaken existing or potential perceptions that a close relationship existed between a particular field and socially undesirable ways of thinking. *Attaching* used the appearance of being scientific to create or strengthen perceptions of similarity between a particular field and some highly respected field such as physics.

Distancing Both political scientists and psychologists employed distancing. Consider political science first.

Distancing in Political Science In the early 1900s, some political scientists feared their discipline would lose creditability if it were perceived as so heavily ideological that it could not speak with one voice. For example, Charles E. Merriam (1921) saw ideological conflict within political science as a problem because it prevented political scientists from speaking with authority. Inability to do so caused political science to lose stature.[2] To distance political science from ideologies, he advocated "a science defined by 'method,' oriented to 'control,' and sustained by organized professional structures to promote research" (Ross, 1991, p. 396).

Distancing in Psychology Psychologists employed scientific appearance to distance themselves from a potential threat to their status. Psychologists perceived being identified with what Coon (1992) called spiritualism (the belief in psychic phenomena and along with belief that one can contact the deceased) and psychic research as a threat to their credibility.

In the mid 1800s, laypeople's tendency to associate psychology with spiritualism threatened psychology's legitimacy. Coon (1992) showed how psychologists of the time turned to positivism to distance psychology from spiritualism. Many psychologists called for gathering evidence about the conditions under which spiritualistic phenomena were observed. They maintained that scientists could do this best, not because scientists were better judges but because "they would be publicly perceived as such" (p. 144).

Sometime in the early 1900s, early industrial/organizational psychologists also turned to science in an effort to gain distance. Zickar and Gibby (2007) wrote, "Applied psychologists' reliance on statistical and scientific methods allowed them to distinguish themselves from the numerous charlatans who offered cheap and easy panaceas for industry's woes" (p. 69).

Such uses of scientism for distancing from unwanted associations are consistent with the neo-institutional account. Even more commonly, psychologists and sociologists attempted to associate themselves with science to gain legitimacy.

Attachment

Attachment in Psychology Psychologists' efforts to gain status for their field by attaching their work to science took several forms. For one thing, their laboratories served as icons. This attachment tactic began with the founding of Wilhelm Wundt's laboratory in 1879 at the University of Leipzig—an event many view as the origin of scientific psychology.

Danziger's[3] (1990) observations about Wundt's laboratory are revealing:

> If one traces the way in which participants in psychological experiments are referred to in the early empirical papers of the Leipzig group, one can detect evidence of a rapid process of institutionalization, which manifests

> itself in two ways. First, the more concrete terms used to refer to experimental participants tend to drop out and to be replaced by more abstract terms. The relatively specific activities that the experimental division of labor had assigned to them—activities like signaling or associating … were soon replaced by labels that refer in a more general way to the function of the participant in psychological investigation. The favored terms that now emerge are "observer", "reactor" (*Reagent*), and "person under experiment" (*Versuchsperson*) on the one hand and "experimenter" on the other. (p. 32)

When American psychologists developed their laboratories, they too used them as symbols to gain stature. Capshew (1992) observed that "the laboratory became a metaphor for scientific psychology itself" (p. 132).

Likewise, Benjamin (2000) noted that early American psychologists pointed to their laboratories to show that they were doing science. Drawing on Popplestone and McPherson (1984), she wrote that psychologists' marketing efforts helped them to gain legitimacy and recruit students. Psychologists pointed to their laboratories as evidence that they were worthy members "in the fraternity of science" (Popplestone and McPherson, 1984, quoted in Benjamin, 2000, p. 321).

Perhaps this early emphasis on the laboratory and the influence of one widely read classic, Boring's *A History of Experimental Psychology* (1929/1950), led psychologists to overemphasize the role of the laboratory and experimental methods in their field. Capshew (1992) wrote:

> The ideology of experimentalism remained strong … and helped to unify an increasingly diverse discipline.… On the undergraduate level, courses in the history of psychology … created a market for textbooks in history (or history and systems) of psychology. Among the most widely adopted texts was *A History of Experimental Psychology* by Edwin Boring (1950). Already considered a classic since its original appearance in 1929, the new edition continued to recount the story of scientific psychology solely from the perspective of the experimental laboratory, practically reifying it in the process. (p. 137)

The emphasis psychologists placed on methods was clearly an attempt to associate themselves with science. The eminent 20th-century psychologist Sigmund Koch (1959) lamented that among new fields of science of the early modern period, "at the time of *its* inception, *psychology was unique in the extent to which its institutionalization preceded its content and its methods preceded problems*" (p. 783).

Robinson (2001) asserted that Koch believed the premium psychologists placed on method harmed psychology because it meant that no matter what aspect of psychology the method was applied to the resulting research was "destined to be simplistic, inauthentic and vapid" (p. 420). Koch (1959) observed that only now (i.e., late 1950s) was psychology "*ready—or almost ready—to assess its goals and instrumentalities with primary reference to its own indigenous problems*" (p. 783). While other sciences had gained their stature by adding to knowledge, psychology had functioned by emulation. Koch continued:

> The history of psychology ... is very much a history of changing views, doctrines, images about *what to emulate in the natural sciences*—especially physics. In the 19th century, this meant the *extension* of experimental method to subjective phenomena; for early behaviorism, it meant the *use* of experimental method exactly as in physics (objectively). By the late 'twenties, there was much objective experimentation but few bodies of clearly stated predictive principles comparable to the crowning achievements of physics: its theories (e.g., Newton's mechanics, relativity theory). Instead, experimentation sometimes seemed aimless, "*theoretical*" hypotheses but loosely related to data, and debate idle. We thus get, beginning around 1930, the emulation of natural science *theoretical* method. (p. 784)

Attachment in Sociology In debating whether or not sociology was a science and whether or not the social sciences could be scientific, like most other social scientists, sociologists held up the natural sciences as the exemplar (Azevedo, 2002). Many of them presumed that if they adhered to the *methods* of the natural sciences, their discipline would also be scientific. Many advanced positivism, because it appeared to provide "certain knowledge of the world" (Azevedo, 2002, p. 717). Pioneering American sociologists such as Herbert Spencer (1873) advocated a Comtean position as a means to make sociology a respectable science (Ross, 1991).

When sociologists tried to gain legitimacy by appearing to be scientific, they often emphasized quantitative methods. They used quantification to pursue external financial support from foundations, government, and business. Turner and Turner (1990) observed that many sociologists believed that members of the Rockefeller Foundation equated "scientific" with "statistical." This belief affected the discipline's internal practices. Proposals made to the foundation emphasized quantification. Journals emphasized quantitative articles. Sociology departments increased emphasis on mathematical sophistication in hiring faculty and training students.

Central in this research were the survey techniques for measuring attitudes that Paul Lazarfeld developed in the 1940s and 1950s. With the help of close personal connections with Frank Stanton of CBS and contacts with advertising executives, Lazarsfeld established the Bureau of Applied Social Research (BASR) to conduct large business-oriented survey projects. The associated emphasis on measurement and quantitative methods led to an increase in the number of people in the field who were skilled in quantitative methods.

Over time, as academic status became contingent upon publication in highly regarded journals, competition for space in these journals intensified. Since many of these journals favored statistical work, positions in graduate schools and on faculties became increasingly dependent on quantitative abilities. Turner and Turner (1990) wrote:

> One … need not adduce any complex intellectual reasons for the rapid increase in the proportion of work of a statistical character in the "best" journals and for the effects of this newly competitive environment on graduate programs. Defendants[4] [*sic*] that sought to maintain their standing in the profession employed young sociologists who could produce these articles, and they argued for changes in graduate requirements that would assure that the graduates of the leading universities would be able to produce articles of this kind. (pp. 172–173)

As the Lazarsfeld approach grew, sociology became increasingly quantitative. The trend gained impetus from advances in sampling techniques that permitted attitude survey research using inexpensive small surveys. Further, the ease of performing significance tests and the feelings of accomplishment associated with finding significant differences that could be replicated induced new confidence that research efforts had indeed achieved results. Turner and Turner (1990) noted that emphasis on measurement and quantification and the "relentless propagandizing for the scientific method and the identification of science with metricization" (p. 125) over time promoted the scientific agenda.

Turner and Turner's (1990) "institutional analysis" suggested that the movement to employ the techniques of natural sciences proceeded with neither any coherently articulated philosophical grounding, nor any convincing evidence of accurate prediction of social phenomena. While some heated discussions about the merits of emulating the natural sciences and about what sociology ought to be did occur, Turner and Turner concluded that the debate lacked philosophical depth. For example, they pointed to Talcott Parsons' assertion that it was fruitless to debate whether the scientific study of social life was possible because it was already in existence. From this Parsons concluded "that fact ends the argument" (1986, p. 110).

Nevertheless, debates continued, and while they did, the view that sociology was a "natural science" prevailed; most of this attachment to science in sociology involved mimetic and resource-seeking activities.

On the other hand, on occasions when resources were contingent on less scientific practices, some sociologists took paths that appeared less scientific. For example, in the 1960s, when financial resources were contingent on student enrollments, some sociology departments taught material that, despite its marginally scientific appearance, was attractive to undergraduate students. Turner and Turner (1990) reported that at this time sociology departments built their enrollments by attracting students from the subpopulation of the "most politically committed students of the era" (p. 138). To some degree, appealing to this audience of socially concerned students conflicted with making sociology a "pure science."

Some noted intellectual leaders created a literature that appealed to these students. Robert Merton (1961) contributed a social problems text. Soon after, in the 1970s and 1980s, major trends that were not highly quantitative emerged and gained stature, in part because they attracted students. For example, symbolic interactionism gained standing partly because it was a basis for some very popular courses. It "was easy to teach and attractive to students" (p. 168).

With this exception, as American sociologists tried to gain resources, they primarily did so by trying to make their discipline appear scientific.

Overview We saw that the quest for legitimacy influenced the shape of social science. In the 19th century the natural sciences had already gained legitimacy, so the social scientists structured their fields in ways that resembled how the natural scientists had structured theirs. We argued that scientism played a major role in this process. We believe that some of scientism's consequences were dysfunctional because scientism meant that features of the inquiry process may have gained their position through somewhat mindless adoption as opposed to informed decisions.

SCIENTISM—THE CURSE THAT KEEPS ON GIVING

Unfortunately, seemingly mindless use of scientific-like practices is continuing in organization studies. We believe it contributed to two currently controversial practices governing inquiry in organization studies. These practices are the heavy emphasis on null-hypothesis significance testing (NHST) and the use of "theory" as a *sine qua non* in evaluating research.

Although both practices may have considerable positive value, recently some scholars' writings have pointed to some important negatives.

Emphasis on Null Hypothesis Testing

Recently, Schwab and Starbuck (2009) became the latest in a long list of critics of the dominant role NHST plays in the social sciences. A much abbreviated list of critics would include Berkson (1942), Bakan (1966), Gigerenzer and Murray (1987), and Danziger (1987). After noting that the use of NHST in management research increased rapidly in the late 20th century, Schwab and Starbuck (2009) reviewed some of the problems associated with using it: (1) Statistical significance can almost always be achieved by increasing sample size (this means that the assessment of scientific findings can depend on the motivation of scientists to roll out more data); (2) NHST can portray effects that are too small to be practically useful as significant and large important effects as not significant; (3) NHST can portray truth as dichotomous and clear-cut; and (4) use of NHST is burying scholarly fields in worthless findings.

Our interest in what Morrison and Henkel (1970) called "the considerable amount of indiscriminate use of significance tests in behavioral research" (p. ix) led us to examine the process through which NHST was adopted by psychologists. How did such a controversial approach become so widely used in the behavioral sciences?

In discussing what they called the inference revolution (1940–1955), Gigerenzer and Murray (1987) noted, "The making of inferential statistics as an indispensable instrument for the psychologist" (p. 19) unified psychology by prescribing a common method in the absence of a common theoretical perspective.

> Prior to 1940, the issue of inductive inference was peripheral both to psychological method and to psychological theory. Between 1940 and 1955, statistical methods were institutionalized in psychology; we have called this the "inference revolution." These methods were in a fact a hybrid of theories that professional statisticians regarded as distinct and even incompatible: Fisher's theory of null hypothesis testing, supplemented by concepts from Neyman and Pearson and sometimes by Bayesian interpretations. Unaware of the controversies within statistics proper, and driven by the hope of mechanizing inductive inference, most psychologists systematically misunderstood and exaggerated the power of these methods. But this did not prevent hybrid statistics from becoming the methodological orthodoxy throughout psychology, governing both the design and publication research. (p. 28)

Gigerenzer and Murray asked how psychologists could have convinced themselves that this statistical theory was the single valid instrument for making inferences from data to hypotheses.

They argued that this conclusion was an illusion. They observed that the illusion was created and sustained by several factors, such as

1. Neglect of controversial issues in statistics (e.g., the intense controversy between Fisher, and Neymen and Pearson, in which Neyman and Pearson pointed to inherent subjective aspects in statistics such as assumptions about the shapes of sampling distributions).
2. Neglect of alternative approaches (e.g., Neyman and Pearson's theory and Bayes's theory).
3. Anonymous presentation of the conflicting components of what became the hybrid theory. (Anonymous presentation deviated from usual scientific practice. One consequence was that readers often did not know who authored the ideas. This step contributed to perceiving the controversy as less intense and fostered the appearance of one true theory.)
4. Institutionalization of the hybrid theory advanced in textbooks through university curricula and the publishing practices of major journals until quality of research came to be judged by level of significance.

5. Confusion. The difficulty of combining the Fisher and Neyman-Pearson approaches resulted in numerous errors in textbook presentations.

Danziger (1987) provided additional support for the role of institutional processes in the history of NHST, by showing the interplay between the institutionalization of analysis of variance (ANOVA) and the special type of knowledge psychologists were pursuing. He argued that psychologists embraced Fisherian analyses rapidly even though they did not understand them fully. A major reason was the kinds of questions they were asking and the particular categories they were using. Noting that only some psychologists adopted Fisherian techniques, Danziger wrote:

> Those who found these statistical techniques congenial formed a subset of psychologists distinguished from other subsets by the way they defined their subject matter and the goals of their activity. Whether the statistical seed fell on stony or on fertile soil depended on the manner in which the soil had been prepared by the work of conceptualization that had already been performed on it. (p. 36)

He explained that for methodological considerations to function as criteria for decisions about production and publication of data, they must have acquired an authority that comes only with institutionalization.

This institutionalization was partially a function of psychologists' preexisting assumptions about the nature of the object they were investigating. These assumptions were closely linked with their goals. One of their chief goals was application of knowledge—often in an administrative context. They intended their research to "provide administrators with a data base from which to make more effective decisions about the programs and individuals under their control" (p. 43). Emphasis on these goals led psychologists to change their focus from individual psychology of the Wundtian tradition to a Galtonian emphasis on establishing qualities of a population. Danziger (1987) wrote, "Analysis of variance and related techniques became popular in psychology because psychological research practice had switched to models that yielded aggregate data of potential usefulness" (p. 45). Over time, the accepted methodology affected the structure of acceptable theories—"it came to be accepted that a scientific psychological theory had to … be capable of generating predictions on the level of group data" (p. 46). Danziger concluded, "There are good grounds for asserting that the adoption of the statistical inference model had theoretical consequences for psychology that far transcend its purely technical significance" (p. 46).

In short, through the institutional lens we see a pattern in which the goals of social scientists to serve particular audiences affected the choice of tools (e.g., statistical procedures), and as these tools became institutionalized in the discipline they influenced the nature of accepted theory. The process involved in this ascendency resembles the pattern of forces that fostered the previously discussed scientism featuring quests for social legitimacy.

An institutional theory account for attraction to statistical tests is supported by observations of leading social scientists, including Bakan (1966) and Meehl (1978).

Bakan (1966) suggested that psychologists' emphasis on significance tests stemmed from their acceptance of a myth that is associated with a general cultural belief, the belief that because something is mathematical, it is precise and valid.

In short, ritualistic use of NHST appears to be, at least in part, a product of institutional and social forces of the sort we saw were associated with scientism. These forces helped lead psychologists to follow what Meehl (1978) described as a "basically unsound, poor scientific strategy, and one of the worst things that ever happened in the history of psychology" (p. 817).

A second core practice that recently has become controversial may also be a function of scientism. We refer here to the practice by leading journals to require that for a manuscript to be published, it must evidence a contribution to theory.

Use of Theory as Sine Qua Non *in Evaluating Research*

We are not arguing against theory. Rather, we are interested in examining the process through which a major feature of contemporary practice gained its standing without agreement on what it is (see Sutton & Staw, 1995; Weick, 1995) and without firm evidence that it advances our understanding and with only limited consideration of possible dysfunctional effects.

It is well known that editorial policies of many of the leading organizational journals demand that to be published, a manuscript must evidence a contribution to theory. For example, the information for contributors statement of the 2007 *Academy of Management Journal* contained the following information: "All articles published in the *Academy of Management Journal* must also make **strong theoretical contributions.** Meaningful new implications or insights for theory must be present in all *AMJ* articles" (p. 1267).

Although, like most of our colleagues, we value good theory and appreciate contributions to it, some scholars have raised some important issues about the scientism the idolization of theory entails.

Bourgeois (1979) commented on the history of the use of theory in the administrative sciences, pointing to a direct link of the high value social scientists place on theory and their esteem for the physical sciences. He suggested that social scientists for a long time had sought to develop theories similar to those of Newtonian physicists. However, "behavioral theory is too immature for such attempts to succeed" (p.

443). Despite this predicament, Bourgeois advised social scientists to continue the quest but for the time being to do so with the limited aspirations of developing middle-range theories. Since then, others advanced the idea that social scientists' attraction to theory may be, at least in part, due to its legitimizing value in a context where being perceived as scientific yields prestige.

In pointing to possible problems associated with what he termed idolization of theory, Hambrick (2007), in his paper "The Field of Management's Devotion to Theory: Too Much of a Good Thing?" observed, "Management's idolization of theory began, harmlessly enough, as an outgrowth of the field's efforts to demonstrate academic worthiness" (p. 1347).

Hambrick argued persuasively that while theory is often useful our field's preoccupation with it may lead us to exclude some interesting and valuable research. He strengthened his case by discussing Miller's (2007) thought-provoking paper. Miller proposed that if the scientist who discovered penicillin had been constrained by the norms about the use of theory that control organization science, his results might not have been published. Hambrick wrote, "If the epidemiologist's paper went to a journal like one of ours, it would be rejected. No matter how important the topic or persuasive the analysis, the message would be: Go away and don't come back until you have a theory" (2007, p. 1348).

Given our attraction to diverse approaches to inquiry, we believe Hambrick's concern is justified and see it as another useful illustration of scientism's continuing impact on organization studies. The dysfunctions Hambrick noted give us further concern about the potential costs to our discipline of the mindlessness that scientism might entail.

CONCLUSION

In this chapter, we presented evidence that ideas from the general culture, the process of professionalization in the social sciences, and social scientists' pursuit of resources all played significant roles in promoting scientism in North American social science. We believe this evidence supports the view that principles from neo-institutional theory provide a meaningful account for the hegemony of scientism in social science.

It is also noteworthy that in reviewing of the history of scientism in North American social science, we did not find any evidence of a carefully thought-out intellectual foundation for scientism.

Two 20th-century developments highlight the absence of foundation. First, in the mid 20th century a new field, philosophy of science, emerged (Turner, 2006) and raised questions about the ability of science to reveal absolute truth. Second, European organization scholars whose work was less governed by scientism than their North American colleagues' became more influential. Together, these two factors set the stage for debates about knowledge in organization studies. The debate was often misguided because few seemed to acknowledge the role of institutional processes in shaping the status quo. The debates were intense because traditional social scientists seemed threatened with a loss of their standing and identity and because challengers of the status quo experienced the chance of a lifetime to promote their agendas.

The above consideration of the origins of scientism in social science contributed to our rethinking of the controversy about knowledge and the process of inquiry in the social sciences that we discuss in the following chapters.

ENDNOTES

1. Note the congruence of Bannister's list with Scott's (1994) ideas about the essential elements of institutional theory.
2. Merriam's (1921) concern about political science resembles Pfeffer's (1997) concern that organization studies does not speak with one voice.
3. We thank Stephen Turner for introducing us to Danziger's work.
4. We assume the word should be *departments*.

REFERENCES

Azevedo, J. (2002). Updating organizational epistemology. In J. A. C. Baum (Ed.), *Companion to organizations* (pp. 715–732). Oxford, UK: Blackwell Publishers.

Bakan, D. (1966). The test of significance in psychological research. *Psychological Bulletin, 66*, 423–437.

Bannister, R. C. (1987). *Sociology and scientism: The American quest for objectivity, 1880–1940*. Chapel Hill, NC:University of North Carolina Press.

Benjamin, L. T., Jr. (2000). The psychology laboratory at the turn of the 20th century. *American Psychologist, 55*(3), 318–321.

Berkson, J. (1942). Tests of significance considered as evidence. *Journal of the American Statistical Association, 37*, 325–335.

Bernard, L. L., & Bernard, J. (1965). *Origins of American sociology: The social science movement in the United States*. New York, NY: Russell & Russell.

Boring, E. G. (1950). *A history of experimental psychology*. New York, NY: Appleton-Century-Crofts. (Original work published 1929)

Bourgeois, L. J., III. (1979). Toward a method of middle-range theorizing. *Academy of Management Review, 4*, 443–447.

Capshew, J. H. (1992). Psychologists on site: A reconnaissance of the historiography of the laboratory. *American Psychologist, 47*(2), 132–142.

Coon, D. J. (1992). Testing the limits of sense and science: American experimental psychologists combat spiritualism, 1880–1920. *American Psychologist, 47*(2), 143–151.

Danziger, K. (1987). Research practice in American psychology. In L. Kruger, G. Gigerenzer, & J. S. Morgan (Eds.), *The problematic revolution: Ideas in the social sciences* (Vol. 2, pp. 35–47). Cambridge, MA: MIT Press.

Danziger, K. (1990). *Constructing the subject historical origins of psychological research*. New York, NY: Cambridge University Press.
Davis, G. F., Diekmann, K. A., & Tinsley, C. H. (1994). The decline and fall of the conglomerate firm in the 1980s: The deinstitutionalization of organizational form. *American Sociological Review, 59*, 547–570.
Dewey, J. (1929). *The quest for certainty*. New York, NY: G.P. Putnam's Sons.
DiMaggio, P. J., & Powell, W. W. (1983). Institutional isomorphism. *American Sociological Review, 48*(2), 147–160.
Fernandez-Alles, M. de la luz, & Valle-Cabrera, R. (2006). Reconciling institutional theory with organizational theories: How neoinstitutionalism resolves five paradoxes. *Journal of Organizational Change Management, 19*(4), 503–517.
Freidson, E. (1994). *Professionalism reborn: Theory, prophecy, and policy*. Chicago, IL: University of Chicago Press.
Gigerenzer, G., & Murray, D. J. (1987). *Cognition as intuitive statistics*. Hillsdale, NJ: Lawrence Erlbaum.
Gordon, R. A., & Howell, J. E. (1959). *Higher education for business*. New York, NY: Columbia University Press.
Hambrick, D. C. (2007). The field of management's devotion to theory: Too much of a good thing? *Academy of Management Journal, 50*(6), 1346–1352.
Haskell, T. L. (2000). *The emergence of professional social science*. Baltimore, MD: Johns Hopkins University Press.
Keveles, D. J. (1978). *The physicists*. New York, NY: Knopf.
Koch, S. (Ed.). (1959). *Psychology: A study of science, study I. Conceptual and systematic. Formulations of the person and the social context* (Vol. 3, pp. 729–788). New York, NY: McGraw-Hill.
McKelvey, B. (2002). Model-centered organization science epistemology. In J. Baum (Ed.), *Companion to organizations* (pp. 752–780). Oxford, UK: Blackwell Publishers.
Meehl, P. E. (1978). Theoretical risks and tabular asterisks: Sir Karl, Sir Ronald, and the slow progress of soft psychology. *Journal of Consulting and Clinical Psychology, 46*(4), 806–834.
Merriam, C. E. (1921). The present state of the study of politics. *American Political Science Review, 15*(2), 173–185..
Merton, R. K. (1961). *Contemporary social problems*. New York, NY: Harcourt, Brace & World.
Miller, D. (2007). Paradigm prison, or praises of alternative research. *Strategic Organizations, 5*, 177–184.
Miner, J. B. (2002). *Organizational behavior: Foundations, theories, and analyses*. New York, NY: Oxford University Press.
Mizrachi, M. S., & Fein, L. C. (1999). The social construction of organizational knowledge: A study of the uses of coercive, mimetic and normative isomorphism. *Administrative Science Quarterly, 44*, 653–683.
Morrison, D. F., & Henkel, R. E. (Eds.). (1970). *The significance test controversy: A reader*. Chicago, IL: Aldine Publishing.
Parsons, T. (1986). Social science: A basic national resource. In S. Z Klausner & V. M. Lidz (Eds.), *The nationalization of the social sciences* (pp. 41–112). Philadelphia, PA: University of Pennsylvania Press.
Peirce, C. S. (1868). Questions concerning faculties claimed for man. *Journal of Speculative Philosophy, 2*, 103–114.

Pfeffer, J. (1997). *New directions for organization theory*. New York, NY: Oxford University Press.

Popplestone, J. A., & McPherson, M. W. (1984). Pioneer psychology laboratories in clinical settings. In J. Brozek (Ed.), *Explorations in the history of psychology in the United States* (pp. 196–272). Lewisburg, PA: Bucknell University Press.

Rice, S. A. (Ed.). (1981). *Methods in social science: A case book*. Chicago, IL: University of Chicago Press. (Original work published 1931)

Robinson, D. N. (2001) Sigmund Koch—Philosophically speaking. *American Psychologist, 56*(5), 420–424.

Ross, D. (1991). *The origins of American social science*. New York, NY: Cambridge University Press.

Schwab, A., & Starbuck, W. H. (2009). Null-hypothesis significance tests in behavioral and management research: We can do better. *Research Methodology in Strategy and Management, 5*, 29–54.

Scott, W. R. (1994). Institutional analysis variance and process theory apparatus. In W. R. Scott & J. W. Meyer (Eds.), *Institutional environments and organizations: Structural complexity and individualism* (pp. 81–99). Thousand Oaks, CA: Sage.

Scott, W. R., & Meyer, J. W. (1994). *Institutional environments and organizations: Structural complexity and individualism*. Thousand Oaks, CA: Sage.

Sorell, T. (1991). *Scientism: Philosophy and the infatuation with science*. New York, NY: Routledge.

Spencer, H. (1873). *The study of sociology*. New York, NY: Appleton.

Starbuck, W. H. (2005). How much better are the most prestigious journals? *Organization Science, 16*, 180–200.

Sutton, R. I., & Staw, B. M. (1995). What theory is *not*. *Administrative Science Quarterly, 40*, 371–384.

Turner, S. P. (2006). The philosophy of the social sciences in organization studies. In S. R. Clegg, C. Hardy, T. B. Lawrence, & W. R. Nord (Eds.), *The sage handbook of organization studies* (2nd ed., pp. 409–424). Thousand Oaks, CA: Sage Publications.

Turner, S. P., & Turner, J. H. (1990). *The impossible science: An institutional analysis of American sociology*. Newbury Park, CA: Sage Publications.

Weick, K. E. (1995). What theory is *not*, theorizing is. *Administrative Science Quarterly, 40*, 385–390.

Zickar, M. J., and Gibby, R. E. (2007). Four persistent themes throughout the history of I-O psychology in the United States. In L. L. Koppes (Ed.), *Historical perspectives in industrial and organizational psychology* (pp. 61–80). Mahwah, NJ: Lawrence Erlbaum Associates.

CHAPTER

5

Origins of the Knowledge Controversy in the History of Organization Studies

Before you read this chapter, it is important for you to be aware of its narrow objectives. It is not intended to be a complete history of organization studies. This chapter covers only one segment of the history of organization studies—the portion most directly related to emergence of the controversy on the subject of what constitutes knowledge. It reflects our experiences from our location as late-20th-century applied social scientists in Anglo-North America. We were socialized to be social scientists whose work was to do what Kuhn (1970) called normal science. Given this background, we found the critique of normal science by some late-20th-century European organization scholars informative.

It was this challenge to what we and most of our colleagues were doing that became what we experienced as the knowledge controversy. The controversy seemed to be rooted in a portion of European organization scholarship known as organization studies. In this chapter, we try to capture the key aspects of this development.

With Nord, Lawrence, Hardy, and Clegg (2006) we view organization studies as including two major streams of inquiry. One is what many now call organization science. This stream features inquiry that was conducted primarily in the 20th century in Anglo-North America under such headings as organization behavior and organization theory. Much of this inquiry took place in the context of the scientism we discussed in Chapter 4.

What we call organization science features scholarship dealing with topics that have a long history in North American applied social science, such as organization behavior, organization theory, and strategic management. Typically, inquirers likely to include themselves under this heading aspire to do science in the sense described by Miner (2002). They emphasize precise definitions, objective data collection, reliable findings, and systematic and cumulative research. They seek to understand, predict, and control.

Organization studies also includes what Nord, Lawrence, Hardy, and Clegg called "contra" science. As we will show in this chapter, the contra science theme came to the fore in the mid 1900s, largely as a result of European scholarship. The contra science theme gained standing with the founding of the journal *Organization Studies* and publication of Burrell and Morgan's (1979) *Sociological Paradigms and Organisational Analysis*.

The controversy we address in this book emerged when the contra science theme confronted the emphasis on science in organization science. Some of this confrontation was manifested in Europe in the so-called paradigm war. It grew in North America as North American scholars became familiar with the contra science theme from Europe.

To understand the origins of the knowledge controversy, it is useful to explore, at least briefly, the history of organization science and organization studies.

The subject matter of what we call organization studies is illustrated by the contents of the journal *Organization Studies* and the editions of the *Handbook of Organization Studies* (Clegg, Hardy, & Nord, 1996; Clegg, Hardy, Lawrence, & Nord, 2006).

The journal *Organization Studies* was founded in Europe to publish scholarly work to promote understanding of organizations while simultaneously challenging the scientism featured in Anglo-North American organization science. By laying down this gauntlet, the journal established itself as a primary outlet for scholars interested in philosophical and value-based aspects of the study of organizations. Many battles of the paradigm war were fought in its pages.

Following the above course, the journal became a combination of somewhat traditional organization science and a platform for questioning scientism.

Similarly, both editions of the *Handbook of Organization Studies* combined treatment of topics popular in organization science, such as leadership, decision making, and culture, with questioning of the scientism of mid- and late-20th-century social inquiry.

The knowledge controversy in organization studies flared up as two different views of inquiry and knowledge about organizations came to coexist in the late 1900s.

HISTORICAL OVERVIEW OF ORGANIZATION STUDIES

As noted, "organization studies" is a relatively new label that refers to an eclectic body of contemporary social science scholarship. This

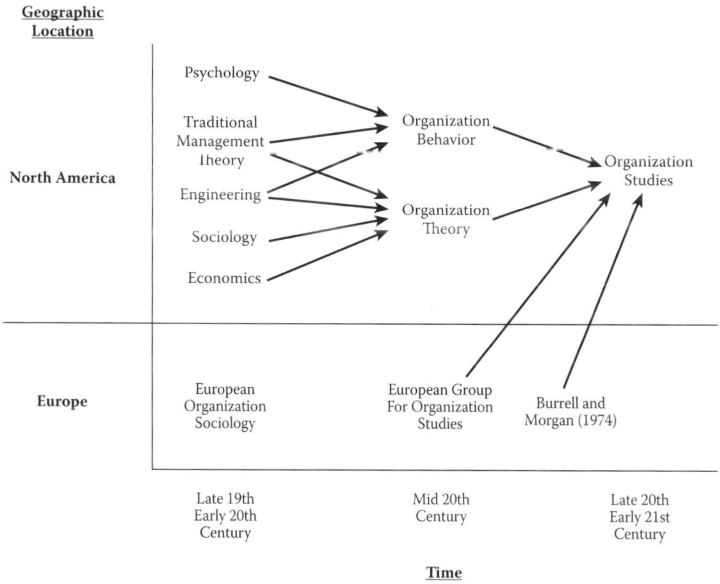

Figure 5.1 Sketch of history of organization studies.

body descended from several sources. Major components stemmed from the scholarship that produced organization science, such as the Anglo-North American social sciences. The term itself and much of the field's contents flowed from late-20th-century European organizational scholarship.

Figure 5.1 provides a rough sketch of the development of organization studies. It partitions organization studies' history into two very general quasi-independent paths. The path in the upper portion of the figure portrays the developments in English-speaking North America during the 20th century when organization behavior and organization theory evolved. This part of the figure describes much of the history of what we are calling organization science. The lower portion shows the flow from European sociology to European organization studies.[1] The figure shows how, over time, the two paths merged to produce what we call organization studies. In this perspective, organization science is part of organization studies.

Although some might argue that Figure 5.1 overstates the independence of North American and European organization scholarship prior to the late 20th century, we believe it does not. There is good reason to believe that throughout most of the 20th century North American organization scholars paid little attention to the work of their European counterparts (with a few exceptions, such as the Aston studies, which were published in the North American journal *Administrative Science Quarterly*, and Marx, Weber, and Crozier's work).

This separation has been widely acknowledged. Palmer (2006), for instance, observed, "Organizational scholarship was more developed in North America than elsewhere and while organization scholars in other parts of the world frequently cited their colleagues in North America, the reverse did not often happen" (p. 54). Similarly, Hickson (1996) noted that in the part of the world where the study of organizations is most developed, "in North America and European Union, the interchange between the two seems uncomfortably more one-way from the former to the latter than it ought to be" (p. 227). Consequently, we feel justified in treating the history of organization science (the upper portion of Figure 5.1) independently of the study of organizations in 20th-century Europe.

Considering the origins of organization science from a North American perspective reveals that organization science evolved rather directly from the applied social science fields of organization behavior and organization theory, which developed in the middle of the 20th century from several Anglo-North American social sciences.

Origins of Organization Theory

People studied how to organize for many centuries. Starbuck (2003) observed that texts about managerial practices existed as early as 2000–3000 B.C. However, contemporary organization theory, with its roots in management theory and engineering, originated primarily in the last half of the 19th and first half of the 20th centuries. According to Starbuck, key moves in developing organization theory included looking at single organizations as integrated systems, recognizing that many organizations resembled each other, and considering interactions among groups of organizations. We limit our discussion to a few elements of this shift in the United States after 1850. (For more comprehensive treatments, we recommend Starbuck, 2003; Shenhav, 2003; and Massie, 1965).

People from diverse backgrounds contributed to organization theory's development: (1) executives and administrators who reported on their organizational experiences (see Massie, 1965, for an excellent summary); (2) the scientific management movement (mainly engineers); (3) sociologists; (4) industrial and social psychologists; (5) political scientists; and (6) economists. In addition to the heavy influence of social science disciplines on organization theory's development, at least one non-social science field was very important.

Shenhav (2003) located the roots of American management theory in mechanical engineering. He noted how the engineering perspective lent support to the view of the natural universe "as a system of clockwork that follows timeless and immutable laws" (p. 160). In adopting this view, people considered social systems and societies as machine-like entities. From the 1860s to the 1960s this view "dominated organization-theoretic writings" (p. 161). Organization theory arose from these ideas. Organization theory's engineering inheritance promoted features of scientism such as application of quantitative techniques, the doctrine of "value-freeness," and using the natural sciences as models. It also led people to focus on the efficiency aspects of bureaucracy.

The strength of engineering's influence in the history of organization theory was quite apparent in James Thompson's (1956/1957) essay in the inaugural issue of the *Administrative Science Quarterly*. He wrote, "An administrative science will be an applied science, standing approximately in relation to the basic science as *engineering stands with respect to the physical sciences*" (p. 103, italics added).

The engineering perspective also influenced the other cornerstone of 20th-century American studies of organization: organization behavior.

Origins of Organization Behavior

What came to be known as organization behavior incorporated information from industrial engineering (scientific management), early I/O psychology, the Western Electric studies, and the work of Kurt Lewin. Early in the 20th century the mechanistic/engineering orientation strongly influenced psychologists' research on organizations. Baritz (1960) wrote, "Scientific management not only conditioned the industrial climate for psychologists; it determined to a large degree the direction, scope, and nature of psychological research" (p. 31). In particular, it led such early I/O psychologists as Hugo Munsterberg, whose work shaped industrial psychology for the coming decades, to focus on employee selection. The associated emphasis on measurement was consistent with the engineering perspective and meshed well with the stress on quantification that the spirit of scientism promoted.

The engineering ethos influenced organization behavior in other ways. For example, it helped to stimulate the most significant studies in the history of American applied social science, the research at Western Electric's Hawthorne plant in the 1920s. Perhaps the most notable outcome of these studies came from a serendipitous result—recognition of the role of social factors in the workplace.

The engineering framework that guided these studies directed the choice of the initial independent variables (e.g., effects of illumination, pay, and rest pauses) and of the dependent variable, output. However, the serendipitous finding spawned interest in topics including group norms and supervision, worker motivation, and related behavioral matters that eventually became the core of organization behavior.

Environmental Pressures Contributing to Scientism in Organization Behavior

At first blush, this shift from the initial engineering variables to a concern with social factors seems to represent a move away from scientism. However, the ultimate effects with respect to scientism were mixed. On the one hand, Landsberger (1958) observed that the Hawthorne studies opened the door for qualitative research, such as William Foote

Whyte's, which appeared to run counter to scientism. But, on the other hand, the interest in leadership that the Hawthorne studies generated also led to quantitative research on leadership.

Finally, the interest in workgroup behavior provided a path along which Kurt Lewin's social psychological studies entered the organizational arena. The ultimate relation of Lewin's work to scientism was also mixed. His experimental studies were consistent with scientism. On the other hand, some of his nonexperimental work stimulated approaches that many might see as running counter to scientism, for example, sensitivity training and action research.

Soon, study of the individual, research on groups and leadership, and study of motivation became the core of what was labeled organization behavior. The new field featured sharply contrasting methodological approaches that varied substantially in their ties to scientism.

Here we need to highlight an important environmental pressure. Until the mid 1900s, organization behavior did not exist. Also, the social sciences that became part of organization behavior's core were not emphasized in business schools. However, in the early 1960s, events combined to induce business schools to give greater attention to social science. This move set the stage for organization behavior's ascendance.

The growth of social science in business schools, as we noted in Chapter 4, stemmed in large measure from pressures to appear more scientific.

In the early 1960s, the 1959 Gordon-Howell report and a parallel report of the Carnegie Foundation pressured business schools to raise their standards. In response, many schools turned to the social sciences to make their curricula and research appear more creditable. Many of them hired faculty with social science PhDs to teach such courses as "human resource management" and "human relations." As the new faculty introduced more behavioral content into the existing courses, a new label, "organizational behavior," emerged that reflected the change.

Since many of the newly hired faculty members received their doctorates from North American psychology departments, they brought with them the scientism of American psychology as well as the ability to publish research in major "scientific" journals, such as *Journal of Applied Psychology*.

Miner (2002) reported that following the turn to the social sciences, business schools gained prestige in their university surroundings. Thus, although Miner (2002) noted there were doubters, once upon a time organization behavior lived reasonably happily in its business school home. But, it did not do so ever after. Soon, developments in Europe challenged its scientism. The lower portion of Figure 5.1 reviews the development of organization studies in Europe.

Contemporary European Organization Studies

Prior to 1973 European organizational sociology was highly diffuse (Lammers, 1998). Organization scholars from various European countries were not familiar with each other's work. However, this began to change in the early 1970s. Eventually these changes produced the European Group for Organization Studies (EGOS).

Development of EGOS

In 1973, informal meetings that produced some coherence and that eventually led to the founding of EGOS occurred. The informality at the early stages makes it difficult to capture exactly what happened. As Lammers (1998) put it, "Formalization of the functions was abhorred in those days" (p. 886). Furthermore, the whole was "kept together by no more than common goals and norms embedded in a certain esprit de corps" (p. 886). Lammers (1998) observed that members of an EGOS colloquium committee prepared general EGOS conferences. Further, autonomous working groups and various "national contacts" kept things alive throughout Europe. The conferences featured impromptu meetings and ad hoc sessions. Lammers (1998) reported that over time the organization became more formalized. Eventually, a contemporary EGOS emerged. In March 2008 its Web page described it as "a scholarly association which aims to further the theoretical and/or empirical advancement of knowledge about organizations, organizing and the contexts in which organizations operate." The Web page reported that on July 31, 2007, EGOS had 1,450 members.

The most visible evidence of EGOS's development was its 1980 founding of the *Journal of Organization Studies* (discussed above). In the journal's first issue its founders, Hickson et al. (1980), described *Organization Studies* as "a supranational forum for ideas in the understanding of organizations" (p. 1). Further, the journal "would be flexible in content and style, open to a diversity of paradigms, and to any and all of the disciplines which contribute to organization theory" (p. 2). Palmer (2006) observed that an implicit motive of Hickson and his colleagues in founding the journal was to correct for the biases of hegemonic American scholarship. At about the same time, Burrell and Morgan's (1979) book played a similar role.

Burrell and Morgan

Burrell and Morgan's (1979) *Sociological Paradigms and Organisational Analysis* helped to provoke the knowledge controversy in Europe, often known as the paradigm war. Further, it served as a conduit that introduced many North American organization scholars to the European challenges to scientism.

In so doing, it played a major role in the rapprochement of European and North American organization scholarship.

At the heart of the paradigm war were disagreements between defenders of the orthodox faith in functionalism and normal science and supporters of alternative contra science views. The latter challenged the possibility of developing the type of "grand narratives" that normal science appeared to promise (Clegg & Hardy, 2006).

Although Burrell and Morgan's book played a central role, it was not alone in fueling the war. Silverman's (1971) *The Theory of Organizations: A Sociological Framework* also stimulated critical discussion of the functionalist view that dominated organizational sociology at the time.

In the paradigm war, scholars such as Lex Donaldson (1996) argued for positivist organization theory against the likes of Burrell and Morgan (1979) and Silverman (1971). Combatants drew on diverse sources for ammunition. Donaldson relied heavily on North American theorists such as Blau (1970), Lawrence and Lorsch (1967), and Thompson (1967). Some on the other side drew heavily on French scholars, including Foucault and Derrida.

As European organization sociology became more prominent, it provided a provocative counterpoint to the hegemonic scientism of North American organizational science.

Blending North American and European Perspectives Into Organization Studies

The developmental process portrayed in Figure 5.1 reflects that while the term *organization studies* originated in Europe, currently it refers to an international enterprise that includes the North American-grown organization science disciplines of organization behavior and organization theory. In our view, organization studies is a blending of late-20th-century European and North American study of organizations. This blending is consistent with the aim of *Organization Studies*' founders to create a supranational forum. It was also reflected in Clegg, Hardy, and Nord's (1996) *Handbook of Organization Studies,* which placed current developments in North American organization behavior and organization theory side by side with conceptual and critical themes of European organization scholarship.

CONCLUSION

The knowledge controversy in contemporary organization studies is the product of two parallel streams: (1) North American organization science (which includes organization behavior and organization theory) that grew out of more basic social science disciplines; and (2) European organizational scholarship. The streams embodied different positions on scientism. The North American stream championed it. The European stream was a bit divided about it. Some European scholars promoted work of the type featured in the North American tradition, whereas others sought to challenge the hegemony of North American scientism in the study of organizations. As these different positions encountered one another, they helped to shape the knowledge controversy.

ENDNOTE

1. The paths in Figure 5.1 are very general. Neither one describes the nature of all of the organization scholarship in either continent.

REFERENCES

Baritz, L. (1960). *The servants of power*. New York, NY: Wiley.

Blau, P. M. (1970). Formal theory of differentiation organizations. *American Sociological Review, 35*, 201–218.

Burrell, G., & Morgan, G. (1979). *Sociological paradigms and organisational analysis*. London, UK: Heinemann.

Clegg, S. R., & Hardy, C. (2006). Representation and reflexivity. In S. R. Clegg, C. Hardy, T. B. Lawrence, & W. R. Nord (Eds.), *Sage handbook of organization studies* (2nd ed., pp. 424–443). London, UK: Sage Publications.

Clegg, S. R., Hardy, C., Lawrence, T. B., & Nord, W. R. (2006). *The sage handbook of organization studies* (2nd ed.). London, UK: Sage Publications.

Clegg, S. R., Hardy, C., & Nord, W. R. (Eds.). (1996). *Handbook of organization studies*. London, UK: Sage.

Donaldson, L. (1996). *For positivist organization theory*. London, UK: Sage Publications.

Hickson, D. J. (1996). The ASQ years then and now through the eyes of a Euro-Brit. *Administrative Science Quarterly, 41*(2), 217–228.

Hickson, D., Agersnap, F., Ferraresi, F., Hofstede, G., Kieser, A., Lammers, C., & Thoenig, J.-C. (1980). Editorial. *Organization Studies, 1*(1), 1–2.

Kuhn, T. (1970). *The structure of scientific revolutions*. Chicago, IL: University of Chicago Press. (Original work published 1962)

Lammers, C. J. (1998). An inside story: The birth and infancy of EGOS. Memories in tribute to Franco Ferraresi*. *Organization Studies*, 19(5), 883–888.

Landsberger, H. A. (1958). *Hawthorne revisited in the management and the worker: Its critics and developments in human relations and industry*. Ithaca, NY: New York State School of Industrial and Labor Relations.

Lawrence, P. R., & Lorsch, J. W. (1967). *Organization and environment: Managing differentiation and integration*. Boston, MA: Harvard University.

Massie, S. (1965). Management theory. In J. G. March (Ed.), *Handbook of organizations* (pp. 387–422). Chicago, IL: Rand McNally & Company.

Miner, J. B. (2002). *Organizational behavior: Foundations, theories, and analyses*. New York, NY: Oxford University Press.

Nord, W. R., Lawrence, T. B., Hardy, C., & Clegg, S. R. (2006). Introduction. In S. R. Clegg, C. Hardy, T. B. Lawrence, & W. R. Nord (Eds.), *Sage handbook of organization studies* (2nd ed., pp. 1–15). Thousand Oaks, CA: Sage Publications.

Palmer, D. (2006). Taking stock of the criteria we use to evaluate one another's work. *Administrative Science Quarterly, 51*, 535–559.

Shenhav, Y. (2003). The historical and epistemological foundations of organization theory: Fusing sociological theory with engineering discourse. In H. Tsoukas & C. Knudsen (Eds.), *The Oxford handbook of organization theory* (pp. 183–209). New York, NY: Oxford University Press.

Silverman, D. (1971). *The theory of organizations: A sociological framework*. London, UK: Heinemann.

Starbuck, W. H. (2003). The origin of organization theory. In H. Tsoukas & C. Knudsen (Eds.), *The Oxford handbook of organization theory* (pp. 143–182). New York, NY: Oxford University Press.

Thompson, J. D. (1956/1957). On building an administrative science. *Administrative Science Quarterly, 1*, 102–111.

Thompson, J. D. (1967). *Organizations in action: Social science bases of administrative theory*. New York, NY: McGraw-Hill Book Company.

CHAPTER

6

Key Themes in the Debate About Orthodox Science in the Study of Organizations

In Chapter 5, "Origins of the Knowledge Controversy in the History of Organization Studies," we saw that in the late 1900s organization studies and the knowledge controversy developed from the interface of North American organization science with European organization scholarship. European scholars appeared to be the first to use "organization studies" to label this interdisciplinary field. Some of them who founded this field sought to provide a counterpoint (what in Chapter 5 we called contra science) to the Anglo-North American scientism that dominated the study of organizations. In this chapter, we see that for some time a similar counterpoint was latent in discussions of methods in North American social science. Development of this counterpoint, along with events in Europe, represented a significant challenge to orthodox science.

By the end of the 20th century, the tension in organization studies between the counterpoint and the previously hegemonic scientism commonly featured the following major themes: (1) positivism versus antipositivism, (2) role of language in organization studies, and (3) modernism versus postmodernism.

POSITIVISM VERSUS ANTIPOSITIVISM

Some critics of orthodox science framed their ideas, perhaps inappropriately (Hunt, 1994), as an attack on positivism. Hunt persuasively argued that many of the attacks on positivism appeared to stem from misunderstanding positivism. In Chapter 8, "Alternative Approaches for the Knowledge Controversy," we discuss positivism in depth.

A noted defender of positivism in organization studies, Lex Donaldson (1996), summarized the central issues in the debate. He wrote:

> Positivism in organization theory has been opposed by anti-positivism (Burrell and Morgan, 1979). *Anti-positivism rejects each of the central tenets of positivism and argues instead for an approach that is the opposite—namely, voluntarist, specific to industries or locales and which explains organizations by complex accounts such as an emphasis on political factors.* Pioneering work in organization theory showed that a positivist approach could be fruitful. However, subsequent scholars turned against positivism and embraced more anti-positivist approaches. Their views have become the present-day accepted theory. Nevertheless, a deeper analysis reveals that their positions are flawed. A *more in-depth consideration shows that the positivist theory is valid.* Accordingly, much contemporary theorizing is founded on error. (p. 1)

We will treat positivism more fully in Chapter 8 when we examine all the major alternatives in the controversy. However, for the present we turn to a second theme feature in the challenge to orthodox science.

ROLE OF LANGUAGE IN ORGANIZATION STUDIES

A second theme common in reactions to the breakdown of orthodoxy centered on the discussion of the role of language that Morgan (1980) provoked. Two sets of interchanges among organization scholars reveal what was involved.

Especially informative was an interchange between Pinder and Bourgeois (1982) versus Morgan (1983) in *ASQ*. Firing the first salvo, Pinder and Bourgeois criticized the overuse of metaphors and other figurative language in organization science and urged greater use of literal language related to observable elements.

Morgan (1983) responded that Pinder and Bourgeois's concerns stemmed from their foundational view. He argued that metaphors stimulate imagination and creativity; he reiterated a call from a paper with Smircich (see Morgan & Smircich, 1980) for organization scholars to make their underlying assumptions explicit. He also argued for a revised understanding of science that realized "science may be able to generate many different and perhaps contradictory knowledges about the same phenomenon, all of which may have some merit" (p. 606). In response, Bourgeois and Pinder (1983) made their philosophical perspective explicit, describing themselves as Kantians who believe in a single reality that causes human perceptions but also believing "that there is no way of knowing whether, or how well, those perceptions map that reality" (p. 610).

From this point on, several organization scholars paid increased attention to language and philosophy. The debate was intense.

Astley (1985) proposed that administrative science was an interpretative exercise, because what we call truth is a product of the rules embedded in theoretical schemata. Therefore, we should relinquish the notion that our theoretical constructs are direct representations of external reality. He predicted that once we do we will recognize that "language itself becomes the essential subject matter of scientific deliberation" (p. 499).

Astley argued that the chief product of organization research was language, not objective knowledge. If accepted, this position would force organization scholars to reconsider how their research should be evaluated. He suggested that, contrary to the traditional emphasis social scientists placed on certainty and precision, managers found knowledge provided by contemporary organization research was valuable because it featured empirically imprecise language. Contrary to what most social scientists were taught, a theory's merits were enhanced not by precision but by linguistic ambiguity. Further, consistent with Davis (1971), Astley emphasized another nontraditional criterion—that a theory's acceptance was determined by how interesting it appeared to be.

In later work, Astley continued to focus on language. His article with Zammuto (see Astley & Zammuto, 1992) elaborated on his explanation of why managers valued the theory and research of organization scholars. The information these scholars provided was useful to managers for several reasons. First, its ambiguous language helped managers to preserve organizational coherence in the face of inconsistent demands. In addition, organization science helped managers for a combination of previously unrecognized reasons, including symbolic value and highly general tools and concepts.

As scholars wrestled with Astley's position, the role that values play in organization studies was evident. Prime examples were Donaldson's (1992) and Beyer's (1992) highly critical rejoinders to Astley and Zammuto. Donaldson based his criticism of "antipositivism" and his praise for positivism on his explicit interest in developing an organization theory that managers would support. This strategy to gain legitimacy was consistent with the historical process associated with institutionalized scientism (see Chapter 4).

This brings us to the third theme in the challenge to scientific orthodoxy, modernism versus postmodernism.

MODERNISM VERSUS POSTMODERNISM

Clegg and Hardy (1996) asserted that much of the questioning of orthodoxy in organizational scholarship resulted from displacement of modernist organizations by postmodernist ones. The concepts of modernism and postmodernism fostered intense debates. (Indeed, we fear some readers of the current volume will classify the controversy we address as one of modernism vs. postmodernism and place our position in the postmodern camp. We believe both of these classifications would be a mistake. We return to this issue in Chapter 10.)

Commonly, postmodernist organization studies are thought to be a counterpoint to the modernist perspective in organization science that preceded it. Gergen and Thatchenkerry (1996) summarized the key contrasts. The modernist view rested on ideas from the Enlightenment that emphasized the individual as a rational agent, techniques to gain empirical knowledge about an objective reality, and language as representational. Postmodernists, in contrast, emphasized communal over individual rationality, social construction over empirical method, and language as social action.

As many scholars jumped on the postmodern bandwagon, numerous others viewed it as a destructive threat to contemporary social science. Friedman (2002), for example, argued postmodernism as portrayed by Gergen (2001) would reduce scientific psychology to "a chaotic nescience, an agnostic void in which hope for any substantial knowledge has been abandoned" (p. 463). Hofman (2002) saw Gergen's postmodernism as the gratuitous adding of philosophy to the already compartmentalized discipline of psychology.

Although we see many problems with the terms *modernism* and *postmodernism* (see endnote 4 in Chapter 3), both have been used frequently in discussions of the state of organization studies. As scholars debated the themes of positivism-antipositivism, the role of language, and modernism versus postmodernism, some radically different perceptions of what constituted knowledge in organization studies emerged.

EVIDENCE OF RADICAL CHANGE IN STUDY OF ORGANIZATIONS IN SPECIAL ISSUES OF THE *ACADEMY OF MANAGEMENT REVIEW*

A convenient way to consider the rethinking is to review the series of special issues concerning theory published by one of the most respected organization journals, the *Academy of Management Review* (*AMR*). Between 1989 and 1999, *AMR* published three special issues devoted to the question, "What is good theory?"

1989 Special Issue

The first of these issues was published in 1989 under the editorship of David Whetten. Authors in this issue treated theory in relatively traditional terms. Van de Ven (1989) emphasized advancing "knowledge to a scientific discipline" (p. 486). Bacharach (1989) treated falsifiability, generalizability, and relationships among constructs, variables, propositions, and hypotheses. Tsoukas (1989) emphasized the realist paradigm, and Osigweh (1989) focused on developing precise concepts and positioning them on a ladder of abstraction.

There were exceptions to this traditional bent, such as Weick's (1989) "Theory Construction as Disciplined Imagination" article. But Weick's challenge to tradition was tame in comparison with what was to follow. The issue contained little, if any, explicit critique of positivism or mention of postmodernism.

1992 Special Issue and Reactions

The second special issue, published in 1992, was edited by Linda Smircich, Marta Calás, and Gareth Morgan. Whereas the first issue appeared to represent traditional concepts of what good theory was, the 1992 issue was intended to stimulate the field to reinvent itself. In an opening essay, the editors used a nontraditional format to suggest new criteria for evaluating management inquiry. These criteria included contributions to emancipation, cleverness, suspense, and entertainment value.

Several themes in the issue were somewhat novel to organization science of the time. Novel themes included aesthetics, critical radical humanism, critical theory, postmodernist and feminist inspired readings of traditional theories, the work of Michel Foucault, and criticism of positivism. As in times past, the articles that treated these topics came to receive much attention.

If the purpose of the special issue was to help introduce new perspectives into the field, it succeeded. In a now famous provocative paper, Jeffrey Pfeffer (1993) called the 1992 issue "an extreme example of the proliferation of theoretical perspectives ranging from feminism to conversation analysis and radical humanism" (p. 615). His paper gives us a sense of the nature of the accumulating tensions in organizational science at the time. Pfeffer concluded from the contents of the issue, that the field had become a very large tent under which "any theoretical perspective or methodological approach is as valid as any other" (p. 615). In sum, the second issue (1992) emphasized some emerging new perspectives that raised concerns by challenging the traditional ways.

To straighten things out, Pfeffer called for a tighter paradigm. We treat this "Pfefferism" in Chapter 8. Pfeffer was not alone in trying to nudge the field closer to how it seemed to function in the orthodox consensus era. Other scholars, writing in other outlets, also called for returning things to the *status quo ante*. For example, Hogan and Sinclair (1996) wrote that one

> ideological barrier to the notion of a cumulative science of social phenomena is the *deconstructionist perspective* of certain writers who, frustrated by the lack of progress in our field, argue that progress is a myth because "social psychology is history." … The argument is epistemological and taken from the deconstructionist school of literary criticism. These writers note that each person sees the world differently and,

> because there are no absolutes in the universe, there is no way to claim that any one version of reality is more valid or true than any other. This leads to the claim that the data based generalizations of social science are no more true than the observations of a poet or a religious mystic. This is an old issue in philosophy; Bishop Berkeley (1685–1753) developed a famous version of deconstruction in the eighteenth century, arguing that our knowledge of the world is idiosyncratic. *Samuel Johnson* responded by kicking a lamppost and remarking, "*Thus I refute you, Dr. Berkeley.*" (p. 383, italics added)

1999 Special Issue

The third issue (1999) illustrated how much had changed in the decade since the first issue. Kimberly Elsbach, Robert Sutton, and David Whetten served as editors for this third issue. The editors' reflections on the contents of this special issue are especially revealing.

In comparing this issue with the earlier ones, the editors revealed the degree to which the orthodox view had waned. Elsbach, Sutton, and Whetten (1999) wrote:

> In 1989, the notion that skilled organizational theorists are not just objective scientists, but also good storytellers who weave convincing tales of cause and effect, was unknown in many corners of the field and ridiculed in most others. It is now accepted by a large proportion of organizational theorists and is often used as an argument—even by some of the most traditional, quantitative, and positivistic researchers we know—about why good theory requires using many of the same methods as good literature. In 1989, the notion that a good theory could be developed that lacked independent and dependent variables was new and controversial; it is now viewed as a trivial truth by many of the same people who found this idea to be absurd. We could name at least fifteen respected organizational theorists who would have rejected process theories as "unscientific" in 1989 but find such theories to be a useful and important way of describing and explaining events in 1999. Finally, in 1989, the notion that there is no objective means of assessing the value of a theory would have been viewed as heresy in many of the same corners that it is now accepted as given truth, or at least a plausible and troubling possibility. (p. 633)

To the degree that contributors to this issue represented events accurately, clearly things had changed dramatically in 10 years. Scientism's dominance about what constituted knowledge and the norms governing work in organization science was substantially weakened. In fact, by 1999 Elsbach et al. reflected favorably on the proposition that the task of organization theorists had shifted from being objective scientists to being good storytellers. Criteria for theory also changed: in 1999, but not in 1989 and before, to be good, a theory did not need to have independent and dependent variables. Similarly, in 1999 but not in 1989, many scholars seemed to accept the view that there was no objective way to assess a theory's validity. In this spirit, Calás and Smircich (1999) explicitly championed postmodernism.

Other contributors to the 1999 *AMR* special issue resonated with these changes; some called attention to the term *incommensurable,* which (see Chapter 11) had become a red flag to defenders of the traditional view. Several writers in the 1999 issue appeared to accept the view that some organization theories were not commensurable. McKinley, Mone, and Moon (1999), for example, wrote:

> Even a brief review of contemporary organization theory suggests that the discipline is composed of multiple, largely incommensurable theoretical frameworks or schools of thought. (p. 634)

The above evidence from the special *AMR* issues and the reactions they stimulated make it clear that by the end of the 1900s, students of what was traditionally called organization science disagreed about what constituted knowledge in their field. We will provide deeper insight into the responses to these tensions in the following chapters, where we consider some of the reactions to the breakdown of consensus and also the alternatives various scholars proposed.

CONCLUSION

Obviously, by the end of the 20th century, the consensus that scientism permitted in the social sciences for much of that century waned significantly. The breakdown produced a number of tensions about the nature of knowledge in organization studies and organization science. Vigorous scholarly debate resulted. We propose generative uncertainty as one possible way to deal with the controversy. Of course, there are others. In Chapter 8, we will analyze several of these proposals.

REFERENCES

Astley, W. G. (1985). Administrative science as socially constructed truth. *Administrative Science Quarterly, 30,* 497–513.

Astley, W. G., & Zammuto, R. F. (1992). Organization science, managers, and language games. *Organization Science, 3*(4), 443–460.

Bacharach, S. B. (1989). Organizational theories: Some criteria for evaluation. *Academy of Management Review, 14*(4), 496–515.

Beyer, J. M. (1992). Metaphors, misunderstandings, and mischief: A commentary. *Organization Science, 3*(4), 467–476.

Bourgeois, V. W., & Pinder, C. C. (1983). Contrasting philosophical perspectives in administrative science: A reply to Morgan. *Administrative Science Quarterly, 28*(4), 608–613.

Burrell, G., & Morgan, G. (1979). *Sociological paradigms and organisational analysis.* London, UK: Heinemann.

Calás, M. B., & Smircich, L. (1999). Past postmodernism? Reflections and tentative directions. *Academy of Management Review, 24*(4), 649–671.
Clegg, S. R., & Hardy, C. (1996). Introduction: Organizations, organization and organizing. In S. R. Clegg, C. Hardy, & W. R. Nord (Eds.), *Handbook of organization studies* (pp. 1–28). London, UK: Sage.
Clegg, S. R., Hardy, C., & Nord, W. R. (Eds.). (1996). *Handbook of organization studies*. London, UK: Sage.
Davis, M. S. (1971). That's interesting: Toward a phenomenology of sociology and a sociology of phenomenology. *Philosophy of Social Science, 1*, 309–344.
Donaldson, L. (1992). The Weick stuff: Managing beyond games. *Organization Science, 3*(4), 461–466.
Donaldson, L. (1996). *For positivist organization theory*. London, UK: Sage.
Elsbach, K. P., Sutton, R. I., & Whetten, D. A. (1999). Perspectives on developing management theory, circa 1999: Moving from shrill monologues to (relatively) tame dialogues. *Academy of Management Review, 24*(4), 627–633.
Friedman, H. (2002). Psychological nescience in a postmodern context. *American Psychologist, 57*, 462–463.
Gergen, K. J. (2001). Psychological science in a postmodern context. *American Psychologist, 56*, 803–813.
Gergen, K. J., & Thatchenkerry, T. J. (1996). Organization science as social construction. *Journal of Applied Behavioral Science, 32*, 356–377.
Hofman, S. (2002). More science, not less. *American Psychologist, 57*, 462.
Hogan, R., & Sinclair, R. (1996). Intellectual, ideological, and political obstacles to the advancement of organizational science. *Journal of Applied Behavioral Science, 32*, 378–389.
Hunt, S. D. (1994). On the rhetoric of qualitative methods: Toward historically informed argumentation in management inquiry. *Journal of Management Inquiry, 3*, 221–234.
McKinley, W., Mone, M. A., & Moon, G. (1999). Determinants and development of schools in organization. *Academy of Management Review, 24*(4), 634–648.
Morgan, G. (1980). Paradigms, metaphors, and puzzle solving in organization theory. *Administrative Science Quarterly, 25*(4), 605–622.
Morgan, G. (1983). More on metaphor: Why we cannot control tropes in administrative science. *Administrative Science Quarterly, 28*(1), 601.
Morgan, G., & Smircich, L. (1980). The case for qualitative research. *Academy of Management Review, 5*(4), 491–500.
Osigweh, C. A. B. (1989). Concept fallibility in organizational science. *Academy of Management Review, 14*(4), 579–594.
Pfeffer, J. (1993). Barriers to the advance of organizational science: Paradigm development as a dependent variable. *Academy of Management Review, 18*(4), 599–620.
Pinder, C. C., & Bourgeois, V. W. (1982). Controlling tropes in administrative science. *Administrative Science Quarterly, 27*, 641–652.
Smicich, L., Calás, M., & Morgan, G. (1992). New intellectual currents in organization and management theory. *Academy of Management Review, 17*(3), 404–406.

Tsoukas, H. (1989). The validity of idiographic research explanations. *Academy of Management Review, 14*(4), 551–561.
Van de Ven, A. H. (1989). Nothing is quite so political as a good theory. *Academy of Management Review, 14*(4), 486–489.
Weick, K. E. (1989). Theory construction as disciplined imagination. *Academy of Management Review, 14*(4), 516–531.
Whetten, D. A. (Ed.). (1989). Special forum on theory building. *Academy of Management Review, 14*(4), 481–625.

CHAPTER

7

Organization Scholars' Responses to the Breakdown of Orthodoxy

In Chapter 5 we argued that as organization behavior and organization theory developed in North America they inherited the scientism that dominated the parent social science disciplines from which they evolved. This lineage contributed to an operational consensus that, following the "scientific method" (i.e., emulating methods attributed to the natural sciences), would lead to valid information about organizations. We call this the consensus about orthodox science.

This consensus fostered unity among students of organization well into the 20th century, even though, as we discussed in Chapter 4 on institutionalized scientism, it developed without benefit of a well-articulated philosophical foundation. Decades later, organization science grew from organization behavior and organization theory and incorporated this heritage of a consensus. Thus, since in our view organization studies includes this organization science, it too has remnants of the consensus on orthodox science.

As organization studies took shape in the latter half of the 20th century, several developments operated in concert and challenged the orthodox consensus. These developments included direct attacks on scientism, increased attention to the effect of personal values on what scholars regarded as knowledge, changes in organizations, changes in how disciplines involved with the study of organizations themselves functioned, and major changes in thinking about uncertainty both inside and outside organization studies.

In this chapter, we elaborate on the developments that weakened the consensus. We suggest the weakened consensus opened space for arguments about underlying issues—issues that the consensus on orthodox science masked. Then, in Chapter 8, we examine alternative perspectives that emerged as the consensus unraveled.

ATTACKS ON SCIENTISM IN THE STUDY OF ORGANIZATIONS

In the mid 1900s, at least in North America, scientism dominated the study of organizations. Some challenges to scientism appeared as concerns about methodology in social science.

Methods-Focused Challenges in North America

In North America, for the most part, early critiques of conventional methodology did not address the philosophical issues. These early debates about method did, however, help to open space for the more philosophically informed discussions that followed.

Within psychology, Paul Meehl's (1954) monograph on statistical versus clinical prediction opened many eyes. Meehl addressed a very specific problem—the predictive capabilities of clinical psychologists. However, his discussion had far-reaching implications. His distinction between clinical versus statistical *collection* and clinical versus statistical *combination* of data foreshadowed future debates about qualitative versus quantitative methods.

Other methodologically focused contributions opened things up further. Perhaps the best known were Orne's (1962) discussion of demand characteristics and Rosenthal's (1964) research on experimenter bias and the Pygmalion effect. Soon, however, more philosophical concerns emerged.

Philosophical Turn

In the mid 1900s, the philosophy of science blossomed as a subdiscipline of philosophy (Turner, 2006). As it did, social scientists began to pay increased attention to epistemological issues. Books such as Kaplan's (1964) and Polanyi's (1964) had questioned the established research process as the path to truth. However, the most influential book was Kuhn's (1962/1970) *The Structure of Scientific Revolutions*. Following Kuhn, social scientists increasingly questioned assumptions about the linearity of the knowledge accumulation process.

Some of Kuhn's popularity may have been due to the support his ideas gave to social scientists who wanted to believe their fields could be sciences. As Fuller (2000) observed, Kuhn's work "was used uncritically by social scientists … to legitimate their activities as paradigms on the same footing as those of the physical sciences" (p. 381).

Fuller (2000) put it this way: What Kuhn said was "in principle at least, it appeared that humanists and social scientists could become proper scientists if they consolidated their efforts ... and constituted themselves as paradigms" (p. 216). In other words, Kuhn "seemed to provide a blueprint for how a community of inquirers can constitute themselves as a science, *regardless* of their subject matter" (p. 234).

On the other hand, Kuhn's demonstration that accumulation of knowledge in the physical sciences was not always linear encouraged some social scientists to question the privileged status of science. Many found it difficult to accept scientism as uncritically as they had previously. Kuhn's book became a vehicle in which the challengers to the status quo could ride quite comfortably. "Paradigm" became, and still is, a key component of the ongoing discussions.

Post-Kuhn Developments in Organization Studies

Management theorists were quick to embrace Kuhn's concerns. According to Turner (2006), one result was an effort to confront the entrenched position with the introduction of phenomenological critique. This effort was associated with interest in Silverman's (1970) book that emphasized how organization participants construct organizations.

In this spirit, other challenges to the hegemonic scientism were brewing. One of the most influential in organization studies was a book that generated intense debates about the nature of knowledge in organization theory: Burrell and Morgan's (1979) *Sociological Paradigms*.[1]

Burrell and Morgan advanced their now famous two-dimensional model to analyze the 1960s debates in sociology and classify theories about organizations into four paradigms. Their model, reproduced here as Figure 7.1, made previously latent philosophical and value issues manifest. Study of this model helps us to better understand what was now at stake.

Burrell and Morgan began with the assumption that all theories of organization rest on both a philosophy of science and a theory of society. Their first dimension—"subjective versus objective"—considered social theories according to philosophical assumptions. Theories of the subjective sort emphasized "the relativistic nature of the social world" (p. 3). Those at the objective end treated the social world as a "hard, external, objective reality" (p. 3).

The second dimension—"regulation versus radical change"—considered theories according to assumptions about society. Those at the radical change end emphasized deep-seated structural conflict and a corresponding concern with human emancipation and potential for development. Theories at the regulation end focused on society's unity and cohesiveness.

In our view, the regulation-radical change dimension was about values. Accordingly, attending to it challenged the "value-free" assumption associated with orthodox scientism.

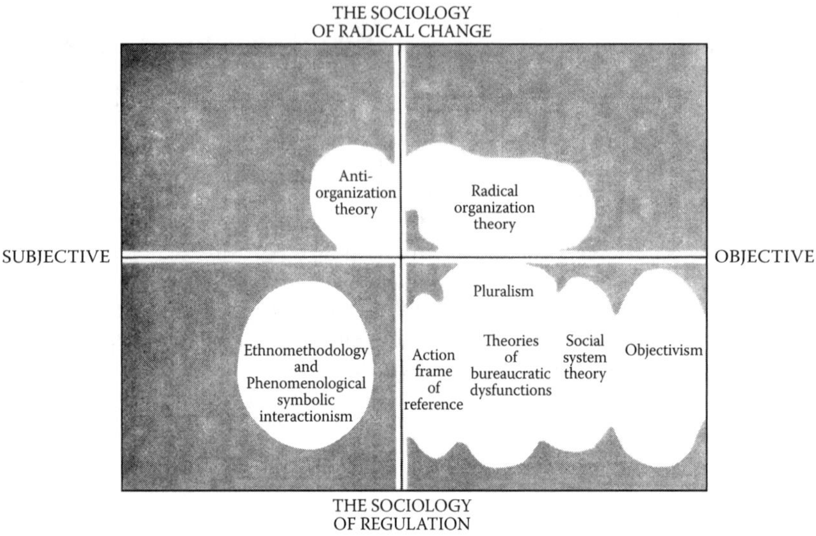

Figure 7.1 Burrell and Morgan's framework.

Guided by the objective–subjective dimension of Burrell and Morgan's framework, social scientists focused more explicitly on ontological and epistemological assumptions than previously. Indeed, much of the "paradigm war" seems to have been fought on this epistemological terrain. In contrast to the attention they gave to these philosophical matters, organization scholars continued to give far less explicit attention to the dimension we view as most closely aligned with values.

Burrell and Morgan's Agitating Effects on Organization Studies Although they used *paradigm* differently than Kuhn, Burrell and Morgan (1979) helped embed the term and its associated questioning of orthodox science in organization studies debates. Their book pointed to the need to reexamine the latent foundations of the field as the issues that are central in the knowledge controversy became salient. In this reexamination, attention to methodological concerns was frequent, especially in North America.

The objective versus subjective dimension resonated with North American concerns about methodology that had moved to the surface in the controversy about the relative merits of qualitative versus quantitative research. In organization studies, these concerns came to the fore in the December 1979 special issue of the *Administrative Science Quarterly* on qualitative methodology edited by John Van Maanen (1979).

Eventually social scientists began to question more widely the assumption that science could be "value-free." Reflecting on the legacy of *Sociological Paradigms* some years later, Burrell (1996) commented,

"What Burrell and Morgan's book may have succeeded in doing was to highlight the breakdown of the field of organization theory into warring encampments and to demonstrate that functionalist approaches ... were by no means the only possible avenues open to organizational analysis" (p. 648).

Although Burrell and Morgan's critique became the most famous, other scholars were challenging scientific orthodoxy in equally profound ways. In our view, one of the most insightful of these lesser known critiques was Mitroff and Kilmann's.

Mitroff and Kilmann's Critique of Science

In the late 1970s, two creative scholars advanced a comprehensive critique of social science. Mitroff and Kilmann (1978), in their book *Methodological Approaches to Social Science*, observed that recent attacks upon the institution of science meant that "science is in serious need of sociological and epistemological reform" (p. 3). Further, "we are ... on the edge of a revolution with regard to thinking about the character of science" (p. 3).

Mitroff and Kilmann demonstrated the importance of individual values and preferences in creating knowledge in social science. They pointed out that ways values and preferences influenced science created problems for the orthodox view of science based on classical Aristotelian logic.

Drawing on Karl Jung, Mitroff and Kilmann developed a four-category typology of scientific inquiry. This typology classified individual scientists into one of four styles of inquiry (analytic scientist, conceptual theorist, conceptual humanist, and particular humanist). Of the four types, Mitroff and Kilmann believed that the analytic scientists (ASs) had impacted on the norms of modern social science most significantly by implanting a view of science as value-free and apolitical and having clear standards for judgment. According to Mitroff and Kilmann, ASs tended to follow John Stuart Mill's (1872) *A System of Logic*. Their strong preferences for certainty, precision, accuracy, and reliability as attributes of knowledge led them to develop an approach to knowledge acquisition that stressed logical construction. In doing so, ASs tended to dismiss features of inquiry that introduced ambiguity or were not cast in a logical form as unscientific, and hence not worth much. In this vein, they excluded values.

According to Mitroff and Kilmann, consequences of the ASs' preferences were great. They observed that the prevailing belief in a value-free science was partially derived "from that aspect of the AS' constitution, which is averse to value judgments" (p. 35). Furthermore, "it is clear that the belief also derives from the failure of value judgments to command the kind of universal assent which scientific statements seem to command" (p. 35).

Mitroff and Kilmann believed that the hegemony of the AS type had not been fully justified intellectually. Its dominance was dysfunctional because the AS perspective led social scientists to overlook important historical, philosophical, psychological, and sociological influences on the inquiry process.

Three other types of scientists (conceptual theorists, conceptual humanists, and particular humanists) complete the Mitroff and Kilmann typology. The preferences of members of these other three groups differ sharply from those of the analytic scientists. For example,

1. Conceptual theorists prefer dialectical logic and indeterminate logics.
2. Conceptual humanists prefer science that generates "valid information in the behavioral or human sense (i.e., information that affects the human condition," that enhances "the ability to make free, informed choices; and … the ability to form commitment to one's choices" (p. 92).
3. Particular humanists seek to capture the uniqueness of each particular individual. Consequently, they prefer the case method.

Given recognition of the lack of appropriate justification for the AS-driven approach and the potential contributions of the other three perspectives, Mitroff and Kilmann wrote that "the entire field of science is in need of revolution and revision.… Anything less than a systemic or holistic approach will fail to capture and do justice to the phenomenon of science" (p. 107). Mitroff and Kilmann's psychologically oriented perspective complements the more sociological account of scientism we advanced in Chapter 4 as well as Burrell and Morgan's call for attending to the value issues reflected in their regulation-radical change dimension.

At about this time, increased attention was given to the influence of values on organization scholarship. As far as we know, the linkage of this growth to Burrell and Morgan and Mitroff and Kilmann was temporal rather than causal. In any case, the belief in value-freeness waned, and values came to be discussed openly.

GROWING ATTENTION TO THE INFLUENCE OF VALUES IN ORGANIZATION STUDIES

In the late 1960s and the 1970s, a number of organizational scholars expressed concerns about their field's scientism.

Chris Argyris authored some of the most widely read of these papers. He attacked what he termed rigorous research head-on in such major journals as the *American Psychologist* (1975) and the *Psychological Bulletin* (1968). He argued convincingly that traditional "rigorous methods" were guided by values that led students of organizations to inadvertently produce information that was self-sealing and promoted "single-loop" learning (i.e., learning that tends to be within the confines of what is currently accepted).

Seemingly a polar example of a Mitroff and Kilmann conceptual humanist, Argyris (1975) charged that by giving heavy emphasis to internal and external validity, social psychologists were unduly guided by Model 1 values. These values included achieving the purposes as I perceive them, maximizing winning and minimizing losing, being rational, and minimizing emotionality. Such pursuits led them to ignore new possibilities and produce research that inadvertently supported the status quo, defensive norms, and low freedom of choice. Accordingly, Argyris called for Model 2 research—research that promotes "double-loop" learning (i.e., learning that confronts the validity of goals or implicit values). Model 2 research generates information that solves problems so that they remain solved.

Even though Argyris framed his argument in terms of method, his concerns seemed value driven. He focused on finding ways to give people control and protect them from harm. As we understand him, his challenge to the existing methods was not rooted in epistemology. Existing scientism was problematic to him, not so much because it failed to describe reality as because it did not yield results that would contribute optimally to human improvement.

Also, in the mid 1900s, a number of other scholars published value-driven challenges. Some of these recognized previously latent values quite explicitly.

Outing Latent Values

In one of the earliest discussions of latent values in modern applied behavioral science, Baritz (1960) described how values influenced industrial psychology throughout its history. In *Servants of Power,* Baritz showed how 20th-century industrial psychology had been shaped by business values and interests.

Soon after, challenges to these underlying values became even more explicit. For example, Marxist-inspired critiques by Benson (1977) and Nord (1974, 1977) called attention to substantive values that had become embedded in studies of organizations and to how these values suppressed other values.

At roughly the same time, other social science scholars discussed the ways that the personal lives of social scientists influenced their work. Perhaps the most noteworthy was Gouldner's (1970) brilliant application of the sociology of knowledge to sociology itself.

CHANGES IN ORGANIZATIONS

Other forces contributing to the challenge of the consensus on orthodox science stemmed from changes in organization studies and changes in the organizations under investigation. Some important changes within organization studies included an increased number and variety of publication outlets and an increased role of European organizational scholars.

Changes Within Organization Studies

Changes in Publication Outlets

In the 1950s and 1960s, most of the highly esteemed outlets available for organization scholars to publish their work required scholars to walk the path of scientism. Soon, however, expansion in the number and type of publication outlets reduced the power of the previously hegemonic "orthodox science" gatekeepers.

Changes included the founding of new outlets as well as older outlets expanding the type of scholarship they published. By the 1980s and 1990s, some of the traditional outlets, such as the *Administrative Science Quarterly* (perhaps because of the leadership of such pioneering editors as Karl Weick and Stephen Barley), became much more open to alternative approaches. For example, under Weick's editorship creative thought pieces such as Pinder and Bourgeois's (1982) critique of metaphor experienced the limelight of publication in *ASQ*.

The prestige of several new publication outlets grew rapidly. Many of them valued a wide spectrum of scholarly endeavors. Some of these, such as the *Academy of Management Review,* valued investigations of contextual and historical matters. In addition, new European-oriented outlets, *Organization* and *Organization Studies,* were founded and gained prestige. As noted in Chapter 5, the founders of *Organization Studies* were explicit in their desire for openness to diverse paradigms. This expansion of intellectual space reduced the hegemony of the orthodox consensus.

Growth of European Influence

A second change within organization studies was that European organizational scholars, most of who were less influenced by scientism, came to exert much greater influence. What is the evidence that European influence increased? The great impact of Burrell and Morgan's (1979) *Paradigms,* alone, provides support for the assertion.

In addition, authorship in leading journals and handbooks demonstrated increased European influence. European scholars published a growing percentage of the papers in major organization journals.

The *Administrative Science Quarterly,* for example, became more global. Palmer (2006) observed that as late as the mid 1990s an overwhelmingly large percentage of articles that *ASQ* published were authored by North Americans. However, soon the magnitude of this dominance diminished. Oliver's (1999) unpublished report showed that about 12% of the articles *ASQ* published between 1978 and 1998 had at least one non-North American coauthor.

In addition, European scholars were much more prominent as authors of chapters in major handbooks. Whereas North American scholars wrote all of the chapters in March's (1965) path-breaking *Handbook of Organizations* and all but one of the chapters in the first edition of Dunnette's (1976) *Handbook of Industrial and Organizational Psychology*, nearly 50% of chapter authors in Clegg, Hardy, and Nord's (1996) *Handbook of Organization Studies* were from universities outside of North America. Even more recently, non-U.S. writers wrote the majority of the chapters in Tsoukas and Knudsen's (2003) *The Oxford Handbook of Organization Theory*. North American dominance waned. In sum, dynamics within the study of organizations changed in ways that favored the decline of the orthodox consensus.

At about the same time, the dynamics of the organizations that students studied changed in ways that also likely displaced the established scientism. The evidence that these changes displaced scientism is a bit circumstantial, but nevertheless we find it convincing.

In Chapter 5 we saw how the mechanical engineering perspective induced people to conceptualize well-functioning organizations as mechanistic efficiency-seeking bureaucracies. This engineering framework was consistent with scientism. In this context, it is reasonable to expect that if the mechanistic view of organizations waned, the associated scientism might also.

Changed Nature of Organizations

Most organization scholars would agree that the major[2] organizations of the late 20th century were less mechanistic than many of those in the middle of the century. Much of the change stemmed from the pressures that globalization and new technologies placed upon organizations to encompass more diversity and be more flexible. Clegg and Hardy (1996) described the change as a move from "modernist" to "postmodernist" organizations. With this shift, they postulated, the functionalist sociological framework of the past became less useful for understanding organizations.

Organizations that require high reliability (e.g., nuclear power plants and aircraft carriers) of the sort Weick and Roberts (1993) discussed demanded more complex models than the older mechanistic ones did. Traditional scientism was less satisfactory for studying such late-20th-century organizations.

While all this was happening, the intellectual culture was changing as well.

CHANGES IN THINKING ABOUT UNCERTAINTY

As we showed in Chapter 3, there was a major change in the late 20th century concerning the way many scholars approached uncertainty.

Some of this change contributed to the breakdown of the orthodox view of science.

In Chapter 3 we saw how in the late 1900s, leading philosophers introduced new approaches for thinking about foundations of knowledge. Philosophers concerned with such matters, such as Baynes, Bohman, and McCarthy (1996), spoke of the "end of philosophy." This new thinking penetrated organization studies.

Intellectual Changes Within Organization Studies

Late-20th-century changes within organization studies included new views about the nature of knowledge and concerns about the role of language.

New Views of the Nature of Knowledge in the Study of Organizations

We can illustrate this change by describing changes in Nord's reactions to the following statement by the organization sociologist Robert Dubin (1976):

> It is exceedingly difficult to say something meaningful about the real world without starting in the real world. Observation and description of the real world are the essential points of origin for theories in applied areas like industrial psychology, if not in all areas. (p. 18)

When Nord first read this statement, soon after it was published, he hardly noticed it. He was not aware of Dubin's assumption about a knowable external reality. However, when he reread it in the mid 1990s in the context of the knowledge controversy, he realized Dubin's assumption of a knowable external reality was controversial. Much changed in the 20 years between the two readings.

Marsden and Townley (1996) captured the essence of the change:

> A systematic critique of normal organization science developed during the 1970s, spurred on by developments in epistemology and ontology, which undermined the prevailing positivist conception of the practice of science.... Over the past twenty years, this critique stimulated an assortment of theories of organizations which oppose normal organization science. (p. 667)

Concerns About Language

Closely related to the above changes, as noted earlier, was the increased attention philosophers gave to language. The new perspectives fueled debates about the use of language, and language itself became a major issue in organization studies.

Gareth Morgan (1983), of Burrell and Morgan fame, deserves much of the credit (or, as some might see it, the blame) for triggering the language debate in organization studies. Morgan pointed out the great influence of metaphor on human thought in general and on the study of organizations in particular. He argued that words and names "do not so much denote external 'things' as conceptions of things activated in the mind by a selective and meaningful form of noticing the world, which may be shared with others" (p. 610). He added that the study of organizations was limited because "the orthodox view in organization theory has been based predominantly on the metaphors of machine and organism" (p. 613).

CONCLUSION

Events of the mid 1900s challenged the once hegemonic scientism. Since scientism was so heavily embedded in the fabric of organization science, it might be expected that established members of the field would rush to its defense.

In fact, many defended it vigorously. This defense and the counterattacks it provoked resulted in tensions in organization studies during the late 20th and early 21st centuries. In the next chapter, we examine how these tensions played out.

ENDNOTES

1. In the spirit of reflexivity and as a note of caution, the strong influence we place on Burrell and Morgan's book reflects how we experienced the origins of the controversy. Undoubtedly others, especially our European colleagues, experienced it differently.
2. Please note the word *major*. More than likely smaller organizations in both eras were organic.

REFERENCES

Argyris, C. (1968). Some unintended consequences of rigorous research. *Psychological Bulletin, 70*, 185–197.

Argyris, C. (1975). Dangers in applying results from experimental social psychology. *American Psycholgist, 30*, 469–485.

Baritz, L. (1960). *The servants of power*. New York, NY: Wiley.

Baynes, F., Bohman, J., & McCarthy, T. (1996). *After philosophy: End or transformation*. Cambridge, MA: MIT Press.

Benson, S. K. (1977). Organizations: A dialectical view. *Administrative Science Quarterly*, 22, 1–21.

Burrell, G. (1996). Normal science, paradigms, metaphors, discourses and genealogies of analysis. In S. R. Clegg, C. Hardy, & W. R. Nord (Eds.), *Handbook of organization studies* (pp. 642–658). London, UK: Sage.

Burrell, G., & Morgan, G. (1979). *Sociological paradigms and organisational analysis*. London, UK: Heinemann.
Clegg, S. R., & Hardy, C. (1996). Introduction: Organizations, organization and organizing. In S. R. Clegg, C. Hardy, & W. R. Nord (Eds.), *Handbook of organization studies* (pp. 1–28). London, UK: Sage.
Clegg, S. R., Hardy, C., & Nord, W. R. (Eds.). (1996). *Handbook of organization studies*. London, UK: Sage.
Dubin, R. (1976). Theory building in applied areas. In M. D. Dunnette (Ed.), *Handbook of industrial and organizational psychology* (pp. 642–658). Chicago, IL: Rand McNally.
Dunnette, M. D. (Ed.). (1976). *Handbook of industrial and organizational psychology*. Chicago, IL: Rand McNally.
Fuller, S. (2000). *Thomas Kuhn: A philosophical history of our times*. Chicago, IL: The University of Chicago Press.
Gouldner, A. W. (1970). *The coming crisis of Western sociology*. New York, NY: Basic Books.
Kaplan, A. (1964). *The conduct of inquiry methodology for behavioral science*. Scranton, PA: Chandler Publishing.
Kuhn, T. (1970). *The structure of scientific revolutions*. Chicago, IL: University of Chicago Press. (Original work published 1962)
March, J. G. (Ed.). (1965). *Handbook of organizations*. Chicago, IL: Rand McNally.
Marsden, R., & Townley, B. (1996). The owl of Minerva: Reflections on theory in practice. In S. R. Clegg, C. Hardy, & W. R. Nord (Eds.), *Handbook of organization studies* (pp. 659–675). London, UK: Sage Publications.
Meehl, P. E. (1954). *Clinical versus statistical prediction: A theoretical analysis and review of the evidence*. Minneapolis, MN: University of Minnesota Press.
Mill, J. S. (1872). *A system of logic* (8th ed.). New York, NY: Longmans Green.
Mitroff, I. I., & Kilmann, R. H. (1978). *Methodological approaches to social science*. San Francisco, CA: Jossey-Bass.
Morgan, G. (1983). More on metaphor: We cannot control tropes in administrative science. *Administrative Science Quarterly, 28*, 601–607.
Nord, W. R. (1974). The failure of current applied behavioral science: A Marxian perspective. *Journal of Applied Behavioral Science, 10*, 557–578.
Nord, W. R. (1977). Job satisfaction reconsidered. *American Psychologist, 32*, 1026–1035.
Oliver, C. (1999). Unpublished report to editorial board. *Administrative Science Quarterly*.
Orne, M. T. (1962). On the social psychology of the psychological experiment. *Academy of Management Review, 17*, 776–783.
Pinder, C. C., & Bourgeois, V. W. (1982). Controlling tropes in administrative science. *Administrative Science Quarterly, 27*, 641–652.
Polanyi, M. (1964). *Personal knowledge: Towards a post-critical philosophy*. New York, NY: Harper Torchbooks.
Rosenthal, R. (1964). Experimenter outcome-orientation and the results of the psychological experiment. *Psychological Bulletin, 61*, 405–412.
Silverman, D. (1970). *The theory of organizations*. London, UK: Heinemann.
Tsoukas, H., & Knudsen, C. (Eds.). (2003). *The Oxford handbook of organization theory*. Oxford, UK: Oxford University Press.

Turner, S. P. (2006). The philosophy of the social sciences in organizational studies. In S. R. Clegg, C. Hardy, T. B. Lawrence, & W. R. Nord (Eds.), *The Sage handbook of organization studies* (2nd ed., pp. 409–424). Thousand Oaks, CA: Sage.

Van Maanen, J. (Ed.). (1979). Qualitative methodology. *Administrative Science Quarterly, 24*(4), 519–712.

Weick, K. E., & Roberts, K. (1993). Collective mind in organizations: Heedful interrelating on flight decks. *Administrative Science Quarterly, 38*, 357–381.

SECTION 3

Alternatives

CHAPTER

8

Alternative Approaches for the Knowledge Controversy

Until fairly recently, many social scientists would have claimed that science can provide a value-free view of phenomena. In the last few decades, as the claim was questioned, social scientists felt some pressure to specify their philosophies and values. Once expressed, such foundational statements often came under attack from opposing theorists. Angry debates ensued and still occur about what the foundation of knowledge in the field should be.

Students of organization studies proposed a number of alternative approaches for dealing with the knowledge controversy. In Chapter 1 we detailed our own alternative, generative uncertainty. It features the acknowledgment of both one's uncertainties and the predictability of some phenomena, such as the sunrise and the boiling point of water.

In this chapter, we summarize specific alternatives that are currently popular among organization scholars. For each alternative, we have selected one or more well-known proponents to serve as spokespersons. We list these perspectives and their spokespersons in Table 8.1.

We describe each alternative and then assess it briefly from our generative uncertainty perspective. One criterion we use in the assessments is how well each perspective succeeds in avoiding problematic assumptions. We prefer perspectives that use assumptions sparingly. As we see it, every assumption closes a door, eliminating one or more degrees of freedom.

The first alternative we consider is positivism. We begin with an overview of positivism's history and then turn to a particular version advanced by Lex Donaldson, our spokesperson for positivism in organization studies.

TABLE 8.1 Major Alternatives for a Framework to Guide Organization Studies to Manage the Current Philosophical Controversy

Name of Alternative	Name of Scholars Whose Work We Use Most Heavily to Summarize the Approach	Some Specific Aspects Considered
Positivism	Lex Donaldson	• Logical positivism • Lex Donaldson's organization studies positivism
Realism	Michael Devitt, Shelby Hunt	• Objectivism • Redesigns that incorporate uncertainty • Scientific realism • Evolutionary natural realist epistemology • Critical realism
Critical realism	Roy Bhaskar, Steve Fleetwood	
Evolutionary epistemology	Donald Campbell	
Evolutionary natural realism	June Acevedo	
New pragmatism	Andrew Wicks, R. Edward Freeman	Hilary Putnam's internal realism
Naturalism	Robert Proctor, E. John Capaldi	
Treat organization studies as a humanity	Meyer Zald	Better humanists
Postmodernism	Kenneth Gergen, Martin Kilduff, Ajay Mehra	
Phronesis	Flyvbjerg	Phronetic science
Objectivism	Edwin Locke, Onkar Ghate	
Pfefferism	Jeffrey Pfeffer	

POSITIVISM

Overview of the History of Positivism

According to Kincaid (2000), positivism originated from separate movements in 19th-century social science and early-20th-century philosophy. Some key ideas of positivism were that metaphysical speculations are meaningless, that there is a universal a priori scientific method that is the same for both natural and social sciences, that the various sciences should all be reducible to physics, and that the theoretical parts of good science must be able to be translated into observation statements.

Key figures in the origin of positivism were Saint Simon and his one-time personal secretary Auguste Comte. These philosophers considered science superior to all other forms of knowledge and distained metaphysics as not scientific. They claimed there is only one scientific method for all sciences. Comte's (1975) positivism rejected as illegitimate what cannot be directly observed. He wrote, "All good intellects have repeated, since Bacon's time, that there can be no real knowledge but that which is based on observed facts" (p. 73)

For Comte, absolute answers about the universe's origin and destiny and inner causes of phenomena were beyond human reach. He noted, however, that Fournier's research produced precise laws about heat without need for any information on the essential nature of heat. Comte saw this approach to knowledge as representative of a higher stage of human development.

A key theme from Comte's positivism played an important role in 20th-century American social science. This theme was his insistence on observation as the only source of creditable knowledge. Kincaid (2000) noted that positivism supported the use of quantitative data and precisely formulated theories in modern social science.

Logical Positivism

A version of positivism, logical positivism, developed in the 1920s from discussions of a group called the Vienna Circle. Events that led up to World War II stimulated many of the logical positivists to move to English-speaking countries, where their influence spread. For a time, logical positivism was part of the conventional wisdom in the philosophy of science.

Major Tenets

Tenets of this view included (1) the verification principle (this principle stated that the meaning of a proposition was identical with the means of verification; a concept that does not have a means of verification is meaningless), (2) metaphysics should be avoided, and (3) what Quine (1951) called reductionism—the belief that all meaningful statements are based on observation or immediate experience.

Logical Positivism's Hegemony

Logical positivism's preeminence in early-20th-century philosophy of science did not last. Several factors contributed to the decline. First, the verification principle was itself not verifiable. In other words, the tenet that a proposition was identical with its means of verification could not be verified.

Second, critique of logical positivism by philosopher Willard Van Orman Quine (1951) influenced many to abandon positivism. Some scholars credited Quine's (1951) critique as the major source of positivism's decline. In our view, Quine's (1951) most telling point was that "the totality of our so-called knowledge or beliefs, from the most casual matters of geography and history to the profoundest laws of atomic physics or even of pure mathematics and logic is a man-made fabric which impinges on experience only along the edges" (p. 40). He added, "If this view is right, it is misleading to speak of the empirical content of an individual statement" (p. 40). This is so because the meaning of any individual statement depends on the system of knowledge in which it is embedded. As Quine put it, "Any statement can hold true come what may, if we make drastic enough adjustments elsewhere in the system" (p. 40).

If what is taken to be true depends heavily on the system in which it is embedded, then the tenet of reductionism, that is, that all meaningful statements are based on immediate experience, suffers a major blow.

Some years later, pragmatist philosopher Hilary Putnam (1981) described the dilemma of positivism as "the idea that the statements of science are translatable one by one into statements about what experiences we will have if we perform certain actions has now been given up as an unacceptable kind of reductionism" (p. 181). Further, "the older empiricism, or phenomenalism, seemed to provide us with a tidy criterion of cognitive significance: a statement is cognitively significant if it is translatable into a statement about sensations. But it turned out that either the notion of 'translation' is hopelessly vague, or else that statements of science itself failed to satisfy this criterion" (p. 182).

In addition, some of logical positivism's decline stemmed from growth in the popularity of other approaches, such as Popper's (1962) falsification criterion, "statements or systems of statements, in order to be ranked as scientific must be capable of conflicting with possible or conceivable observations" (p. 39). We will discuss two competing approaches, instrumentalism and scientific realism, later.

Following this decline, logical positivism left a legacy.

After the Fall

Legacies of logical positivism are widespread in both philosophy of science and the social sciences; behaviorism and operational definitions are both prime examples.

Also, for some people, following its decline, positivism became a derogatory term. Hunt (1994) observed that in management research *positivist* is short for *logical positivist* or *logical empiricist*. He noted how apparently historically misinformed advocates of qualitative methods ritualistically bashed positivism. Similarly, Kincaid (1996) noted that positivism, like other bygone intellectual movements, was misunderstood by its detractors.

We now look at positivism in contemporary organization studies.

Lex Donaldson's Positivism and Organization Studies

Since Lex Donaldson has been the most prominent advocate of positivism in organization studies, we chose him as our spokesperson for positivism. Mir and Mir (2002) called him the "patron saint of positivist inquiry in organizations" (p. 109). Donaldson's championing of positivism was closely aligned with his commitment to structural-contingency theory. As we will see, his version of positivism shares important features with traditional versions of positivism (e.g., emphasis on quantitative data and precisely formatted theories) but rejects others (e.g., neglecting concepts that are not observable).

According to Donaldson (2003), "Positivism takes the natural sciences as a role model" (p. 40). "The aim [of positivism in organization studies] is to reveal causal regularities that underlie surface reality" (p. 41). It advocates use of the hypothetico-deductive method and aims to create valid explanations about how the world really operates.

In addition, Donaldson (1996) advanced Newtonian physics as an exemplar for inquiry in organization studies. Although he acknowledged that some 20th-century developments in physics, such as issues of indeterminacy, and explanations that "seem to have outgrown linear concepts of time and Cartesian geometry" (p. 55) raise problems for the use of physics as a role model, he continued to believe that Newtonian physics "is still an established body of knowledge which offers reliable explanations of many phenomena such as motion and light" (p. 55). Likewise, "the rate at which steel balls roll down wooden slopes is still predicted by the laws of motion. These scientific laws remain valid and useful knowledge" (p. 55).

Consequently, Donaldson (1996) advised his organization studies colleagues to, at least for now, continue to follow the Newtonian course. In his words:

> Surely present attempts at administrative enquiries parallel studies of reflection or falling bodies more than they do the physics of black holes.

> Bodies of knowledge have to begin with simple, validated models and then proceed to more refined, complex formulations. Thus, in so far as social scientists take natural sciences as an inspiration, Newtonian physics may be more helpful than quantum physics. The associated conceptual building blocks of cause leading to effect, past preceding present and general laws, also command continuing respect (Behling 1980)—at least until alternative postulates of proven greater explanatory power are available. (pp. 55–56)

Epistemology

Donaldson (2003) asserted that the view of science as a hypothetico-deductive activity was "probably the epistemology that is most common among contemporary positivists" (p. 50).

Ontology

Donaldson (2003) provided a mixed view of ontology. At one point, he was explicit that "there is no ontological claim being made" (p. 54). In partial contradiction, however, earlier in the same chapter, he appeared to assume an underlying reality when he wrote: "Underlying the surface appearance of the natural world there are deeper structures of regularities of causes and effects" (p. 40).

Values

Donaldson claimed that positivist organizational science "aims to create valid explanations that capture how the organizational world really operates, rather than to broadcast views that may better accord with values but are not accurate characterizations of the world as it exists. In addition, organizational science is value-free and may be quite tough-minded in some of its aspects" (p. 42). Furthermore, it is "objective" in that the objects of inquiry "are observed from without by detached observers" (p. 40).

Social Facts as Explanations

Donaldson believed that social facts are adequately explained by other social facts. He wrote:

> In positivist organizational theory, the reason why the ideas in the minds of the social actors make no independent contributions to the explanation is not that they have no effect, but rather lies in the logic of functionalism. Clearly, most organizational changes occur because of decisions by the management or other parties. Thus ideas in the minds of these social actors are part of the process that produces the changes. The decision-makers may consider a range of choices and then choose between them. However, as Blau (1972: 13fn) insightfully states, the decision-makers

> will choose the option that is most effective. Given that only one option is the most effective, then it is predetermined that the decision-makers will choose that one. Thus positivism gains force when united with functionalism, so that the option that is chosen has to be chosen because of its functionality, that is, with respect to its beneficial outcomes. (p. 44)

Donaldson's Distinction Between Logical Positivism and Positivism in Organization Studies

Frequently, there has been confusion about what positivism is. Often the confusion arises from differences among people who call themselves positivists. Donaldson (2003) recognized this problem and explicitly distinguished positivism in organization studies from logical positivism. Thus, the version of positivism that figured so heavily in the organization studies knowledge controversy and the paradigm war was of a somewhat special sort.

In Donaldson's positivism, theoretical concepts "are seen as legitimately being abstract and therefore unobservable" (p. 51). Several processes (e.g., thinking and feeling), while unobservable, are believed to exist and to be legitimate topics for study. Donaldson summarized:

> Positivism seeks objectivity, which is to say high levels of inter-subjective agreement between two or more observers ... and this tends to inhere in observables or other data that are colloquially called objective. This leads to the positivist strategy of seeking to study phenomena by studying objective social facts and then approaching more subjective aspects within that framework. (p. 51)

Assessment of Donaldson's Positivist Alternative

Features We Especially Like About Donaldson's Positivism Students of organizations using approaches like the positivism Donaldson advocates have reported useful findings, such as linkages between organization size and other variables. Another major plus for us is that this positivism, like logical positivism for the most part, refrains from taking a position on the nature of reality.

Features We Have Problems With in Donaldson's Positivism We see three features of Donaldson's positivism as limiting its merits: (1) unnecessary assumptions; (2) claim of freedom from values; and (3) view of science as hypothetico-deductive activity.

Let us examine each of these in turn.

1. Concerning unnecessary assumptions, Donaldson introduced a number of assumptions. Consider three of them: (1) Only one option that is most effective is available to decision makers; (2) it is predetermined that decision makers will choose this most effective option when they are able to; and (3) deeper regularities

of causes and effects underlie surface appearances. We see all of these assumptions as problematic. Each one closes off a potential avenue of exploration rather than encouraging further inquiry.

2. With respect to being value-free, we don't see how positivists, or any other scientists, can avoid enacting values in their work—hence our preference for reflexivity about values as opposed to fighting a losing battle to remain value-free. In fact, Donaldson's own writings reflect the influence of values. For example, Donaldson (1992) referred to the "positivist mission of creating, refining and testing theories of organizations whose concepts are specific enough to be capable of giving, deductively, practical guidance to those who are seeking to manage in the real world" (p. 465).
3. Concerning the view of science as a hypothetico-deductive activity, we believe that the social sciences overemphasized this approach.

Although much of the research reported today still appears to have a positivist foundation, recently advocacy of positivism has declined among scholars. Kincaid (1996) said it was put to rest in the 1950s. Positivism's popularity also declined in organization studies, while realism and postmodernism have gained adherents. We will now examine four varieties of realism that have found favor with organization scholars: objectivism, scientific realism, evolutionary natural realist epistemology (ENRE), and critical realism.

REALISM

A number of perspectives that differ from each other in some important ways embody a commitment to realism. Here we consider some of the ones that figured in the recent knowledge debate in organization studies. We include objectivism, scientific realism, evolutionary naturalist epistemology, and critical realism.

Objectivism

We see objectivism as a form of realism, although when organization studies scholars discuss realism they frequently fail to mention objectivism. In fact, to date, objectivism has not been widely discussed in the organization studies literature.

Edwin Locke (2003) has been its major advocate, and we turn to him as our spokesperson. To understand this perspective, we drew heavily on Locke's writings with Onkar Ghate (Ghate and Locke, 2003). Further, we used the work of objectivism's founder Ayn Rand and contributions from Leonard Peikoff on the ethics of objectivism. These sources revealed five major features of objectivism: axioms, reliance on sensory information, focus on conceptualization, high regard for thinking, and values orientation.

Axioms

Axiom refers to a self-evident truth that cannot be coherently denied. Objectivism is based on three axioms: existence (i.e., what is, is); consciousness (i.e., one is aware that something exists); and identity (i.e., what exists has a specific nature). Ghate and Locke (2003) argued that the three axioms add up to a corollary principle, which Rand called the primacy of existence: "Existence comes first: what exists exists and is what it is independent of any consciousness" (p. 261).[1] Thus, consciousness depends on existence. In order for consciousness to occur, something must first exist.

Reliance on Sensory Information

For objectivists, again quoting Ghate and Locke (2003), "all knowledge (including knowledge of the axioms) begins with the evidence of the senses. To claim that the senses are invalid is a contradiction. On what basis could one claim the senses were invalid except on the basis of sensory evidence? The senses give us automatic knowledge of reality" (p. 262).

Focus on Conceptualization

Sensory data serve as the raw material for concept formation. Ghate and Locke (2003) observed that for objectivism, concepts are "*the form in which a conceptual consciousness grasps reality*.... The mind attains objectivity by connecting every concept to perceptual data and therefore to the facts of reality" (p. 264). It accomplishes this by means of logic, primarily inductive logic.

High Regard for Thinking

The cardinal virtue in objectivism is rationality. "'The virtue of Rationality means the recognition and acceptance of reason as one's only source of knowledge, one's only judge of values and one's only guide to actions" (Rand, 1964, p. 28).

Ghate and Locke were troubled by postmodernist attacks on reason. They countered with the argument that there is no reasoning process that can lead one to the conclusion that reason is invalid.

Values Orientation

Objectivism values egoism, as opposed to altruism, is based on the following thinking: The continued existence of a living organism depends upon its reaching certain goals that are set by its nature. A "gazelle, for instance, must obtain grass to live, a lion must obtain gazelles or the like to live. For animals other than man, the standard of value is built in: within the range of their power; they act automatically to pursue the goals needed to further their lives" (Ghate & Locke, 2003, p. 265). However, this is not true of human beings, who need ethics to teach them how to live. Ghate and Locke claimed, following Rand, that the only objective standard of value is "man's life, which means each individual's life."[2] They contended, "Thus does Rand refute Hume's view that you cannot get an 'ought' from an 'is'" (p. 266). Finally, "Since the purpose of morality is to teach a man how to live, the individual is the proper beneficiary of his moral action. Thus Rand advocates egoism as against altruism.... A moral code that tells an individual to sacrifice himself to others tells him to disregard his life, to renounce his own values, to value his own destruction" (p. 266).

Assessment of Objectivism

Features We Like About Objectivism The chief things we like about this perspective are its support for induction and for thinking and its explicit statement of values. We also appreciate seeing principles presented as axioms, even when we don't agree with them, rather than seeing them presented as the result of proofs that don't ultimately succeed.

Concerns About Objectivism Objectivism is based on commonsense realism, which as we said in Chapter 1 ("Generative Uncertainty") entails major problems.

Further, when Ghate and Locke asked what possible basis one could use to say the senses are invalid, they bypassed the complementary question of what basis one could use to say that the senses are *valid*. Using sensory evidence to prove the validity of the senses is highly questionable. For this reason, we prefer to acknowledge uncertainty about the senses, even as we continue to use sensory data.

Ghate and Locke used the same type of logic on the validity of reason as they did on that of the senses. They said there was no reasoning process that could result in the conclusion that reasoning was invalid. That statement makes sense to us, but it doesn't justify concluding that reason is *valid*. Certainly, it would be pointless to try to use reason to demonstrate its own validity. As we did with the senses, we prefer to admit we don't have a solid justification for the tool of thinking, even as we continue to use it.

We disagree with Ghate and Locke that Rand refuted Hume's principle that you can't get an "ought" from an "is." She insisted that each individual's life was "the only objective standard of value." We're not exactly sure what "objective" means in this context, but it seems safe to say that for objectivists, each individual life is the primary standard of value, and therefore each individual should pursue his or her own best interests, allowing the principle of survival of the fittest to do its job, as it does with the lion and the gazelle.

We have two problems with this position. We do not see any particular reason that human beings should model their standard of value on the behavior of other animals. Second, treating other animals as exemplars does not rule out altruism as a possible standard for humans. Altruism, defined by Masson and McCarthy (1995) as "behavior that benefits another but reduces the altruist's ability to survive" (p. 163), has been extensively documented in nonhuman animals (Masson & McCarthy, 1995; Connor & Norris, 1982; Marais, 1969). Consequently, we do not believe that Rand succeeded in deriving an "ought" from an "is."

It is interesting that critical realists (who on many matters differ sharply from objectivists), as we show later in this chapter, also claim to refute Hume by generating an "ought" from an "is." The value they claim to have generated is quite different from Rand's "individual life." They propose that other things being equal, false consciousness, an obstacle to emancipation, ought to be remedied.

The way that scholars from such widely differing perspectives both claim thinking in support of their theories illustrates the point we made in Chapter 1: that scholars do not agree about universal rules for thinking. Even if universal correct rules of thinking happen to exist, scholars do not agree about what they are.

At any rate, objectivism advances a number of positions we consider problematic:

1. The three axioms of objectivism that, together, represent a commonsense realist position cannot be coherently denied.
2. Consciousness depends on the existence of objects of consciousness.
3. Sensory data are valid.
4. Reason is valid.
5. The behavior of nonhuman animals is an appropriate model for human values.
6. Nonhuman animals do not exhibit altruism.

While to date objectivism has not been widely discussed by organization scholars, some other varieties of realism that incorporate a greater degree of uncertainty have fared better.

Realisms That Incorporate Uncertainty

Most organization studies scholars reject commonsense realism as no longer viable. However, many currently entertain a variety of more sophisticated realisms. Here we treat three of them: scientific realism, evolutionary natural realist epistemology (ENRE), and critical realism. These versions of realism have at least four things in common. They all claim that entities can exist independently of human perception; they all reject the assumption that reality can be known completely; they all strongly reject relativism; and they all recognize the role of values in inquiry.

Scientific Realism

Hunt (2005), following Leplin (1984, p. 1), saw scientific realism as "a majority position whose advocates are so divided as to appear a minority" (p. 131). In spite of the differences among proponents, Hunt asserted that scientific realists all share four fundamental tenets.

Classical realism "holds that the world exists independently of its being perceived" (p. 131). *Fallibilistic realism* "maintains that though the job of science is to develop genuine knowledge about the world, such knowledge will never be known with certainty: There is no 'God's eye' view" (p. 131). *Critical realism*, while "recognizing the fallibility of our perceptual (measurement) processes, maintains that science must critically evaluate and test its knowledge claims to determine their truth content." *Inductive realism* maintains that "the long-term success of a scientific theory gives reason to believe that something like the entities and structure postulated by the theory actually exists (McMullin, 1984, p. 26)" (p. 131).

Three features of this approach deserve special comment. First, the emphasis on fallible human perceptions in fallibilistic and critical realism indicates that human knowledge of reality must remain incomplete. Second, Hunt treated critical realism as a component of scientific realism; however, some organization scholars identify themselves simply as critical realists. We discuss their position below.

Third, in making his case for realism, Hunt (2005) advanced two different arguments:

> Trust is essential in science … because scientific knowledge is a shared form of knowledge; it is shared with its clients. The clients of academic management researchers include not just other academics but also practicing managers, students, government officials, and the public in general … philosophies such as relativism, constructivism, and postmodernism, when they deny the reality-theory connection, are self-defeating for the researchers who adopt them. Who could trust the output of research guided by such philosophies? (p. 136)

In other words, realism inspires client trust, which is in the interest of the scientist. In fact, following Harré (1986), "Any view of science that claims that scientific knowledge is constructed or created by the scientific community independent of some external reality is to be rejected on moral grounds" (p. 136). The crux of the moral issue seems to be that with client trust comes responsibility on the part of management academics to produce knowledge their clients will find believable.

Hunt's second argument in his case for realism echoed McMullin's (1984) position, mentioned above, that long-term success of a theory gives reason to believe in the existence of something like the entities and structures postulated by the theory.

Reflections on Scientific Realism We like the fallibilism, and we like Hunt's attention to values. However, his implication that relativists, poststructuralists, and postmodernists endangered clients' trust in management science because they were immoral appears inconsistent with the value he expressed elsewhere in the same article that scholars should tell the truth as they see it. Did Hunt think that none of the "wrong thinkers" he listed could possibly be sincere? Or did he think, like the medieval church, that holding wrong beliefs, however sincerely, is in itself immoral? Or did he think that wrong thinkers have a right to hold their opinions but not to express them? These are the only possibilities we can imagine, and we disagree with all of them.

We think science has earned considerable trust through centuries of scientists (e.g., Galileo, Darwin, Einstein) honestly expressing their sometimes unpopular beliefs rather than saying what they thought "clients" wanted to hear or would find believable. At any rate, the agenda of favoring realism because of its credibility to clients does not seem especially "moral" to us.[3]

Turning to Hunt's second argument for realism, that the long-term success of a theory gives reason to believe in the existence of the entities and structures it postulates, we consider Larry Laudan's (1984) critique of realism. For Laudan, the "success" argument "seems hard to square with the fact that the central terms of many relatively successful theories (e.g., ether theories, phlogiston theories) are evidently non-referring" (p. 112). (By "evidently non-referring," we assume Laudan meant that those once successful theories postulated entities that today's realist would deny exist.) Of course, the realist might still maintain that "the success of a theory warrants the claim that at least some (but not necessarily all) of its central concepts refer" (p. 115). However, such a weakening of the principle would merely solve one problem while creating another, since it "would leave the realist with no warrant for giving a realist construal of the deep-structure claims of a theory—and that would be to undo realism itself" (p. 115).

To summarize, in spite of the positive features of scientific realism, we don't think the arguments Hunt advanced for realism hold up well; furthermore, Hunt's first argument violates our—and seemingly even his—value of intellectual integrity. Specifically, Hunt appears to advocate that scientists hide their true beliefs to gain political advantage.

Now consider our next realist approach, evolutionary natural realist epistemology, a perspective that developed out of the evolutionary epistemology championed by Donald Campbell (1987). ENRE uses Campbell's (1987) analogy between biological evolution and scientific progress to help explain the successes of science.

Evolutionary Natural Realist Epistemology

Jane Azevedo (2002) explained ENRE well. This approach presumes that people can have knowledge of their world, which exists externally to and independently of themselves, and that this knowledge is a joint function of how the world is and human cognitive processes.

We consider several core features of ENRE: assumptions, the need to be scientific, concern with fragmentation in sociology, criteria for theory, approaches to rationality and methodology, and scientific values.

Assumptions

The first assumption is realism. According to Azevedo (1997), "The basic ontological position of realism is that a world exists independently of our knowledge of it, and that the nature of that world is such that we can have knowledge of it" (p. 65).

Second, ENRE assumes a *unified* reality in which every aspect is capable of causal interaction with every other aspect. For a relation to be causal it has to occur in space-time, involve an exchange of energy, and show a mechanism or state of affairs that leads to a consequent state of affairs.

Third, ENRE assumes that "natural selection wouldn't have left us with eyes that regularly deceive us, at least not grossly. Otherwise, we would not have survived as a species to be deceived by them. So despite its theory-ladennness, which is a biological phenomenon, there is reason to believe that human perception is reliable" (p. 84).

Fourth, ENRE assumes the feasibility of objective (meaning perspective-neutral) criteria for the validity of theories. (Azevedo preferred to talk about validity, in the sense of "well-foundedness" rather than truth (1997, p. 260).) ENRE regards perspective-neutral criteria as necessary in order to combat relativism, and as possible because reality imposes constraints on the content of theories. ENRE goes on to assume that the entities, including the theoretical entities, of any valid causal theory actually exist.

Finally, ENRE assumes that, given the connectedness of reality, "the unification of science is achieved by showing the causal connections that exist" (Azevedo, 1997, p. 166). To be scientific, "a discipline ought to place the highest value on unified knowledge" (p. 211).

Need to Be Scientific

ENRE's quest to be scientific raises two questions. First, what did Azevedo mean by *scientific*? Following Campbell, she thought of science as an institution characterized by the following: (1) It "opens a window on the world through which nature can speak"; and (2) "its norms function to channel consensus in a way that maximizes the opportunity for reality to influence that consensus" (Azevedo, 1997, p. 265). Second, why was being scientific so important to Azevedo? It was important because she posited sociology needed to be considered a science in order to be taken seriously and receive funding. Her insistence that her field be and appear scientific, like Donaldson's, demonstrates that the institutional scientism in the social sciences discussed in Chapter 4 lives on.

Fragmentation of Sociology

Since Azevedo thought science had to be unified, she saw the fragmentation of sociology as an obstacle to its being or becoming a science. Using the metaphor of maps, she showed how ENRE could deal with fragmentation. She began by noting that there can be different types of maps of the same area, for example, street maps, topological maps, geological maps, and aerial maps. Each type serves a different purpose and is evaluated according to how well it serves that purpose. Taken together, the maps provide fuller knowledge of the area than does any one of them alone. Sociological theories, like maps, can work together to provide fuller information than does any one of them alone, especially if theorists avoid the error of assuming they each have the only correct map.

Evaluation of Theories

Also like maps, sociological theories can be evaluated according to how well they serve their purposes. Given that ENRE postulates a unified reality, it considers "explanatory and predictive success and the criteria of internal and external consistency and coherence" (Azevedo, 1997, p. 140) as appropriate, perspective-neutral criteria for validity.

Rationality and Methodology

ENRE uses the same approach to models of rationality that it does to sociological theories, seeing different types of rationality as having different purposes and as potentially complementary rather than necessarily competitive. ENRE's approach to methodology seems mixed. At times, ENRE appears to advocate allowing sociology to "model its methodology on that of the obviously successful natural sciences" (Azevedo, 1997, p. 63). At other times, methodology is treated as something to investigate rather than take as given.

Scientific Values

ENRE sees a need for "a critical and ethical science of society" (Azevedo, 1997, p. xiv). Consequently, it considers both the value-free stance of positivism and the relativism attributed to postmodernism and post-structuralism to be highly unsatisfactory.

Reflections on ENRE

Patterns We Like in ENRE First, we like the map metaphor a lot. It promotes eclecticism and integration of theories, rationalities, and presumably, methods. Second, we like the acknowledgment of the fallibility of human perception and reason. Third, we like ENRE's attention to values, and we like the specific values it holds for science, with one exception, which we will get to shortly.

Concerns About ENRE

Problematic Assumptions ENRE bases claims to objectivity on assumptions of realism and unity that at present its exemplar, the natural sciences, does not support. Azevedo (1997) acknowledged, "The embarrassment to realism caused by the seeming impossibility of a realist interpretation of quantum theory" (p. 204), which she considered "arguably the most successful theory humans have had in terms of predictive success" (p. 198). (We discuss this theory and the problems it causes for some versions of realism in Chapter 9.) Regarding the unity issue, she acknowledged that "there may be no direct way to unify quantum theory and the theory of special relativity" (p. 204).

On top of that, we see the assumptions of realism and unity as violations of ENRE's own norms for science. It's as if ENRE opens a window for nature to speak, but then tells nature what to say. This leads to our concerns about ENRE's scientific values.

Problems With Scientific Values The assertion that a discipline ought to place the highest value on unified knowledge prejudges the matter too much for us—that was the only statement of scientific values we took exception with.

For Azevedo (1997), a major benefit of ENRE was its ability to counteract the relativist idea that one value is as good as another. She felt that the relativism of postmodernists and poststructuralists left them with "nothing to underpin their defense of the powerless" (p. xiii). However, we don't see anything about ENRE either that especially underpins defense of the powerless.

Certainly realist ontology does not in itself entail such a value, or any particular moral value. In fact, as we discussed above, Objectivism, another realist approach, argues firmly that, rather than defending the powerless, each person should constantly seek to advance his or her individual interests.

We know of only two ways to underpin a value. The first is through logic, but in our experience that method always depends on the acceptance of some other value as a primary value from which to derive the target value. The second is through allegiance to a set of teachings, such as a religion, that spells out values. Both methods rely on some value or values as a starting point. Both methods are available to—and used by—realists and nonrealists alike. It's not clear to us how ENRE relates to either of the above methods or to any other method of underpinning values, though Azevedo wrote as though the relationship were obvious to her.

The next realism we discuss, critical realism, like objectivism, attempted to use logic to generate values from facts alone. Since we share the chief value of critical realism, emancipation, we are sorry to report that in our opinion the attempt to ground emancipation in logic fails. Regardless of possible logical difficulties, critical realism has become very popular among some organization scholars today.

Critical Realism

Critical realism's primary path into the organization studies literature was through the work of philosopher Roy Bhaskar (1975, 1986). Recently, Fleetwood (2005) championed critical realism as a way to deal with the controversy introduced by postmodernism.

Bhaskar (1975) argued that an adequate theory of science must deal satisfactorily with a central paradox that knowledge is a function of both social activity *and* the objects of knowledge. Critical realists, like other realists, claim that objects of an independent physical world are the basis for knowledge. They also acknowledge that human activity plays a central role in the generation of knowledge. Bhaskar defined science as "a social activity whose aim is the production of knowledge of the kinds and ways of acting of independently existing and active things" (p. 24).

According to Fleetwood (2005), while not all critical realists have the same ontological commitments, most of them agree that (1) an entity can exist independently of our knowledge of it, but saying that it *can* does not mean that it *does*; (2) "there is no (defensible) theory-neutral observation, description, interpretation, theorization, explanation or whatever" (p. 199), because humans' access to the world is always mediated through their senses, and these are always mediated by the preexisting stock of conceptual resources that people use to interpret and make sense of things; and (3) an entity is said to be real if it has "*causal efficacy; has an effect on behaviour; makes a difference*" (p. 199). For example, "God may or not be real, but the idea of God is as real as Mount Everest, because the *idea* of God makes a difference to people's actions" (p. 199). Critical realism recognizes that people's preconceptions influence what they take to be knowledge. It demands explicit statements of ontological positions, suggesting that such explicitness can foster dialogue among students of organization studies. Fleetwood noted that critical realism and postmodernism overlap concerning the role of social processes in constructing knowledge. He claimed that the failure of many postmodernists to state their ontological assumptions has been a barrier to synergy.

Reflections on Critical Realism

What We Like About Critical Realism We like the heavy emphasis on the potential of social science to expose unfounded beliefs that retard emancipation. We like the acceptance of induction. And we like both the use of practice to support theory development and the assertion that there is no defensible theory-neutral point of view.

Problems We Have With Critical Realism We think critical realism could benefit from admitting a lack of certainty in two areas: the nature of reality and values.

In regard to the nature of reality, most scholars, including critical realists, agree that we cannot access reality directly. Whether or not we assume an independent external reality, we believe all we have to work with are appearances. Even the complex, layered patterns that critical realism favors are still simply patterns of phenomena; they do not necessitate a leap into faith in some external reality. Consequently, we prefer to keep matters simpler by not taking that leap.

The second area where we think critical realists make excessive claims to knowledge is that of values. Bhaskar (1994), for example, expressed the supposedly universal value that "not to concede to others the rights and benefits one appropriates to oneself or otherwise enjoys is to be guilty of theory/practice inconsistency, and to be untrue to oneself, heterological, heteronomous [*sic*] and alienated" (p. 146). We're not convinced this is a universal value.

Not only do many critical realists claim to know universal values, but they also claim that they can generate values logically, starting with facts.

We treat this issue in some depth here because some scholars (e.g., Locke, 2002; Bhaskar & Collier, 1998) assumed, we believe erroneously, that values could be derived rationally. We think this problematic assumption requires critical analysis.

Bhaskar and Collier (1998) tried to refute, we believe unsuccessfully, Hume's principle that one cannot distinguish between moral good and evil by means of reason or, as Bhaskar and Collier put it, generate values from facts. They started with a hypothetical situation in which false consciousness was known to occur. False consciousness was their fact. From it, they wanted to generate the value that, other things being equal, false consciousness ought to be remedied. They argued as follows: "It may be that a social scientific study can show that a given society necessarily generates, and relies on for its own reproduction, certain false beliefs about itself. But that is something *wrong* with that society, which (other things being equal) ought to be put right" (p. 387).

We think the above argument entails two implicit value judgments or value premises: (1) False consciousness is a wrong, or in the words of Bhaskar and Collier (1998), "one ought to believe what is true"; and (2) wrongs ought to be put right.

Regarding the first premise, Bhaskar and Collier (1998) acknowledged, "It might be said that the view that one ought to believe what is true is itself a value judgment" (p. 387). However, if they had treated this judgment as a premise in their argument, they would have introduced a value and they could not then claim to have generated their conclusion from facts alone.

They offered the reader two different, apparently independent, paths around this difficulty: (1) Bring in the value premise as part of a definition; and (2) blur the distinction between the *rules for* discourse and the *content of* discourse, thereby enabling a rule *applicable to* the argument (the rule that discourse should be truthful) to take on the additional function of premise *in* the argument.

Let us look at these two approaches in more detail.

Bhaskar and Collier (1998) included the premise that one ought to believe what was true in their definition of belief. They maintained that while the principle that one ought to believe the truth was a value judgment in one sense, it was "not an optional value judgment" (p. 387) because it followed from the nature of belief: "One does not even know what belief is if one does not know that you should believe what is true" (pp. 387–388). In other words, the idea that one should believe what is true (as opposed to having false consciousness) was part of the *definition of belief*. We find their introduction of a premise as part of a definition to be problematic.

Later, they listed several cases in which some might not agree that a person always should believe what is true. For example, Plato, in his *Republic*, advocated that citizens believe a "noble lie" about the origin of classes. However, in defense of their premise, they disputed Plato's approach, claiming, "A free and equal society would not need lies" (p. 389).

Giving another example, Bhaskar and Collier (1998) wrote, "It is best if an assassin have false beliefs about his victim's whereabouts" (p. 388). They countered this and other possible exceptions with the claim that "none of this proves that knowledge is not a good or false belief an evil; only that … most things, including true or false belief, are only good or evil 'other things being equal'" (p. 388).

These and other possible exceptions lead us to question the universality of Bhaskar and Collier's definition of *belief*. Moreover, even if one accepts this universality, there is another problem. Their definition includes a value, that is, that one should believe what is true. This raises a problem concerning their position on generalizing values from facts alone, because by using this definition, Bhaskar and Collier began with a value that was not reasoned from fact.

The other attempt that Bhaskar and Collier made to avoid direct introduction of "belief in truth" as a good was to identify truth as a condition for discourse. Quoting Bhaskar (1998, p. 63) they argued:

> That truth *is* a good (*ceteris paribus*) is not only a condition of moral discourse, it is a condition of any discourse at all. Commitment to truth and consistency apply to factual as much as to value discourse and so cannot be seized upon as a concealed (value) premise. (p. 388)

We do not agree that the concept of truth as a good is a condition of *all* discourse. However, even if we did, we wouldn't agree that commitment to truth as a *principle of discourse* makes "Truth is good" into a *premise* of discourse itself.

Bhaskar and Collier did not even deal with the second value premise that is implicit in their argument, namely, the assumption that wrongs ought to be put right. We do not know how one can get from "false consciousness is a wrong" to "false consciousness ought to be put right" without that additional premise.

Given what we see as Bhaskar and Collier's implicit interjection of value into the argument and also the step they omitted, we do not agree with their claim to have generated a value from facts alone.

Without a doubt, positivism and realism are the most frequently mentioned perspectives for attempting to ground organization studies knowledge philosophically. However, a number of others deserve attention.

PRAGMATISM

Andrew Wicks and R. Edward Freeman are our spokespersons for pragmatism. Pragmatism has a relatively long history in American philosophy. Its founders included Charles Sanders Peirce, William James, and John Dewey.

Contributions of Pragmatism

Pragmatism provides insights that are useful for thinking about the knowledge controversy in organization studies. These include ideas about knowledge and the world and Putnam's internal realism.

Knowledge and the World

Pragmatism posits a world "out there." Wicks and Freeman (1998) wrote, "It would be foolish to suggest that reality or the world is simply an illusion in which people can do whatever they choose within it" (p. 126). On the other hand, pragmatism rejects both the privileged status of science and the notion of an objective understanding of an underlying reality.

In general, pragmatism holds "that an ideology or proposition is true if it works satisfactorily, that the meaning of a proposition is to be found in the practical consequences of accepting it, and that unpractical ideas are to be rejected" (McDermid, 2006, p. 1).

Ultimately, Wicks and Freeman wanted to shift the goal of the study of organizations from foundational knowledge to the generation of hope about possibilities for the future. Pragmatism accepts that certain metaphysical and epistemological questions are vexing and seemingly irresolvable. It offers to move beyond them by focusing on one central matter—whether or not information is "useful in the sense of helping people to better cope with the world or to create better organizations" (Wicks and Freeman, 1998, p. 129). In fact, it proposes that the value of research in serving human needs or purposes is the fundamental criterion for judging its worth.

Although they suggested usefulness as the criterion for evaluating information, Wicks and Freeman noted that pragmatism is not utilitarianism. Rather, "the pragmatic value of usefulness simply requires those engaged in research or decision-making to scrutinize the practical relevance of a set of ideas as defined by their purposes and those shared by their community" (1998, p. 129). Thus, members of a research community should begin by asking what set of goals can be agreed on.

In recommending pragmatism for organization studies, Wicks and Freeman (1998) pointed to two advantages. First, by helping to reorient the foundation of organization studies so as to emphasize human purposes, it creates space in organization studies to treat ethics, thereby increasing the relevance of the field's research. Second, it would offer an attractive alternative to the two warring choices, positivism and antipositivism. They claimed that pragmatism was clearly better than a return to positivism, which, by holding that inquiry, should be value-free, positivism-excluded ethics. It was also better than simple antipositivism, which had helpfully revealed the absence of objectivity in the positivist approach, but had not, to date, offered a viable alternative.

Putnam's Internal Realism

Although some pragmatists may disagree with this idea, Hilary Putnam (1987) provided a way of thinking that avoids enmeshment in a conflict between realism and relativism. He called this idea internal realism. To Putnam, internal realism was "at bottom, just the insistence that realism is not incompatible with conceptual relativity. One can be *both* a realist and a conceptual relativist. Realism (with a small 'r') is a view that takes our familiar commonplace scheme as well as our scientific and artistic and other schemes at face value without helping itself to the notion of the thing 'in itself'" (p. 17).

Meanwhile, conceptual relativism maintains that our views depend on the conceptual (linguistic) schemes in which we formulate them. For example, a table can be conceptualized in different ways. The average person views it as solid, but in the scheme of modern physics, it consists of very tiny particles separated by proportionately huge empty spaces.

Putnam claimed that his type of realism was compatible with conceptual relativism, since what is in one sense the same world

> can be described as consisting of "tables and chairs" (and these described as colored, possessing dispositional properties, etc.) in one version *and* in another version, as consisting of open space-time regions, particles, and fields, etc. in other versions. To require that all of these *must* be reducible to a single version is to make the mistake of supposing that "Which are the real objects?" is a question that makes *sense independently of our choice of concepts*. (p. 20)

For Putnam, so long as we limit ourselves to one conceptual scheme, some specific questions such as "How many chairs are in this room?" can have correct answers.

Reflections on Pragmatism for Organization Studies

We like pragmatism a great deal. We especially appreciate its acceptance of uncertainty, its focus on values, and the way it holds its realism lightly. In fact, what some pragmatists call "the world" may be fairly close to what we call "appearances" or "phenomena." We also like Putnam's internal realism, which seems a valuable pattern for integrating the regularities of experience with the role of culture and language in shaping that experience.

We do, however, have concerns about pragmatism. We find the assumption of realism problematic. We also question pragmatism's involvement with "truth." Truth is a prime example of what we call a quicksand term because so many people use it to mean different things and, in doing so, precipitate dysfunctional argument.

To make our concern clear, we consider what two leading pragmatists wrote about truth. In *Truth and Progress* (1998), Richard Rorty referred to his protest that "my pragmatic views still allow me to call some statements 'true' and others 'false' and to argue for so calling them" (p. 2). However, instead of defining "true," he explained why he didn't need to: "The greatest of my many intellectual debts to Donald Davidson is that nobody should even try to specify the nature of truth.... Davidson has helped us realize that the very absoluteness of truth is a good reason for thinking that no theory of the nature of truth is possible. It is only the relative about which there is anything to say. (This is why the God of orthodox monotheists, for example, remains so tiresomely ineffable)" (p. 3). Here Rorty seemed to present truth as a sort of Platonic form with an essence so ineffable that trying to pin it down would be futile.

To give another example, pragmatist Putnam (1990) wrote that "to claim of any statement that it is true, that is, that it is true in its place, in its context, in its conceptual scheme, is roughly, to claim that *it could be justified were epistemic conditions good enough*" (p. vii).

But what does this mean? Putnam explained what would be good epistemic conditions for determining if there was a chair in his study. These included good lighting, good eyesight, and an unconfused mind. However, he stopped short of telling what he meant by truth, with the disclaimer that "for a variety of reasons" (p. viii), what he was offering was *not* a definition of truth.

Thus, while we like pragmatism a great deal, we are bothered by the way some leading pragmatists use a key word like *truth* while appearing unwilling or unable to define it.

Our next alternative, naturalism, is an approach that shares much with pragmatism. It has become popular with some psychologists. We will go into considerable detail about this perspective, because it illustrates several points we want to make about uncertainty.

NATURALISM

E. John Capaldi and Robert W. Proctor championed naturalism in an excellent book (1999) and a fine article (Proctor & Capaldi, 2001). To date, they have directed their work primarily at psychologists; as of this writing, naturalism has not appeared to play a major role in organization studies. However, the approach offers interesting insights for our field, especially in the area of methodology. But first, what is naturalism?

Proctor and Capaldi quoted Callebaut's (1993) description:

> Naturalism as a philosophical movement claims that whatever exists or happens in the world is susceptible to explanation by natural scientific methods; it denies that there is or could be anything which lies in principle beyond the scope of scientific explanation ... naturalism is firmly rooted in the philosophical tradition (materialism, empiricism) (p. xv). (p. 765)

Because Proctor and Capaldi favored the *normative* naturalism of Larry Laudan, we will focus on that specific variety of naturalism. Laudan (1996) wrote:

> I have proposed both a criterion for selecting methodological rules and some principles for evaluating cognitive aims. I have dubbed the combination of these two "normative naturalism". The approach is naturalistic because it regards epistemology and methodology as coextensive with the sciences; it is normative because, unlike many forms of naturalism, it retains a significant role for methodological advice and appraisal. (p. 173)

Laudan (1984) was primarily concerned with cognitive rather than ethical values. He wrote:

> I have nothing to say about ethical values as such, for they are manifestly not the predominant values in the scientific enterprise. Not that ethics plays no role in science; on the contrary, ethical values are always present in scientific decision making and, very occasionally, their influence is of great importance. But that importance fades into insignificance when compared with the ubiquitous role of cognitive values. (p. xii)

Capaldi and Proctor and Laudan expressed strong resistance to relativism. Capaldi and Proctor (1999), for example, saw Pfeffer's (1993) recommendation to study how social sciences achieved paradigm consensus as a malodorous, insidious variety of relativism. Capaldi, Proctor, and Laudan were especially bothered by Kuhn's implication that individual preferences of scientists play a role in theory selection. Laudan challenged Kuhn's position that choices among competing theories depended upon a mixture of objective and subjective factors. He defended sciences as both rational and progressive. Laudan (1996) tried to "rescue the notion of scientific progress" (p. 81). To do so, he took what we see as a relativistic turn when he asked: "Successful according to whom?" or "Progressive according to what standards?" and answered: "Successful by *our* lights; progressive according to *our* standards" (p. 138).

NORMATIVE NATURALIST APPROACH TO METHODOLOGY AND THEORY

Normative naturalists maintain that all issues, including questions of methodology, should be settled empirically. Capaldi and Proctor argued that methodological statements were empirical statements and therefore should be evaluated in the same way as any empirical statement—in terms of usefulness. Drawing on Laudan (1996), they asserted that methodological rules express means-ends relations (e.g., if one's goal is Y, one ought to do X). Since methodological rules can be tested only by their empirical adequacy, ontological commitments are not sufficient justifications for method. In fact, in the chapter "Downplaying Ontology," Capaldi and Proctor (1999) noted that "even a cursory examination of the historical record will serve to show that great scientists often produced monumental accomplishments that not only had little to do with some of their more important ontological assumptions but were actually contrary to those assumptions" (p. 172).

Naturalists consider that methodological commitments may sometimes be dysfunctional. Proctor and Capaldi (2001) pointed to Oreskes's (1999) observation that American geologists were slow to accept plate tectonics because their strong commitment to some methodological beliefs interfered with their appreciation of relevant evidence.

Proctor and Capaldi (2001) claimed naturalism could help deal with the problem that "in American mainstream psychology, the scientific method is identified almost exclusively with hypothesis testing" (p. 759). They observed that this methodological bias has generated serious disagreements that naturalism can help to resolve by calling scholars to evaluate research in terms of its value for advancing specified interests, to pay greater attention to the philosophy of science, and to engage in dialogue with those who seem to hold extremely different perspectives.

Laudan offered some interesting insights regarding theory and method, such as

> Axiological differences can co-exist with factual-level and methodological agreement. (1984, p. 45)
>
> We must simply drop Kuhn's insistence on the integral character of world views or paradigms ... *the various components of a world view are individually negotiable and individually replaceable in a piecemeal fashion* (that is ... replacement of one element need not require wholesale repudiation of all the other components). (1984, p. 73)

> I hold that it is crucial to recognize that there is a whole spectrum of cognitive stances that scientists can adopt toward their theories (suggested by phrases like "entertain", "consider", and "utilize as a working hypothesis"). "Accept" and "reject" are but two (rather remote) points on this spectrum; yet they virtually alone have received serious attention from epistemologists and philosophers. (1996, p. 111)

Reflections on Naturalism

What We Like About Naturalism

Normative naturalism contributed to our thinking in the areas of theory and method. We liked Laudan's insights on these topics both for themselves and for the new ways they gave us to think about Kuhn's offerings. Furthermore, we liked the openness of normative naturalism to methods other than hypothesis testing. We especially liked the idea of settling methodological questions empirically.

Problems We Have With Naturalism

We have two major differences with the values of naturalism. First, we disagree with Laudan's normative naturalist position that ethical values (compared with cognitive values) play an insignificant role in scientific decision making. This position seems like a remnant of the old idea that science can and should be value-free. We think ethical values, such as the values associated with political-economic systems, heavily influence scientific decisions, for example, decisions about what to investigate. We'd like to see such values routinely made explicit.

Second, according to our values about inquiry, naturalism places too much emphasis on certainty instead of trying to maintain an open mind. For one thing, the assumption that all phenomena can be explained by natural scientific methods appears superfluous. Rather than being based on reliable information, it seems to reflect an unnecessary act of faith.

The most significant indication of the quest for certainty was the effort to refute relativism. We think the best way to approach inquiry (in either science or philosophy) is with open-minded willingness to let the chips fall where they may rather than by striving for a previously targeted outcome.

In their zeal to refute relativism, we think Laudan, Proctor, and Capaldi neglected some important considerations, including the following:

1. Some research indicates that personality factors play a role in theory preference (see Mitroff & Kilmann, 1978).
2. Anecdotal evidence indicates that political factors play a role in theory preference. Examples are the apparent effect of Niels Bohr's powerful leadership in the rapid acceptance of the Copenhagen interpretation of quantum mechanics (see Chapter 9) and the

largely unquestioned acceptance of scientism by social scientists (see Chapter 4).

3. Scholars disagree about what they consider rational. Laudan (1984) finessed this point by referring to "*our* intuitive standards of rationality" (p. 64, italics added) as if the scientific community reached consensus about such intuitions. However, we see no evidence that it ever has. Consider the differences in thinking between Einstein and Bohr regarding the Copenhagen interpretation, and the differences between Kuhn and normative naturalists regarding relativism. This point is important because Laudan based a great deal of his argument against Kuhn's relativism on supposedly shared intuitions of rationality.
4. The normative naturalist position on progress in science entails the same kind of relativism as Laudan's approach to rationality, in that both issues ultimately come down to individual intuitions. However, relativism is what the normative naturalists are trying to avoid. Laudan said we can define progress "by our lights." But who does *we* and *our* refer to? Different scholars have different "lights." Postmodernists commonly define *progress* differently from Laudan and consider progress in science a myth (see Kilduff & Mehra, 1997). Furthermore, even Laudan had to tinker a little with the definition of progress in order to make his desired claim. We quote his rationale:

> What is required, if we are to rescue the notion of scientific progress, is a breaking of the link between cumulative retention and progress, so as to allow for the possibility of progress even when there are explanatory losses as well as gains. (1996, p. 81)

By now, our unhappiness with trying to rescue the notion of progress rather than letting the chips fall where they may will come as no surprise. We suspect that politics, individual preferences, and even individual differences in thinking all play some role in theory choice. We'd like to see these potential factors researched further. We think it's better to try to make sense of what's happening even if the information might lead to some uncertainty about science. After all, the information might also help us do better inquiry.

We believe it's possible to maintain that both individual and political factors may influence theory choice, without advocating either radical relativism about science or an anything goes approach. We do not share either of those views. Instead, we see regularities among appearances and think that inquiry can give us numerous useful patterns based on those regularities. Furthermore, we agree with Laudan that some methods are better suited than others for investigating specific problems and that both thinking and scientific norms play major roles in theory choice.

On the other hand, we cannot demonstrate unequivocal progress in science or consensual rules for scientific methodology or scientific thinking. To our minds, it's best to acknowledge such areas of uncertainty and then proceed as best we can.

Now, we will consider what has recently been the most controversial of our alternatives, postmodernism.

POSTMODERNISM

In recent decades, many critics of the dominant scientism marched under the banner of postmodernism. Indeed, postmodernism's popularity and notoriety have been major contributors to the controversy we address here. In order to introduce the influence of the postmodernist perspective in organization studies, we review two different sources: Gergen (2001) and Kilduff and Mehra (1997).

We start with Gergen.

Gergen

Gergen (2001) proposed that the postmodern perspective can help transform latent modernist themes or assumptions prevalent among psychologists. Table 8.2 summarizes three potential transformations.

Incidentally, the three modernist themes in the table were actually embedded in Western culture long before modern times. Plato emphasized individual rationality and saw language as a carrier of truth, and all three themes appeared in the work of Aristotle.

Gergen asserted that postmodern constructionism claims neither truth, nor objectivity, nor universality, nor moral superiority. Elaborating, he wrote:

> To be sure, certain arguments of the traditional kind are put forth (e.g., they follow certain conventions of rational argument, they make reference to an assumed reality, etc.), but this is not to impress them with the stamp of truth. It is only to engage in a cultural practice of sense making. One can scarcely stand outside one's traditions and still communicate effectively. (2001, p. 807)

Moreover, the fact that humans live in a world that is socially structured does not mean that world is any less significant or that people's

TABLE 8.2 Gergen's (2001) Proposed Transformation of Modernist Themes to Postmodernist Themes in Psychology

From (Modernist Theme)	To (Postmodernist Theme)
Centrality of individual knowledge	Communal rhetoric
World as objectively given	World as socially constructed
Language is truth bearing	Language as pragmatic practice

emotions to it are null and void. To illustrate this point, Gergen observed, "To know that a home run is only part of a game does not lessen the thrill of hitting one when the bases are loaded" (2001, p. 807).

In addition, postmodernism focuses on pragmatic outcomes. It opens space for values, as demonstrated by the fact that adopters of the postmodern perspective often do advance a particular standpoint (e.g., Marxist or feminist).

Reactions to Gergen's Postmodernism

Positive Reactions We have a number of positive reactions to Gergen. We like his acceptance of empirical research, the way he challenged scientism head on, and his focus on values. We also like his questioning of modernist assumptions.

Concerns About Gergen's Postmodernism Even though we like his questioning of modernist assumptions, we do not like his next step. Unfortunately, he filled in the gaps left by the questioned assumptions with assumptions of his own rather than leaving openings for exploration, as we would have preferred. For example, he stated, "The postmodernist proposes that language is the child not of the mind but of cultural process" (p. 806). Construing this matter as either/or finesses the possibility that both cultural and neurological factors play a role in language development. We'd like to keep that door open for further inquiry.

As another example, Gergen stated, "One of the most significant vistas opened by the postmodern dialogues lies in the refiguring of theoretical potentials. If scientific descriptions and explanations of the world are not demanded by the nature of the world itself, then one is released from the shackles of the taken for granted" (2001, p. 810). We agree that social construction apparently plays a major role in determining people's views, but we're not ready to consider it the only factor. Perhaps something like "the nature of the world" also plays a part.

In spite of great diversity among cultures at present and over history, there seem to be constancies among reports of some patterns, such as the patterns called stars. These constancies suggest, to us at least, possible limitations on the role of that social construction in the creation of human worldviews.

We would prefer it if Gergen and other scholars, as members of fields concerned with inquiry, treated their own and others' assumptions as assumptions and treated those assumptions with more skepticism than we see now.

Such skepticism would be in the spirit of the founders of both modern science and postmodernism. More skepticism about assumptions might even decrease the amount of dysfunctional debate in organization studies. We should note, however, that harmony in the field is not the goal of this recommendation. We consider discussion of differences essential for any field. On the other hand, we don't think the cause of inquiry is well served by extensive debate over unnecessary, unsubstantiated assumptions.

This brings us to our second treatment of postmodernism, that of Kilduff and Mehra (1997).

Kilduff and Mehra

Unlike Gergen, who directed his paper at psychologists, Kilduff and Mehra (1997) targeted organizational research specifically. Their postmodern approach shares several features with Gergen's, including respect for empirical science, a pragmatic approach, appreciation of diversity, and a social constructionist bent.

Kilduff and Mehra identified some features that they believed were common among postmodernists:

1. Postmodernists reject "overarching propositions" (p. 456).
2. Postmodernists "prefer the interesting over the obvious and place a high value on paradox, contrast, counterintuition, and humor" (p. 473).
3. Postmodernists problematize a number of assumptions that many scholars take for granted. These include:
   a. Greater paradigm unity is achievable or desirable.
   b. It's appropriate for the vast majority of scientists to do "normal science," that is, solve puzzles within accepted theoretical frameworks.
   c. Scientists are unable to shift back and forth between competing paradigms.
   d. Organization studies should privilege middle-range narratives.
   e. The pursuit of truth is a reasonable goal for social science.
   f. It's possible to achieve an unmediated, objective representation of the facts.

According to Kilduff and Mehra (1997), postmodernists seem to make some assumptions of their own, including:

1. Following Cronbach (1982), "general, lasting definite 'laws' are in principle beyond the reach of social science" (p. 465).
2. The idea of progress in science is a myth. This is so because "the more we know, the more we realize we don't know. We progress toward ever greater knowledge of our own ignorance" (p. 466).
3. Rhetoric and aesthetics help determine theory acceptance.
4. Following Wittgenstein, "Certainty is only possible within the boundaries of a particular language game" (p. 463).

Specifics of Kilduff and Mehra's Perspective

Kilduff and Mehra argued "for an epistemology that combines a skepticism toward metanarrative with a commitment to rigorous standards of enquiry in pursuit of radical challenges to accepted knowledge" (1997, p. 453).

Unlike some postmodernists, Kilduff and Mehra followed the tradition of pragmatism in making the seemingly innocuous assumption that there is a real world that can be systematically investigated.

Like the original postmodernism, which developed in architecture as a reaction to the modern style, Kilduff and Mehra were "eclectic rather than exclusive" (1997, p. 457). They sought to "include and use techniques, insights, methods, and approaches from a variety of traditions, reaching backwards, forwards, and sideways with little regard for academic boundaries or the myth of progress" (p. 457). Consequently, they did not oppose modernity and the achievements of modern science.

Reflections on Kilduff and Mehra's Postmodern Approach

Positive Features We like this approach a great deal. Of all the alternatives we reviewed, this seems to us the most compatible with our own generative uncertainty. We especially like the list of assumptions that Kilduff and Mehra said postmodernism "problematizes." We agree that these assumptions need a thorough reassessment.

We also like the combination of a high degree of eclecticism and a willingness to apply standards. This is not an "anything goes" approach. Furthermore, we liked the excitement about research we felt in reading Kilduff and Mehra's paper.

Some Concerns About Kilduff and Mehra's Approach We question some of their assumptions:

1. General, lasting laws are beyond the reach of social science. (Our view is that this position may be a self-fulfilling prophecy. We don't see any reason to close that particular door at present.)
2. The pragmatism-based realist assumption. (As noted earlier in this chapter, we view the assumption of realism as problematic.)
3. Progress is a myth. (We see *progress* as a quicksand term in that it is used in different ways by people on different sides of an argument. By some definitions, progress is a myth. By others, it is not.)
4. Certainty is possible only within a particular language game. (We don't think total, absolute certainty makes sense in any language game, but a high degree of certainty seems possible in some cases, even *across* language games. For example, people can probably be fairly certain in predicting the phenomena we call sunrise, the rate of falling bodies, and the boiling of water.)

FLYVBJERG—*PHRONESIS*

Phronetic Science

Recently, Bent Flyvbjerg (2001, 2006) proposed reemphasis on one of Aristotle's knowledge virtues—*phronesis*—as a path to more meaningful social science. He reasoned from the assumption that contemporary social science was losing to the natural sciences in the science wars (illustrated by recent attempts, e.g., the Sokal hoax by natural scientists to denigrate the social sciences). He had little hope of significant gain if social scientists continued to emulate the natural sciences because they were not likely to be able to produce the cumulative and predictive theory of those sciences. Flyvbjerg (2001) believed that the social sciences currently could not provide the type of knowledge esteemed by the modern ideal science project, that is, knowledge that was "universal, invariable, context-independent." At present, theories of this sort do not exist in the social sciences. He acknowledged they might exist in the future; however, because the results of social science research depend heavily on the context in which phenomena are studied, it is "probable" (p. 46) that social science can never be explanatory and predictive. Further, social science research is unlikely to provide the type of cumulative knowledge that earned natural sciences their high esteem. Driving home the probability idea, he wrote that the fact that no one has found the elements that could make the study of human activity predictive "does not rule out the possibility that these elements might exist" (p. 46).

Social scientists, including such greats as Marx, Comte, and Freud, idealized the sort of knowledge the natural science paradigm offered and sought to emulate natural scientists. However, in view of the problems noted above, modern social scientists should abandon this ideal and turn their attention to research that is directed toward one of Aristotle's three virtues of knowledge (*phronesis*) that was supressed by the Enlightenment's emphasis on Aristotle's other knowledge virtues (*episteme* and *techne*). Flyvbjerg (2006) wrote, "Research practiced as *episteme* is concerned with uncovering universal truths about organization and organizing" (p. 372). This sort of knowledge differs from the two other intellectual virtues that Aristotle proposed, one of which was *techne*, or craft/art, which is concerned with pragmatic knowledge or instrumental rationality.

Whereas the natural sciences have a comparative advantage with respect to the latter two virtues, social sciences have one with respect to *phronesis*.

Phronesis concerns ethics. It is concerned with values, interests, and power. It "goes beyond both analytical, scientific knowledge (*episteme*) and technical knowledge or know-how (*techne*) and involves judgments and decisions" (p. 2) resembling those made by social and political actors. It concerns analysis of "things that are good or bad for man"

(Flyvbjerg, 2001, p. 57). Its main objective is to provide input for social dialogue and praxis.

Phronetic researchers focus on values, for example, "Where are we going?" and "Is it desirable?" (p. 130). They reject the view that central values that can be rationally and universally grounded exist. However, they are not left normless; they assume that values are produced socially and historically and thus are situational and contextual.

Flybjerg noted, as we have in our treatment of some social scientists' reactions to postmodernism, that many fear that abandoning faith in the possibility of theory and epistemology that the idealized modern science project appears to offer paves the way for relativism and nihilism. However, Flybjerg noted that "the door is already wide open for relativistic and nihilistic tendencies, insofar as epistemically oriented social scientists ignore the fact that epistemic theory cannot serve as a bulwark against relativism and nihilism since such theory … does not currently exist and can probably never come to exist" (2001, p. 48).

Following these ideas, Flyvbjerg (2001) triumphantly concluded, "We have repealed the conventional normal science ideal for social science" (p. 48). On the basis of what he called the deconstruction of the conventional scientific ideal for the social sciences and its emphasis on theory and context independence, Flyvbjerg advised that social scientists take new direction by returning to Aristotle's *phronesis,* which the Enlightenment suppressed.

Aristotle believed that one of the major goals for studying the social and political dimensions was to develop society's value rationality *vis-à-vis* its scientific and technical rationality. Aristotle attached great importance to value rationality, but Flyvbjerg lamented that since the Enlightenment modernity installed instrumental rationality (emphasis on means without attention to ends) in both science and society.

To recover from this loss stemming from modernity, Flyvbjerg urged social scientists to concern themselves with the analysis of values. Doing so, they would ask: What things are good for humans? Three specific questions (the classic value-relational questions) need to be addressed: Where are we going? Is it desirable? What should be done? Flyvbjerg (2001) sketched the main features of a phronetic social science that could deal with such questions in which he proposed some methodological guidelines. He advanced these guidelines as "cautionary indicators of direction" (p. 129).

Methodological Guidelines

1. *Focus on values.* Focusing on values begins with attending to the above three classic value-rational questions. Such inquiry demands considering foundationalism vs. relativism. Phronetic researchers reject both of these "isms" in favor of contextualism or "situational ethics" (p. 130). Grounding judgments in the relevant sociohistorical context guards against nihilism and relativism. Validity is open to other interpretations. Every interpretation must be built

on claims of validity, and these claims depend on basic ground rules of a community of social scientists. The objective is always to come to a "better" interpretation. To arrive at "better" interpretations, social scientists dialogue with one another using established ground rules.

2. *Place power at core of analysis.* This emphasis directs attention to another series of questions, including:
   a. Who gains and who loses?
   b. What possibilities are available to change existing poor relations?
   c. Is it desirable to do so?
3. *Getting close to reality.* This involves centering one's research in the context studied and getting very close to the phenomenon. A phronetic researcher becomes part of the phenomenon studied. Achieving the goal of getting close to phenomena can involve getting away from the theoretical and scientific literature.
4. *Emphasizing little things.* This can involve what Clifford Geertz and Gilbert Ryle called "thick description." Such research demands exacting attention to detail.
5. *Looking at practice before discourse.* Focus is on the actual daily practices that constitute a given field of interest.
6. *Study cases and context.* Emphasis on study of concrete cases. Importantly, cases exist in contexts, and it is vital to recognize the context dependence.
7. *Asking "how."* By focusing on "how," phronetic researchers are able to develop "descriptions and interpretations … from the perspective of participants, researchers, and others" (p. 137).
8. *Joining agency and structure.* Study attends at both the actor and structural levels. Actions of people are analyzed in relation to organization structures.
9. *Dialoguing with a polyphony of voices.* Successful phronetic research includes many voices, including the researcher's, without the researcher's voice claiming final authority (Flyvbjerg, 2001, p. 129).

Overview of Phronetic Social Science

Phronetic research does not try to develop either theory or universal method. Flyvbjerg (2001) summarized: One task of phronetic research is "to provide concrete examples and detailed narratives of how power works … and to suggest how power might be changed" (p. 140).

Our Reactions to Phronesis

Positive Reactions to Flyvbjerg

Several aspects of Flyvbjerg's view are very appealing to us. For instance, we applaud Flyvbjerg for calling attention to the possibility that the idealized model of science of the modern project and the natural sciences themselves may not be the appropriate examples for social scientists. Furthermore, his observation that attention to power and the social nature of inquiry, at least sometimes, even in the natural sciences fall short of the scientific ideal of providing cumulative, universal knowledge is important in view of the concerns that people have about postmodernism opening the door to nihilism and relativism. Flyvbjerg (2001) observed the door was always open; it was just that the natural science ideal was so strong that implications of the difficulties of realizing it were overlooked. Likewise, we appreciated his acknowledgment of uncertainty, for example, his use of the word *probably* to refer to the limits of the possibilities of human knowledge and his proposal of methodological guidelines as cautionary indicators.

Further, we appreciate his recognition of how attention to values was suppressed by achievements of the natural sciences and his drawing attention to the importance of power. We also appreciate his questioning of the idea that central values can be rationally and universally grounded.

One of the other things we like about Flyvbjerg is that he appears to make very few assumptions. Undoubtedly, his ability to avoid assumptions was aided by his willingness to live with uncertainty, as reflected when he wrote that things were "probable" and introduced his guidelines for research as "cautionary indictors of direction." Also, the emphasis he placed on situational dependence enabled him to avoid the assumptions that more absolutistic stances often entail.

Overall, we find much to like about phronetic research as developed by Flyvbjerg. Among other things, it embodies the agnostic spirit about human knowledge we find attractive. In addition, it calls attention to how, in recent centuries, scientism suppressed awareness that interests and values influence inquiry. Moreover, the call for researchers to get close to the phenomena and look at context resonates with us. These insights stimulate the questioning of the value of emulating natural sciences such as physics—an issue to which we devote the next chapter.

"PFEFFERISM"

"Pfefferism" is not a fully developed alternative like others we have discussed. Rather, it is a shorthand term to refer to ideas from a paper by Jeffrey Pfeffer (1993) that have been widely discussed in connection with the controversy about knowledge in organization studies.

Pfeffer made few, if any, explicit philosophical assumptions. Instead, he focused on helping the field to gain influence and resources. The major tactic he advanced for accomplishing this was development and institution of a "strong" paradigm (i.e., a paradigm on which there was consensus).[4] To accomplish this, he proposed that influential members in the field control venues of access and dissemination. He thus implied that paradigm consensus could be socially created. He wrote:

> Members of high-paradigm fields enforce both theoretical and methodological conformity. They do this by reserving the most desirable places only for those who conform to the disciplinary orthodoxy and criticizing, regardless of their power or the validity of their ideas, those who depart from the established paths. (1993, p. 614)

Reflecting on Pfefferism

Pfeffer's view has stimulated many critical comments, including at least two article-length rejoinders (Canella & Paetzold, 1994; Van Maanen, 1995).

Pfefferism seems silent on the type of philosophical issues that concern us in this book. In fact, the substance and philosophy that underlie application of Pfeffer's pragmatic advice could be almost anything. However, today, if one implemented Pfeffer's suggestion for development of a single tight paradigm, realism and positivism might be likely candidates to take over organization studies, at least in terms of number of current influential supporters. Perhaps that explains why so many of Pfeffer's critics have filled the vacuum in his paper by attributing (we believe misattributing) realist or positivist positions to him.

In any case, we like Pfeffer's suggestion for students of organizations to examine the process of consensus formation in various fields. However, his proposal for organization scholars deliberately to make paradigm decisions on the basis of political goals violates our value of intellectual integrity. This practice would require some organization scholars to endorse a paradigm that they didn't assent to intellectually or to pressure others to endorse a chosen paradigm. While we think some influences of personal and political factors on scientific thinking may be unavoidable, we still value intellectual integrity in the form of efforts to examine such influences, to be honest about possible biases, and to avoid introducing deliberate biases. We also think the practice would do harm in the long run by corroding people's trust in organization studies.

We now turn to another suggestion for improving organization studies, that of Zald, who called for students of organizations to become better humanists.

ZALD—BECOMING BETTER HUMANISTS

Although Zald's (1993) proposal to become better humanists is not an alternative philosophical perspective in the same way that realism and pragmatism are, the idea is related to many of the issues (e.g., the privileged position of science) that concern us in this book.

Zald's (1993) fundamental concern was that social scientists, by focusing so strongly on presenting their disciplines as physics-like sciences, neglected the fact that their disciplines are also partly humanities.

He proposed that efforts to appear to be doing science were associated with accepting a problematic dichotomy, that is, science or humanity. However, he argued that inquiry in social science is better viewed as a continuum with science at one pole and humanities at the other. Unfortunately, acceptance of the problematic dichotomy resulted in social scientists emphasizing the scientific end of the continuum and thereby making their disciplines, at best, "*poor* humanities" (p. 514).

Zald, consistent with our discussion of scientism in Chapter 4, argued that the emphasis on science did not come from reflections upon philosophical foundations but rather from the social practices of academicians.

Zald suggested that if social scientists followed his advice and gave more explicit attention to the humanities, they would become more sensitive to context and would recognize that their theories, rather than being representations of general truth, are better interpreted as conceptualizations of concrete historical trends.

At the same time, Zald (1993) insisted that information generated from the science end of the field is still valuable. Thus, the issue is not one of humanities versus science but rather "how we *combine* a positivistic programme of theoretical and empirical accumulation with the enriching possibilities of the humanities" (p. 516). If social scientists follow this path, they will pay more attention to the role of values in inquiry.

Reflections on Becoming Better Humanists

Insights from the humanities could be useful in conjunction with many of the alternatives we have discussed. We especially like Zald's recognition of the influence of values and his recognition that the widespread emulation of the natural sceinces was based upon neither reflection nor relevant philosophy.

CONCLUSION

In this chapter, we reviewed what we believe to be the major current alternative perspectives for dealing with the knowledge controversy in organization studies. While from our generative uncertainty standpoint we saw merit in each perspective, we also found problems with each one, often in the form of unnecessary assumptions.

In Chapters 1 and 2, we described our own alternative, generative uncertainty. We believe our perspective incorporates many of the advantages of the alternatives considered above while avoiding many of their problematic assumptions.

ENDNOTES

1. The opposite of the primacy of existence would be the primacy of consciousness, according to which consciousness would come first and create existence. However, for objectivists, this principle must be false, because consciousness lacks the power to create reality.
2. Peikoff (1991) elaborated on this concept by asserting, "For any living organism, the course of action that survival demands is continuous, full-time, *all-embracing.* No action an organism takes is irrelevant to its existence" (p. 215).
3. Hunt is one of three scholars we discuss in this book who recommended making theory choices for the sake of personal or political advantage. (The other two are Burrell and Pfeffer.) We think it's a very bad idea!
4. There is an obvious similarity between Pfeffer's proposed tactic and Merriam's (1921) proposal for political science in the early 1900s. Rorty (2002) noted that the founders sought to save philosophy from "metaphysical idealism" (p. 704) and also save moral and religious ideals from empiricist and positivist skepticism. We have encountered different explanations of the origin of the term *pragmatism*. Peirce was known to believe that the purpose "or inquiry is not to represent reality, but rather to enable us to act more effectively" (p. 704).

REFERENCES

Azevedo, J. (1997). *Mapping reality: An evolutionary realist methodology for the natural and social sciences*. Albany, NY: State University of New York Press.

Azevedo, J. (2002). Updating organizational epistemology. In J. A. C. Baum (Ed.), *The Blackwell companion to organizations* (pp. 715–732). Oxford, UK: Blackwell Publishers.

Bhaskar, R. (1975). A *realist theory of science*. Leeds, UK: Leeds Books Ltd.

Bhaskar, R. (1986). *Scientific realism and human emancipation*. London, UK: Verso.

Bhaskar, R. (1994). *Plato etc*. London, UK: Verso.

Bhaskar, R., & Collier, A. (1998). Introduction: Explanatory critiques. In M. Archer, R. Bhaskar, A. Collier, T. I. Lawson, & A. Norrie (Eds.), *Critical realism: Essential readings* (pp. 385–394). New York, NY: Routledge.

Blau, P. M. (1970). A formal theory of differentiation in organizations. *American Sociological Review*, *35*(2), 201–218.

Blau, P. M. (1972). Interdependence and hierarchy in organizations. *Social Science Research*, *1*, 1–24.

Callebaut, W. (1993). *Taking the naturalistic turn or how the real philosophy of science is done*. Chicago, IL: University of Chicago Press.

Campbell, D. T. (1987). Evolutionary epistemology. In G. Radnitzky & W.W. Bartley III (Eds.), *Evolutionary epistemology, rationality, and the sociology of knowledge* (pp. 47–89). La Salle, IL: Open Court.

Canella, A. A., Jr., & Paetzold, R. L. (1994). Pfeffer's barriers to the advance or organizational science. *Academy of Management Review*, *19*, 331–341.

Capaldi, E. S., & Proctor, R. W. (1999). *Contextualism in psychological research? A critical review*. Thousand Oaks, CA: Sage Publications.

Comte, A. (1975). Cours de Philosophie Positive (1830–1842). In G. Lenzer (Ed.), *Auguste Comte and positivism: The essential writings*. New York, NY: Harper.

Connor, R. C., & Norris, K. S. (1982). Are dolphins reciprocal altruists? *American Naturalist, 119*, 358–374.

Cronbach, L. S. (1982). Prudent aspirations for social inquiry. In W.H. Kruskal (Ed.), *The social sciences: Their nature and uses* (pp. 61–81). Chicago, IL: University of Chicago Press.

Donaldson, L. (1992). The Weick stuff: Managing beyond games. *Organization Science*, 3(4), 461–466.

Donaldson, L. (1996). *For positivist organization theory*. London, UK: Sage Publications.

Donaldson, L. (2003). Organization theory as a positive science. In H. Tsoukas & C. Knudsen (Eds.), *The Oxford handbook of organization theory: Meta-theoretical perspectives* (pp. 39–62). Oxford, UK: Oxford University Press.

Fleetwood, S. (2005). Ontology in organization and management studies: A critical realist perspective. *Organization, 12*, 197–222.

Flyvbjerg, B. (2001). *Making social science matter: Why social inquiry fails and how it can succeed again*. Cambridge, UK: Cambridge University Press.

Flyvbjerg, B. (2006). Making research matter: Power, values and phonesis. In S. R. Clegg, C. Hardy, T. R. Laurence, & W. R. Nord (Eds.), *Sage handbook of organization studies* (pp. 370–387). London, UK: Sage Publications.

Gergen, K. J. (2001). Psychological science in a postmodern context. *American Psychologist* 56(10), 803–813.

Ghate, O., & Locke, E. A. (2003). Objectivism: The proper alternative to postmodernism. In E. A. Locke (Ed.), *Postmodernism and management: Pros, cons and the alternative* (pp. 249–278). Amsterdam, Netherlands: JAI.

Harré, R. (1986). *Varieties of realism*. Oxford, UK: Basil Blackwell.

Hunt, S. D. (1994). On the rhetoric of qualitative methods: Toward historically informed argumentation. *Journal of Management, 3*, 221–234.

Hunt, S. D. (2005). For truth and realism in management research. *Journal of Management Inquiry, 14*(2), 122–138.

Kilduff, M., & Mehra, A. (1997). Postmodernism and organizational research. *Academy of Management Review, 22*, 453–481.

Kincaid, H. (1996). *Philosophical foundations of the social sciences*. New York, NY: Cambridge University Press.

Kincaid, H. (2000). Positivism in the social sciences. In *Concise Routledge encyclopedia of philosophy* (p. 696). London, UK: Routledge.

Laudan, L. (1984). *Science and values: The aims of science and their role in scientific debate*. Berkeley, CA: University of California Press.

Laudan, L. (1996). *Beyond positivism and relativism: Theory, method and evidence*. Boulder, CO: Westview.

Leplin, J. (1984). *Scientific realism*. Berkeley, CA: University of California Press.

Locke, E. A. (2002). The dead end of postmodernism. *American Psychologist*, 57(6/7), 458.

Locke, E. A. (Ed.). (2003). *Postmodernism and management: Pros, cons and the alternative*. Amsterdam, Netherlands: JAI.

Marais, E. (1969). *The soul of the ape*. New York, NY: Atheneum.

Masson, J. M., & McCarthy, S. (1995). *When elephants weep: The emotional lives of animals*. New York, NY: Delacorte Press.

McDermid, D. (2006). Pragmatism. In *Internet encyclopedia of philosophy*. Retrieved from www.jep.utm.edu/p/pragmati-39k
McMullin, E. (1984). A case for scientific realism. In J. Leplin (Ed.), *Scientific realism* (pp. 8-40). Berkeley, CA: University of California Press.
Merriam, C. E. (1921). The present state of the study of politics. *American Political Science Review, 15*(2), 173–185.
Mir, R., & Mir, A. (2002). The organizational imagination: From paradigm wars to praxis. *Organizational Research Methods, 5*, 105–125.
Mitroff, I. I., & Kilmann, R. H. (1978). *Methodological approaches to social science*. San Francisco, CA: Jossey Bass.
Oreskes, N. (1999). *The rejection of continental drift: Theory and method in American earth science*. New York, NY: Oxford University Press.
Peikoff, L. (1991). *Objectivism: The philosophy of Ayn Rand*. New York, NY: Penguin Books.
Pfeffer, J. (1993). Barriers to the advance of organizational science: Paradigm development as a dependent variable. *Academy of Management Review, 18*(4), 599–620.
Popper, K. R. (1962). *Conjectures and reflections: The growth of scientific knowledge*. New York, NY: Basic Books.
Proctor, R. W., & Capaldi, E. J. (2001). Empirical evaluation and justification of methodologies in psychological science. *Psychological Bulletin, 127*(6), 759–772.
Putnam, H. (1981). *Reason, truth and history*. New York, NY: Cambridge University Press.
Putnam, H. (1987). *The many faces of realism: The Paul Carus lectures*. LaSalle, IL: Open Court.
Putnam, H. (1990). *Realism with a human face*. Cambridge, MA: Harvard University Press.
Quine, W.V. (1951). Main trends in recent philosophy: Two dogmas of empiricism. *Philosophical Review, 60*(1), 20–43.
Rand, A. (1964). *The virtue of selfishness: A new concept of egoism?* New York: New American Library.
Rand, A. (1990). *Introduction to objectivist epistemology* (expanded 2nd ed.). New York, NY: Penguin Group.
Rorty, R. (1998). *Truth and progress.* New York: Cambridge University Press.
Rorty, R. (2002). Pragmatism. In *Concise Routledge encyclopedia of philosophy* (pp. 704–705). London, UK: Routledge.
Van Maanen, J. (1955). Fear and loathing in organizational studies. *Organizational Science, 6*, 687–694.
Wicks, A. C., & Freeman, R. E. (1998). Organization studies and the new pragmaticism: Positivism, anti-positivism, and the search for ethics. *Organization Science, 9*(2), 123–140.
Zald, M. N. (1993). Organization studies as a scientific and humanistic enterprise: Toward a reconceptualization of the field. *Organization Science, 4*(4), 513–528.

SECTION

4

Letting Go

CHAPTER

9

Letting Go of Misguided Attempts to Emulate Physics

In Chapter 4, we showed that for over 100 years Anglo-North American social scientists shaped their inquiry by attempting to follow in the footsteps of natural scientists. In recent years, "physics envy" has been used to refer to this phenomenon. Tapp (2007) described the situation in these words: "Physics envy implies a hierarchy of disciplines with physics at the top. Economists are probably most prone to it, with biologists and psychologists not far behind" (p. 229). Among social scientists, physics envy has been associated with attempts to emulate physics. Given what appears to be physics' success, there seems to be good reason for such emulation.

However, there is reason to believe this emulation rests on a shaky foundation. Campbell (1990) suggested that the admiration many psychologists have for physics is associated with a misunderstanding of the practices of physics. Support for this view came from Secord (1986), who observed that much of the admiration for physics is based on Newtonian physics. This is a problem because, as Secord noted, most contemporary physicists recognize that "Newtonian physics is an anomaly—other areas of physics have little resemblance to it" (p. 200).

Newtonian physics' value for dealing with human experiences in the medium-sized world between the quantum and cosmological levels induced many to believe physics produced knowledge that was certain. The generative uncertainty perspective encouraged us to examine the matter in modern physics. This examination revealed much less certainty about knowledge and even doubts about whether certain knowledge is possible.

Most of what we humans think of as our everyday experiences appears to take place in what Jeans (1981) termed the human-sized world, the Newtonian world of billiard balls and inclined planes. When we humans consider experiences in this world of medium-sized objects, such as stubbing a toe in the dark, the existence of an independent, knowable external reality seems obvious. Our perceptual patterns appear to us as the pictures, sounds, smells, taste, and touch of reality itself. Likewise, the consistent, repeatable results of much research physicists report seems to be about that same "real" world of our perceptions. Thus, it is tempting to think that physicists are what we call commonsense realists. However, as we will see, commonsense realism is not consistent with many well-known observations of modern physics.

Some phenomena of quantum physics, for example, (1) the Heisenberg uncertainty principle connected with the results of the double-slit experiment, and (2) what Einstein called "spooky action at a distance," all pose major challenges to the seemingly simple assumption of commonsense realism.

The possibility that physics envy is associated with lack of understanding of the practice of physics stimulated our curiosity about that practice. In this chapter, we explore two questions: (1) Do physicists generally espouse commonsense realism? (2) What do physicists actually do?

Even though our friend, philosopher Kristin Schrader-Frechette,[1] assures us that today in scholarly circles commonsense realism is dead, our experiences as Anglo-North American social scientists led us to sense vestiges of commonsense realism in organization studies. Given these vestiges of commonsense realism in organization studies, we ask: Do physicists espouse commonsense realism? Let us explain. Our experiences as Anglo-North American social scientists led us to suspect that some of our colleagues may be latent commonsense realists. These suspicions were strengthened when we read some recent publications of highly regarded organization studies writers McKelvey (2002), Ghate and Locke (2003), and Hunt (2005).

McKelvey (2002) wrote, "The natural sciences are held in high esteem because they are OBJECTIVIST—their use of external reality serves as the ultimate criterion" (p. 753). Similarly, in advancing the case of objectivism in an argument we described in some depth in the previous chapter, Ghate and Locke (2003) observed that if the concepts are formed by the correct method, they are "… based in reality" (p. 264).

Yet another vestige of commonsense realism appeared in Hunt (2005). On one hand, Hunt was clear that at present realism cannot satisfactorily explain many phenomena of contemporary quantum physics, such as wave-particle duality. On the other hand, in the same article, while describing a model of truth and scientific realism, he wrote, "A high proportion of successes, relative to failures, gives reason to believe that something similar to the entities, attributes, and structures posited … actually exist in the world external to the theory" (p. 134).

After considering the matter of commonsense realism in physics, we try to answer our second question: What do physicists do? Following these efforts we consider what, if any, aspects are worth emulating.

QUESTION 1: DO PHYSICISTS ESPOUSE COMMONSENSE REALISM?

Many phenomena discussed in contemporary physics involve far more obvious uncertainties than those studied in Newtonian physics. We consider a few examples, beginning with the Heisenberg uncertainty principle.

Heisenberg Uncertainty Principle

Quoting Lightman (1997):

> The basic idea behind the Heisenberg uncertainty principle is that all matter and energy behave partly like a wave and partly like a particle. For the moment, we will use the word "particle" to describe a bit of matter, such as an electron or photon. Let's measure the position and motion of a particle at the moment it passes through a small hole, such as a pinhole in a window shade. It is a fact of nature that the particle acts partly like a wave. When a wave passes through a narrow hole, it spreads out in a series of outgoing ripples…. Analogously, a water wave moving past a branch on a pond breaks up into many ripples and goes outward in all directions…. As a result of such spreading out "downstream" of the hole, we cannot tell exactly the direction of any particular particle when it emerges from the hole. Thus, we cannot accurately specify the initial conditions of the particle at the hole. Consequently, we cannot accurately determine the particle's future trajectory. The amount of spreading out gets bigger the smaller the hole. If we make the hole very small, so that we know very accurately the initial *position* of the particle, the uncertainty in the particle's initial *direction* becomes very large, because the particle could begin its trajectory anywhere inside the area enclosed by the hole. So, the wave-particle duality leads to an unavoidable tradeoff: we can accurately measure the initial position *or* the initial motion of a particle, but not both. Unfortunately, an accurate determination of the future trajectory requires that we accurately specify both. We are stuck with an unavoidable uncertainty. (pp. 209–210)

This is a famous example of how, at the quantum level, we encounter a degree of uncertainty that limits claims to accessing a knowable external reality.

The famous double-slit experiment illustrates the wave-particle duality of nature.

The Double-Slit Experiment

In this famous experiment, the physicist beams photons (the smallest unit of detectable light) through a screen with two slits in it. Again, we quote Lightman (1997) on the results:

> When we don't check to see which slit each photon goes through, each photon behaves as if it went through both slits at the same time, as a spread out wave would do. When we do check, each photon goes through *either* one slit *or* the other and behaves as a particle. Light behaves sometimes as a wave and sometimes as a particle.... Astoundingly ... the behavior that occurs in a given experiment depends on what the experimenter chooses to measure. Evidently, the observer and the knowledge sought by the observer, play some kind of a fundamental role in the properties of the thing observed. The observer is somehow part of the system. These results call into question the long-held notion of an external reality, outside and independent of the observer. (p. 200)[2]

The above phenomena challenged worldviews of physicists that worked well up until the 20th century. Shankar (1980) described the experience this way: "Qualitatively we know that the deterministic world of classical mechanics does not exist. Once we have bitten the quantum apple, our loss of innocence is permanent" (p. 189).

Quantum theory pressured physicists to question the certainties of pre-20th-century physics, and to favor perspectives that entail more ambiguity and uncertainty. In this regard, John Bell (1989) commented that quantum theory "introduces an essential ambiguity into fundamental physical theory, if only at a level of accuracy and completeness beyond any required in practice. It is the toleration of such an ambiguity, not merely provisionally but permanently, and at the most fundamental level, that is the real break with the classical ideal" (p. 362).

"Spooky Action at a Distance"

Einstein used this label derogatorily to refer to the phenomenon in which two particles, for example, two photons in the nucleus of a calcium atom, can become entangled so that after they separate, an action performed on one, such as measurement of polarization, will instantaneously affect measurements of the other. This influence happens so quickly (more rapidly than it could if it did not move faster than the speed of light), unmediated, and not diminished with increasing distance between the particles. Bell's famous theorem treats this phenomenon. This theorem refers to a family of results demonstrating that a local realistic interpretation of quantum mechanics is impossible (Shimony, 2004). In this context, Felder (1999) noted that locality is the principle that an event, which happens at one place, cannot *instantaneously* affect an event some place else. Instantaneously, in this perspective, refers to a time span shorter than that required for light to travel between the two places involved. Many physicists accept the validity of this theorem and believe locality, at the quantum level, is dead.

Such an interpretation seems inconsistent with the belief in the universal certainty of Newtonian mechanics. Phenomena of this sort led physicist-philosopher Sir James Jeans (1981) to assert that Newtonian mechanics was valid only for what he called the "man-sized" world—the portion of the universe about halfway between the world of the electron and the world of the nebulae.[2]

Physicists devised a number of ways to deal with these counterintuitive, seemingly bizarre, phenomena. We begin with Einstein, who seemingly attempted to maintain realism in the face of quantum phenomena. Then we discuss some recent interpretations of quantum mechanics, giving special attention to two widely different approaches that handle the phenomena but do not include commonsense realism. Finally, we give examples of two modern physicists who called themselves realists, showing that even their approaches differ greatly from commonsense realism.

Einstein

Quantum mechanics disturbed Einstein in a number of ways: For one thing, he believed in an external world, independent of the observer, as a basis for all natural science. Quantum theory did not mesh well with that foundation. In addition, his famous statement often quoted as "God does not play dice"[3] revealed his disdain for the uncertainty principle. Furthermore, he did not like the fact that the equations of quantum mechanics predicted "spooky action at a distance," which potentially violated his belief that nothing can travel faster than light.

Einstein, Podolsky, and Rosen (1935) challenged quantum mechanics with a thought experiment, called the EPR experiment, which dealt with entangled protons. The experiment presumably showed that what appeared to be changes in one proton resulting from changes in the other merely reflected characteristics that were present in the first proton from the start.

Years later, after Einstein's death, John Bell (1964) demonstrated conceptually that the EPR argument did not hold up. Later still, in the 1970s, actual experiments verified Bell's argument. However, even before the conceptual and experimental evidence became available, Einstein's realism had lost out among physicists, to the Copenhagen interpretation of quantum physics.

Copenhagen Interpretation

Few, if any, physicists argue with the equations of quantum mechanics; most agree that these equations yield accurate results. Current disagreements have to do only with *interpretations* of those equations. For many years, the Copenhagen interpretation easily led all others in popularity, but according to Tegmark (1997) this situation has begun to change.[4] He stated:

> A (highly unscientific) poll taken at the 1997 UMBC quantum mechanics workshop gave the once all-dominant Copenhagen interpretation less than half the votes. The Many Worlds Interpretation (MWI) scored second, comfortably ahead of the Consistent Histories and Bohm interpretations. It is argued that since all the above-mentioned approaches to nonrelativistic quantum mechanics give identical cookbook prescriptions for how to calculate things in practice, practical-minded experimentalists, who have traditionally adopted the "shut-up-and-calculate interpretation" typically show little interest in whether cozy classical concepts are in fact real in some untestable metaphysical sense. (p. 855)

Here Tegmark raised the question of whether or not it matters which of the four interpretations one prefers, since all give the same results and no test is presently available for selecting among them. Tegmark's four interpretations comprise just a few of the many available. Wikipedia (2006), for example, lists 16 of them. Tegmark's "shut up and calculate" (1997) is an extreme version of instrumentalism, an approach frequently adopted by proponents of the dominant Copenhagen interpretation. We now discuss the first and the second most popular interpretations in Tegmark's survey, instrumentalism and the many worlds interpretation. Can physicists who hold either of these positions be called commonsense realists?

Two Approaches to Quantum Phenomena

Instrumentalism

Physicists of this persuasion are called instrumentalists because they believe that physical theories are best seen as instruments for predicting the results of observation. Instrumentalism offers no definition of or discussion of independent reality. A knowable, independent reality does not even have a place in this approach.

As d'Espagnat (1989) explained, the ontological position of instrumentalism has a social constructionist tinge. Proponents of this interpretation point out that experimenters arrange conditions to make results intelligible not only to themselves but also to all human beings. In other words, scientists force nature to express itself in human language. Thus, the assertion that scientific research yields knowledge of the very structures of independent reality goes too far.

Many Worlds

In the late 1950s, Hugh Everett, then a graduate student in physics at Princeton, postulated that the whole of physical reality contains many worlds. Within each universe, the particles interact with each other, just as they do in the portion of the universe we know. However, each universe also affects the others, but only weakly, through interference phenomena (Deutsch, 1997).[5] To explain the results of some experiments, Everett envisioned two sorts of photons: tangible photons and shadow photons. Tangible photons are the ones that we can see and detect using instruments, "whereas shadow photons are intangible (invisible)—detectable only through their interference effects on tangible photons" (p. 44). Physicists call the collection of tangible protons the universe, and collections of intangible protons, parallel universes. Obviously, the many worlds interpretation, with its intangible, interfering protons from other universes, places limitations on our ability to know *our* universe and thus conflicts with commonsense realism.

Three Contemporary Versions of Realism in Physics

Some physicists still do call themselves realists, but theirs is not commonsense realism. Instead, their realism takes into account the phenomena of quantum mechanics, just as the instrumentalist and the parallel universes approaches do. To show you how this can work, we will consider two self-proclaimed contemporary realist physicists, d'Espagnat and Weinberg, and physicist-philosopher David Albert.[6]

d'Espagnat French physicist d'Espagnat (1989) referred to himself as a realist but asserted that if we are to use "reality" in contemporary physics, we must distinguish two meanings, empirical reality and independent reality. Empirical reality refers to "the totality of phenomena—a reality which we understand better with each day that passes" (p. 7). However, "unless we discard altogether the very idea of a reality that is independent of our knowledge, we have to accept that [independent] reality cannot be identified with the ensemble of phenomena" (p. 15). For d'Espagnat, "independent reality" referred to "everything that *is*" (p. 7). If God exists, God is part of independent reality. However, present-day physics has shown that independent reality is distant or veiled. d'Espagnat chose the term *veiled* to indicate a midpoint between knowable and unknowable: Independent reality is not totally impenetrable to us, but *knowable* is too strong a word.

Since independent reality is veiled, there may be more than one way to glimpse its nature. Science provides just one possible glimpse but may nevertheless reflect something of its structure. At any rate, we need to distinguish carefully "between the *real* and the *observable*" (p. 15). Clearly, the independent reality of d'Espagnat differs considerably from that of commonsense realism.

Weinberg Nobel laureate physicist Steven Weinberg (1993) based his realism on his own experience. He wrote, "The experience of listening to a discussion of quantum field theory or weak interactions in a seminar room in Tsukuba or Bombay gives me a powerful impression that the laws of physics have an existence of their own" (pp. 47–48). In other words, physical phenomena (e.g., gravity) operate the same way in these places or even on the moon. He argued for "the reality of the laws of nature, in opposition to the modern positivists, who accept the reality only of that which can be directly observed" (p. 46). Continuing,

> When we say a thing is real we are simply expressing a sort of respect. We mean that the thing must be taken seriously because it can affect us in ways that are not entirely in our control and because we cannot learn about it without making an effort that goes beyond our own imagination.... As a physicist I perceive scientific explanations and laws as things that are what they are and cannot be made up as I go along ... and I therefore accord the laws of nature ... the honor of being real. (pp. 46–47)

However, Weinberg qualified even that seemingly tentative case for realism by stating, "But I have to admit that my willingness to grant the title of 'real' is a little like Lloyd George's willingness to grant titles of nobility; it is a measure of how little difference I think the title makes" (p. 47). In this spirit, he commented that his use of the term *realist* is consistent with the view of Victorian George Gissing, who wished that the words *realism* and *realist* might never be used again. Then, ultimately returning to his own experience, Weinberg wrote, "It certainly *feels* to me that we are discovering something real in physics, something that is what it is without any regard to the social or historical conditions that allowed us to discover it" (p. 188, italics added).

In short, study of the positions of leading contemporary physicists, even those identifying themselves as realists, makes it clear that the attribution of commonsense realism to physicists in general is unwarranted. In this sense, Jeans's (1981) description of physics over a half century ago seems appropriate today:

> Physics tries to discover the pattern of events which controls the phenomena we observe. But we can never know what this pattern means or how it originates; and even if some superior intelligence were to tell us, we should find the explanation unintelligible. Our studies can never put us into contact with reality, and its true meaning and nature must be for ever hidden from us. (p. 76)

Albert David Albert (1992), working at the interface of philosophy and physics, offered a provocative way to address quantum mechanic's challenge to realism. Albert and Barry Loewer (1988) developed the "many minds view" to address a problem they saw in the many worlds solution to the measurement problem in quantum mechanics. The problem arises in attempting to measure the spin of an electron. It appears that two seemingly accepted approaches to measuring the spin yield results that are "flatly inconsistent with one another" (p. 196). Albert and Loewer were dissatisfied with the many worlds account of this contradiction. In response, they developed the many minds view, which attributes multiple mental states to each observer of measurement.

Although the details of their approach need not concern us here, the essence of their conclusion combines belief in realism with acceptance of the uncertainty of human knowledge. They wrote that the many minds view is "*realist* in the sense that it entails that there is a uniquely correct state for the whole universe and … does not suppose that the state of the universe in any way depends on a consciousness or on what observables an observer decides to measure" (pp. 208–209).

The many minds view postulates that "every observer has associated with it not a single mind but rather an infinite set of minds" (p. 206). One can never be sure that a given observation reveals the postulated, uniquely correct state. In fact, the realism involved implies "that a mind's beliefs about the state of a system after measurement are typically false" (p. 209).

Cordero (2000) observed that Albert's view suggests that "scientific imagination is simply too fertile and obtrusive … to allow for any significant distinction between illusion and reality concerning the quantum domain" (p. 197).

Conclusion

Based on these findings, the essence of our answer to the first question, "Do physicists claim to study an independent knowable reality?" is that many contemporary ones do not. Even the position of many who call themselves realists differs greatly from the commonsense realism some social scientists appear to attribute to physicists. In short, their perspective leaves considerable room for uncertainty about human knowledge.

We are now ready to address our second question about the practice of modern physics.

QUESTION 2: WHAT DO PHYSICISTS ACTUALLY DO?

We believe that often when social scientists say that physicists use the scientific method, they have a specific idea in mind. They are referring to what Kaplan (1964) called the hypothetico-deductive method, according to which

> the scientist, by a combination of careful observation, shrewd guesses, and scientific intuition arrives at a set of postulates governing the phenomena in which he is interested; from these he deduces observable consequences; he then tests these consequences by experiment, as so confirms or disconfirms the postulates, replacing them, where necessary, by others, and so continuing. (p. 9)

Kaplan pointed out that this description of method was based on reconstruction after the fact.

To explain what physicists actually do, we discuss (1) some additional ideas of Weinberg on the methods employed by some famous physicists, (2) essays of some contemporary physicists commenting on the scientific method in physics, (3) some ways that physicists use mathematics, and (4) the ways by which some physicists make important discoveries. We then use this information to develop a tentative list of some things physicists actually do and conclude by assessing the value of emulating them for our colleagues who wish to emulate physics.

Weinberg on Methods in Physics

In *Dreams of a Final Theory* (1993), Nobel laureate physicist Steven Weinberg observed that many physicists rely on aesthetics in a couple of ways that are inconsistent with conventional textbook wisdom about method. For one thing, "scientists tend to choose problems that are likely to have *beautiful* solutions" (p. 160, italics added).[7] For another, aesthetic feelings influence acceptance of theories. Weinberg stated:

> There is no logical formula that establishes a sharp dividing line between a beautiful explanatory theory and a mere list of data, but we know the difference when we see it—we demand a simplicity and rigidity in our principles before we are willing to take them seriously. Thus not only is our aesthetic judgment a means to the end of finding scientific explanations and judging their validity—it is part of what we mean by an explanation. (p. 149)

According to Weinberg (1993), some of the most important theories of modern physics originally achieved acceptance more because of perceived beauty than because of demonstrated validity. Einstein's theory of relativity provided an excellent example of this. The most crucial early converts to general relativity were "the British astronomers, who became convinced not that general relativity was true but that it was plausible enough and *beautiful* enough to be worth devoting a fair fraction of their own research careers to test its predictions" (p. 103, italics added).

Momentum for the theory continued to develop even though the 1919 solar eclipse, which was expected to provide definitive data, yielded only limited support for Einstein's theory. Then discrepant observations during subsequent eclipses triggered questions about possible biases among the 1919 observers. In fact, it was not until World War II that technological developments enabled accurate tests that confirmed general relativity. By then, the theory had already become accepted textbook truth. Perceptions of the theory's beauty appeared to complement limited evidence in prompting the acceptance of this theory. Such an outcome may be common in physics. Weinberg wrote, "Consensus in favor of physical theories has often been reached on the basis of aesthetic judgments before the experimental evidence for these theories became really compelling" (1993, p. 130). This possibility does not seem to be part of the reconstructed logic scenario; the physics community seemed to become convinced of the reconstructed logic account of the scientific method. Systematic observation may play less of a role than one would expect. In fact, Weinberg wrote, "Starting with … [an] analogy between gravitation and curvature, Einstein *leaped* to the conclusion that gravitation is nothing more or less than an effect of the curvature of space and time" (p. 101, italics added). Goldberg (1983) also indicated that Einstein's faith in experimentation was less than absolute: "He could be so sure of himself that in the face of seemingly contrary evidence, he could reject the results of experimental tests at variance with his own conclusions. In fact, he did this in at least two instances" (p. 236).

Incidentally, Weinberg's view of the role of aesthetics in scientific methodology supports our belief that scientific work depends on other criteria than simply the desire to model, predict, and make sense of observed phenomena. Such criteria include aesthetics, increased power for one's chosen field, and individual prestige.

Weinberg distinguished between two types of physicists: sages and magicians. "The sage-physicist reasons in an orderly way about physical problems on the basis of fundamental ideas of the way nature ought to be" (1993, p. 67). In contrast, there are the magicians; "magician-physicists … do not seem to be reasoning at all, but … jump over all intermediate steps to a new insight about nature" (p. 68). For example, in Weinberg's view Planck acted as a magician in inventing his 1900 theory of heat radiation, and Heisenberg's 1925 paper on quantum mechanics was "pure magic" (p. 68). He added that such behavior presents a problem for textbook writers. "The authors of physics textbooks are usually compelled to redo the work of the magicians so that they seem like sages; otherwise no reader would understand physics" (p. 68).

This suggests that the ways some leading physicists worked cannot be captured by the program portrayed by reconstructed logic. (Such a view is consistent with Kaplan's position that the reconstructed logic account describes the outcome of a sort of retrospective sense-making effort rather than a valid description of scientific inquiry.)

The insights we gain from reading Weinberg into what physicists do suggest the hypothetico-deductive method of Kaplan's reconstructed logic framework does not describe how at least some of the great physicists of the past did their work. Since this tells us more about what they do not do than what they do, we probed further.

We considered what a group of contemporary physics professors said about method in the *American Journal of Physics* concerning a quotation from Weinberg's *Dreams of a Final Theory.*

Essays on Scientific Method From Contemporary Physicists

A series of essays by physicists on the scientific method began when Ralph Baierlein, a professor at Wesleyan University, published a letter in that journal asking for reader response to Weinberg's discussion of method. He said, in part:

> Most of my students come with the baggage that I learned in junior high school: The scientific method consists of a long list of steps. Somewhere along the way a hypothesis is generated and then tests are carried out. But that's not how our subject really works. A quotation from Steven Weinberg in this journal pointed out that the method *cannot* be reduced to a formal set of steps, to be followed mechanically; in essence, doing science is an art, not a science. That being said, how do we describe what we actually do? (p. 751)

The journal printed eight responses from physics professors to Baierlein's letter. Two of the writers, Deveney (1999) and LoPresto (1999), defined the scientific method in terms of steps. Although Deveney did not list the steps, LoPresto's four-step list closely resembled the traditional junior high model and Kaplan's (1964) description of the reconstructed logic model. However, both writers indicated that a rote approach to the steps does not work, LoPresto insisting that science is a creative process and Deveney stating, "The scientific method works best when used with a sense of humility, flexibility, and even sport" (1999, p. 273).

Responses of other professors varied, but none of them defined the scientific method in terms of steps of the reconstructed logic model. The commonalities among them well summarized the two-item list that Baierlein (1998) suggested in his original query: "1. Turn to nature for information. 2. Keep testing your theories" (p. 751). Individual responders added various elements to this core, treating the use of creativity, thinking, and tools such as scientific instruments and mathematics as part of what physicists do.

These comments provide some insight into what physicists actually do. They are consistent with Weinberg's position that scientific investigation cannot be reduced to a list of mechanical steps. We use the ideas of these physicists to begin a list of things physicists do in their research:

1. Turn to nature or, as we prefer to say, phenomena for information.
2. Keep testing theories.
3. Use creativity.
4. Think.
5. Use tools such as scientific instruments and mathematics.

The emphasis physicists place on mathematics is, of course, well known and is a large part of what many social scientists envy about physics. As part of understanding what physicists do, we give some attention to their use of mathematics.

Use of Mathematics in Physics

Tabak (2004) noted that often in physics laws are formulated mathematically. Frequently, in communicating their work physicists begin with the governing equations, that is, mathematical statements that describe the basic properties of the systems being considered. In addition, many times physicists deduce previously undiscovered properties of physical systems by study of mathematical laws themselves and of mathematical consequences of previous discoveries.

We gained additional insights into physicists' use of mathematics from writings of noted chemist Henry H. Bauer (1992) and Weinberg (1993).

Bauer (1992) indicated that often physicists appear to favor using mathematics over observation. He wrote:

> One learns physics as a set of mathematically formulated laws more than as a set of observed phenomena; theory serves as a substitute for individual facts. Most physicists asked about the attraction between two of the planes will look up their masses and do a calculation; it would not occur to them to seek direct observational data.... Naturally, then, physicists tend to regard quantitative theory as the epitome of science and scientificity. (p. 27)

Weinberg also indicated the centrality of mathematics. He pointed out that sometimes the mathematical structures survive even when "the underlying principles are found to be wrong" (p. 151). To support this assertion, he pointed to Dirac's theory of electron spin. This theory was very influential and was used successfully in the 1930s and 1940s. However, the electron does not have the spin Dirac's theory required. "Yet the *mathematics* of Dirac's theory has survived as an essential part of quantum field theory" (p. 152). Weinberg continued, "The mathematical structures that physicists develop in obedience to physical principles ... can be carried over from one conceptual environment to another and serve many different purposes" (p. 152). Physicists are led to beautiful structures by physical principles; however, "the beauty sometimes survives when the principles themselves do not" (p. 152).

Examination of Great Discoveries in Physics

We already touched on Einstein's methods. Now we will consider those of some discoveries of other renowned physicists.

Sir Isaac Newton

Composition of Sunlight Crease's (2003) comments on Newton's discoveries about sunlight indicated that Newton did not follow the steps outlined by Kaplan:

> A common stereotype, inflicted on generations of schoolchildren, is that the scientific method is a robotic enterprise: forming, testing, and reforming hypotheses. A vaguer-sounding but more accurate account of what scientists do would be to say they "look at" a phenomenon—they examine it from different angles, understanding it by tweaking it this way and that to see what happens. In his converted laboratory, Newton "looked at" light, using various configurations of prisms and lenses, and eventually arrived at the conclusion that white light was not pure but a mixture of light of different colors. Newton would write later, "For the best and safest method of philosophising [*sic*] seems to be, first to inquire diligently into the properties of things, and establishing those properties by experiments and then to proceed more slowly to hypotheses for explanations of them." (p. 62)

James Clerk Maxwell (1831–1879)

Kinetic Theory of Gases C. W. F. Everitt (1983) rated Maxwell one of the three "supreme creative geniuses" (p. 71) of modern theoretical physics, along with Newton and Einstein.

Among Maxwell's contributions were the electromagnetic theory of light, introduction of statistical methods in physics, and significant advancements in the kinetic theory of gases. Maxwell valued cross-fertilization among sciences. For example, he became intrigued with the information that after many years a glacier begins to flow like a viscous liquid. An analogy between this eventual viscosity of some solids and the behavior of rarefied gases led him to a major insight about the conduction of heat in gases. However, as Everitt pointed out, Maxwell's paper of 1867 on gas theory had more to it than just this "startling analogy." In that paper, Maxwell also generalized a set of hydrodynamical equations, studied the scattering of particles under a repulsive force, invented a notation, developed a new derivation of an existing law, and provided formulas that delivered "result upon result" (p. 131). This complex combination of achievements entailed several different methods, and this does not fit smoothly into Kaplan's reconstructed logic model.

Work of Leaders in Developing Quantum Theory and Nuclear Fission

Quantum Theory MacKinnon (1980) examined the processes involved in the development of quantum theory in the 1920s by three physicists: De Broglie, Heisenberg, and Schrodinger. He concluded that each of them

> had a fairly clear idea of the same underlying problem, the inadequacy of the Bohr-Sommerfield theory of the atom. Each also had a fairly clear idea of what would constitute a solution, a new theory in which established experimental results could be derived and new results predicted through the application of consistent rules, without the *ad hoc* hypotheses, patchwork corrections, and the rather arbitrary mixture of classical and quantum laws that characterized the final stage of the Bohr theory. Finally, the men involved, particularly Heisenberg and Schrödinger, developed their

> positions through a sustained critical dialogue with such physicists as Albert Einstein, Niels Bohr, Wolfgang Pauli, Max Planck, Pieter Debye, Hermann Wehl, Pierre Langevin, and H. A. Lorentz. (p. 267)

Let us put the "sustained critical dialogue" among these physicists of the 1920s and 1930s in context. At that time, the physics community centered in Bohr's Institute for Theoretical Physics at the University of Copenhagen and Rutherford's laboratory at Cambridge. The two groups communicated with each other constantly through papers, letters, and visits. Work would get started in one center and finished in the other. Fun and humor balanced intense late-night discussions of current issues in physics. According to Moore (1966), the two centers "in many ways not only functioned as one but served as a nucleus to bind the world's physicists into a cooperating, close community of physics" (p. 112). Thus, members of that community had constant access to high-level feedback.

MacKinnon (1980) told a story about Heisenberg's desire for favorable feedback from Pauli. Heisenberg liked model-based approaches and had worked out a series of equations describing the motions of electrons within the atom, using a type of oscillator as a model.

He wanted the scientific community to accept his equations and thought if he could convince Pauli, his severest critic, he should be able to convince the rest. But Pauli did not like models, insisting that theories be tied to observable phenomena. So Heisenberg worked out a new justification for his equations, one that relied on observation plus something like the hypothetical-deductive approach. This Pauli accepted (pp. 263–264). Here we see the hypothetical–deductive approach in use but with the motivation to use it coming *after* the original discovery.

Nuclear Fission After physicist Lise Meitner fled Berlin in 1938 to escape the Nazis, she spent Christmas in Sweden with her nephew, Otto Frisch, also a physicist (Moore, 1966). Meitner showed Frisch a letter from her colleague, Otto Hahn, describing an unknown substance he and Fritz Strassmann had produced by bombarding uranium with slow neutrons. The substance appeared to be barium, an impossible result, according to conventional wisdom.

Amazed and puzzled, the aunt and nephew went walking in the snowy woods to clear their heads. They raised the possibility that a uranium nucleus could divide in two, with barium as one of the resulting parts, just as a drop of water divides by elongating until a neck forms in the middle and splits. "In this moment of high creativity, they almost automatically sat down on a log. It was as though their legs would not hold them, for they both anticipated what was coming" (Moore, 1966, p. 225).

Meitner did some calculations. She determined that the charge of a uranium nucleus was adequate to destroy the surface tension, and also that the matter lost in the splitting process would translate exactly into the amount of energy with which the drop would tear apart. The two "looked at one another.... Never before had this insight been given to any humans. They were ... looking into a new world" (p. 226).

They checked and rechecked their conclusion. Then Frisch rushed to Copenhagen to tell Niels Bohr, catching him just as he was embarking for the United States. On hearing the news, Bohr exclaimed, "Oh what idiots we all have been. But this is wonderful. This is just as it must be!" (p. 226). Bohr tried to keep the information quiet until Frisch could do a confirming experiment and publish the discovery. Meanwhile, Bohr had a blackboard installed in his stateroom. He and a colleague spent their voyage in discussion and calculation. They could find no fault with Meitner and Frisch's conclusion.

When Bohr finally felt free to release the news, he announced it at a conference at the Carnegie Institution in the United States. Immediately, physicists at the conference rushed to phone their home laboratories all across the country. By the next morning, laboratories at Baltimore, Berkeley, Columbia, and the Carnegie Institution had all split the atom.

The discovery of nuclear fission did not happen through a prolonged repetition of the steps of hypothesis generation, experiment, and refinement of hypothesis. Meitner and Frisch experienced a flash of insight, did the math, and then realized that, in Bohr's words, "This is just as it must be." Furthermore, other physicists accepted the discovery even before experimental confirmation became available.

In conclusion, *none* of the above major discoveries resulted from strictly following the hypothetico-deductive method of reconstructed logic as described by Kaplan. However, descriptions of the discoveries do suggest adding the following to the list we derived above, from Baierlein and his responders, of things physicists actually do: (1) become deeply preoccupied with a specific problem; and (2) share ideas, information, and mutual criticism extensively with colleagues.

We now have a tentative list:

Some Things Physicists Actually Do

1. Turn to nature (i.e., the phenomena) for information.
2. Keep testing theories.
3. Use creativity.
4. Think.
5. Use tools such as scientific instruments and mathematics.
6. Become deeply preoccupied with specific questions.
7. Share ideas and information with colleagues.

Please note that this list does not include any one method that physicists use exclusively, such as the hypothetico-deductive method. We hope our review of how physicists approach inquiry will help debunk misguided efforts by social scientists to emulate physics by showing that a key belief associated with physics envy—the idea that slavish adherence to any one method is the one true path to scientific discovery. We use Kaplan's (1964) definition of the hypothetico-deductive method to exemplify what we think many people mean by the "scientific method," for Kaplan this was part of a reconstructed logic that did not describe what scientists actually did. He did not think there was only one scientific method. He thought behavioral science should "stop trying to imitate only what a particular reconstruction [the hypothetico-deductive method] claims physics to be" (p. 11). Kaplan (1964) liked P. W. Bridgman's assertion that "the scientist has no other method than doing his damnedest" (p. 27). After our brief look at what physicists actually do, we think Bridgman's statement captures their method fairly well. This concludes our treatment of the second misattribution connected with physics envy—the oversimplified, rule-bound perspective many social scientists appear to have about how physicists work.

CONCLUSION

We respect what physicists have accomplished. However, their achievements do not mean that social scientists—or any scientists—should imitate them mindlessly. On the other hand, at least some of the things they did in the past may be worth considering mindfully as practices social scientists might profitably adapt. At this point, our understanding of what physicists think and what they do permits us to advance some guidelines for such thoughtful consideration. The guidelines fall into two categories: misguided steps to avoid and insights worth exploration.

Avoiding Misguided Steps

Based on the evidence considered in this chapter, we conclude that physicists' accomplishments did not stem from agreement upon any one scientific method, such as the one exemplified in Kaplan's (1964) reconstructed logic. Apparently, lack of consensus on method did not prevent physics from becoming highly successful. It is very clear that at this point in time, the physicists' accomplishments do not depend on commitment to a mechanistic method. Second, if any social scientists are associating commonsense realism with contemporary physics, they are misguided.

Physics and Commonsense Realism

The current beliefs of some leading physicists about reality do not seem compatible with the assumption of an independent knowable external reality. With the exception of Einstein, whose arguments have not held up conceptually or experimentally, none of the physicists we discussed were comfortable asserting the existence of such a reality. The dominant Copenhagen interpretation does not even take a position on reality, though it predicts phenomena with great accuracy. Consequently, we believe uncertainty about the nature of reality makes a great deal of sense at present, not only philosophically but also in the light of current information—or lack of information—about quantum phenomena.

In light of our study of what physicists believe and do, those social scientists who attempt to emulate physics by adopting commonsense realism seem to be misguided. We suggest letting go of that effort.

However, our study of what physicists do and believe revealed some general ideas students of organization studies might consider.

Inquiry as Social Process

First, they should recognize that consistent with Longino's (1990) view, scientific inquiry is a social process. The nuclear fission discoveries we described above are an especially interesting example. The study of a "life sciences" laboratory by Latour and Woolgar (1979) provides additional evidence of such social aspects. It is noteworthy that both Longino, and Latour and Woolgar pointed out that the way we punctuate developments in science as individual achievements may lead us to overlook the social processes involved. Increased awareness of the social nature of inquiry might stimulate some reengineering or deliberate redesign of the process through which we collectively conduct inquiry. The following chapter on limiting agonism and our concluding chapter on improving conversation in organization studies illustrate such deliberate efforts.

A second aspect of physicists' thoughts and practices we think deserves consideration is to take seriously Bridgman's (1955) statement that "the scientific method is nothing more than doing one's damnedest" (p. 535). To us, this involves passionate pursuit of answers to questions deemed important without being rigidly controlled by scientific norms that might constrain inquiry.

ACKNOWLEDGMENTS

We gratefully acknowledge the help of two colleagues in the University of South Florida Physics Department, Dr. Robert Flynn and Dr. Dennis Killinger, for their guidance in our work on this chapter.

To a physicist, beautiful solutions mean obtaining (1) simplest possible math postulate or equation, and (2) widest possible applications to different phenomena (Killinger, 2007, personal communication).

ENDNOTES

1. Personal communication.
2. Sir James Jeans (1981) noted that traditional or Newtonian physics dealt with the "man-sized" world, with the phenomena of everyday human experience. This is the world of falling apples and billiard balls typically studied in high school science courses. However, in the early 20th century, study of both micro-level phenomena (the quantum world) and the macro-level phenomena of cosmology made scientists aware that findings based on person-sized phenomena might be associated with different ways of thinking than needed for other levels.
3. As best we can determine, what Einstein actually said about the matter was in a December 4, 1926, letter to Bohr, in which he discussed quantum mechanics: "The theory yields much, but it hardly brings us close to the Old One's secrets. I, in any case, am convinced that *He* does not play dice" (Calapice, 2000, p. 245).
4. For explanations *other than* intrinsic merit for the hegemony of the Copenhagen interpretation, see Norris (2000, pp. 74–81).
5. For details about the role of interference in the parallel universes interpretation, we refer you to Chapter 2 of Deutsch's (1997) book.
6. We thank Elizabeth Victor for introducing us to Albert's work.
7. To illustrate this point, Weinberg (1993) noted that in the past physicists have studied the phenomenon of smooth phase transitions (e.g., the spontaneous disappearance of magnetism when a magnet is heated above its Curie point, a temperature of 770°C). Although one might think that calculating the precise Curie point would have been of compelling interest, physicists gave it relatively little attention. Instead, the quest for beauty led many of them to devote most of their efforts to calculating critical exponents. They did so because they judged that it would entail a beautiful solution, believing that in marked contrast to the messy problem of calculating precise temperatures of phase transitions it would have simplicity and inevitability.

REFERENCES

Albert, D. (1992). *Quantum mechanics and experience*. Cambridge, MA: Harvard University Press.

Albert, D., & Loewer, B. (1988). Interpreting the many worlds interpretation. *Synthese*, *77*(2).

Baierlein, R. (1998, September). Question #77: The scientific method. *American Journal of Physics*, *66*, 751.

Bauer, H. H. (1992). *Scientific literacy and the myth of the scientific method*. Chicago, IL: University of Illinois Press.

Bell, J. S. (1964). On the Einstein-Podolsky-Rosen paradox. *Physics*, *1*, 195–200.

Bell, J. S. (1989). Six possible worlds of quantum mechanics. In S. Allén (Ed.), *Possible worlds in humanities, arts and sciences* (pp. 359–373). New York, NY: de Grayter.

Bridgman, P. W. (1955). *Reflections of a physicist*. New York, NY: Philosophical Library.
Calapice, A. (2000). *The expanded quotable Einstein*. Princeton, NJ: Princeton University Press.
Campbell, J. P. (1990). The role of theory in industrial and organizational psychology. In M. D. Dunnette & L. M. Hough (Eds.), *Handbook of industrial and organizational psychology* (2nd ed., pp. 39–73). Palo Alto, CA: Consulting Psychologists Press, Inc.
Cordero, A. (2000). Realism, and the case of rival theories without observable differences. In E. Agazzi & M. Pauri (Eds.), *The reality of the unobservable: Observability, unobservability and their impact on the issue of scientific realism* (pp. 191–206). Dordrecht, The Netherlands: Kluwer Academic.
Crease, R. P. (2003). *The prism and the pendulum: The ten most beautiful experiments in science*. New York, NY: Random House.
D'Espagnat, B. (1989). *Reality and the physicist: Knowledge, duration and the quantum world* (J. C. Whitehouse, Trans.). Cambridge, UK: Cambridge University Press.
Deutsch, D. (1997). *The fabric of reality: The science of parallel universes—and its implications*. New York, NY: The Penguin Press.
Deveney, E. F. (1999, April). Answers to question #77: The scientific method. *American Journal of Physics*, *67*, 273.
Einstein, A., Podolsky, B., & Rosen, R. (1935). Can quantum-mechanical description of physical reality be considered complete? *Physical Review*, *47*(10), 777–780.
Everitt, C. W. F. (1983). Maxwell's scientific creativity. In R. Aris, H. T. Davis, & R. H. Stuewer (Eds.), *Springs of scientific creativity* (pp. 71–141). Minneapolis, MN: University of Minnesota Press.
Felder, G. (1999). *Spooky action at a distance: An explanation of Bell's theorem*. Retrieved from http://www4.ncsu.edu/unity/lockers/users/f/felder/public/kenny/papers/bell.html
Ghate, O., & E.A. Locke. (2003). Objectivism: The proper alternative to postmodernism. In E. A. Locke (Ed.), *Postmodernism and management: Pros, cons and the alternative* (pp. 249–278). Amsterdam, Netherlands: Elsevier Science.
Goldberg, S. (1983). Albert Einstein and the creative act: The case of special relativity. In R. Aris, H. T. Davis, & R. H. Stuewer (Eds.), *Springs of scientific creativity* (pp. 232–253). Minneapolis, MN: University of Minnesota Press.
Hunt, S. D. (2005). For truth and realism in management research. *Journal of Management Inquiry*, *14*, 127–138.
Jeans, J. (1981). *Physics and philosophy*. New York, NY: Dover Publications.
Kaplan, A. (1964). *The conduct of inquiry: Methodology for behavioral science*. Scranton, PA: Chandler Publishing Company.
Latour, B., & Woolgar, S. (1979). *Laboratory life: The social construction of facts*. Beverly Hills, CA: Sage.
Lightman, A. (1997). *Great ideas in physics* (2nd ed.). New York, NY: McGraw-Hill.
LoPresto, M. C. (1999, April). Answers to question #77: The scientific method. *American Journal of Physics*, *67*, 275.

MacKinnon, E. (1980). The discovery of a new quantum theory. In T. Nickles (Ed.), *Scientific discovery: Case studies* (pp. 261–272). Boston, MA: D. Reidel Publishing.

McKelvey, B. (2002). Model-centered organization science epistemology. In J. E. Baum (Ed.), *The Blackwell companion to organizations* (pp. 752–780). Malden, MA: Blackwell Publishers.

Moore, R. (1966). *Niels Bohr: The man, his science, and the world they changed.* New York, NY: Alfred A. Knopf.

Norris, C. (2000). *Quantum theory and the flight from realism: Philosophical responses to quantum mechanics*. London, UK: Routledge.

Secord, P. F. (1986). Explanation in the social sciences and in life situations. In D. W. Fiske & R. A. Shweder (Eds.), *Metatheory in social science pluralisms and subjectivities* (pp. 197–221). Chicago, IL: University of Chicago Press.

Shankar, R. (1980). *Principles of quantum mechanics.* New York, NY: Plenum Press.

Shimony, A. (2004). Bell's theorem. In *Stanford encyclopedia of philosophy*. Retrieved from http://plato.stanford.edu/search/searcher.py?query=Bell%27s+Theorem

Tabak, J. (2004). *Mathematics and the laws of nature: Developing the language of science*. New York, NY: Facts on File.

Tapp, A. (2007). Physics envy. *Marketing Intelligence and Planning, 25*(3), 229–231.

Tegmark, M. (1997). The interpretation of quantum mechanics: Many worlds or many words. *Fortschr Physics*, *46*(6–8), 855–862. Retrieved from http://space.mit.edu/home/tegmark/index.html

Weinberg, S. (1993). *Dreams of a final theory: The scientist's search for the ultimate laws of nature*. New York, NY: Vintage.

CHAPTER

10

Letting Go of Agonism

We believe that a number of forces contributed to the knowledge controversy in organization studies and to our field's failure to deal with it effectively. We discussed some of these forces as we examined the history of the field. These included a philosophically questionable scientism and associated physics envy.

In this chapter, we explore one additional force that contributed to the problem—the dominance of agonism in intellectual discourse. We argue that our intellectual heritage from ancient Greece included the idea that argumentative debate (i.e., what we call agonism) almost automatically leads to the discovery of truth. This idea is so firmly embedded in our culture and our field that it is seldom questioned.

To be clear, by questioning agonism we are not questioning critical assessment of scholarly work. We value thoughtful analysis of context, logic, and assumptions by scholars about their own work and about the work of other scholars. What we are questioning is privileging of the idea that what Tannen (2002) called "ritualized adversetiveness" (p. 1651) can be counted on to lead to truth.

The purpose of this chapter is to examine the tradition of agonism and consider any dysfunctional effects it might have for intellectual discourse in general and the knowledge controversy in particular. This analysis will provide a foundation for the next chapter, in which we consider ways of improving communication among organization scholars. For now, we assert that we see no reason agonism is necessary for critical thinking, and we see several reasons to view it as detrimental to critical thinking.

We begin by looking at the history of the reliance on argumentation in Western intellectual discourse.

AGONISM IN WESTERN INTELLECTUAL DISCOURSE

Communication scholar Deborah Tannen's (2000) treatment of "Agonism in Academic Discourse" provided valuable insights. She wrote:

> Many aspects of our academic lives can be described as agonistic.
>
> For example, in our scholarly papers, most of us follow a conventional framework that requires us to position our working opposition to someone else's, which we proved wrong. The framework tempts—almost requires—us to oversimplify or even misrepresent others' positions; cite the weakest example to make a generally reasonable work appear less so; and ignore facts that support others' views, citing only evidence of her own positions.
>
> The way we train our students often reflects the battle metaphor as well. We assign scholarly work for them to read, and then invite them to tear apart. That is helpful to an extent, but often means they don't learn to do the hard work of integrating ideas, or of considering the work's historical and disciplinary context. Moreover, it fosters … a stance of arrogance and narrow-mindedness, qualities that do not serve the fundamental goals of education. (p. B7)

Similarly, Gouldner (1965) observed that the contest mode as we derived it from the Greeks encourages people to seek debater's points. He wrote that to win truth individuals "must partially extricate themselves from the contest system … the conventional contest system is in certain ways, inimical to wisdom" (p. 262).

Tannen (2002) drew on the work of Walter Ong, who also traced the fascination with adversarial language and thought back to the Greeks. Although probably all cultures have some adversarial relationships, Ong (1981) suggested that "with logic, ancient Greece formalized adversativeness as no other culture had done" (p. 22). The ancient Greeks institutionalized agonism in formal education; this tradition, Ong argued, became a core feature of education in the West. "The oral and agonistic roots of Western academicism are identifiable in antiquity and the dialectical procedures of the Socratic dialogues" (p. 125).

Tannen (2002) observed that the adversarial method featured in modern academic discourse is a perverted version of the Socratic method. Drawing on Moulton (1983), she argued that in the true Socratic method counterargument is not designed to show people that they are wrong, but rather it is to shake them from their cherished convictions, so they can approach a matter with a more open mind.

After Socrates, Aristotle showed how the Socratic style of reasoning could help win arguments. From Aristotle's time on, dialectics combined with logic was perceived in the West as an important way of finding truth. Later, Augustine (354–430) integrated Plato and dialectics into Christianity, and the method remained part of European culture during the Middle Ages. Thomas Aquinas, the most renowned Western philosopher-theologian of the Middle Ages, reinforced the emphasis on dialectics when he incorporated a substantial amount of Aristotle into Christianity. For Aquinas (1952), reason and faith were the paths to truth. In describing the path of reason, he emphasized the dialectic. He wrote his major work, *Summa Theologica*, in dialectical style, first presenting and then arguing opposing views.

Please consider the dysfunctional effects of agonism in academe that Tannen pointed out. First, it may discourage potentially good scholars who are not comfortable with agonistic discourse; second, by making scholars feel vulnerable and defensive, it may reduce the willingness of some to suggest new ideas, offer new perspectives, or question received wisdom (Tannen, 2000). Tannen (2002) added a third dysfunction. The process means that any work that is considered is opposed immediately. Consequently, it is difficult for those outside a field (as well as those inside) to gauge the accuracy of published research.

Study of the recent knowledge controversy in organization studies suggests adding a fourth dysfunctional outcome to Tannen's list. The combination of defensiveness and the desire to score debater's points that the argumentative mode produces leads communicators into a vicious cycle of nonlistening and distortion of the rivals' views. When this happens, the argumentative tone grows and communication becomes increasingly distorted.

Two examples from the recent organization studies literature relating to the knowledge controversy, one from each side of the controversy, demonstrate the results of this dysfunctional cycle. The first example concerns Weiss's (2000) interpretation of French philosopher Jacques Derrida's (1976) statement "*Il n'y a pas de hors-texte*" (p. 237). The second example concerns "positivism bashing." We begin with Weiss and Derrida.

Weiss and Derrida

A prime example of distortion associated with agonism in organization studies appeared in Weiss (2000). Weiss seemed to direct his efforts at debunking postmodernism.

To show why we view Weiss's use of Derrida (*Il n'y a pas de hors-texte*) as off the mark, we examine the statement in context. Derrida was concerned with interpreting texts. The statement appeared in his discussion of Rousseau, where Derrida made the point that every writer "writes *in* a language and *in* a logic whose proper system, laws, and life his discourse by definition cannot dominate absolutely. He uses them only by letting himself, after a fashion and up to a point, be governed by the system" (p. 158). Thus, for Derrida, it is "impossible to separate, through interpretation or commentary, the signified from the signifier" (p. 159), and there is no "signified outside the text" (p. 158), no "transcendental signified" (p. 158). In other words, Rousseau's content (the signified) is inextricably interwoven with his system of language and logic (the signifiers).

Based on several factors, (1) our own reading of the pertinent section of Derrida's *Of Grammatology* in French, (2) our reading of G. C. Sprivac's translation of the same material, (3) our reading of Derrida scholars (Norris, 1987; Caputo, 1997; Madison, 1993; Willard, 1993), and (4) Kearney's (1984) interview with Derrida, we think in Derrida's statement he meant to assert that, for any given text, there is no outside text (a literal translation of *hors-texte*) in the sense of a "transcendental signified" to which the text refers. Caputo (1997) elaborated on this interpretation as follows:

> Literature is an *exemplary* example. There *really is* no Jane Eyre (alas, I love her madly) outside the text of *Jane Eyre* whom we may consult, say, to find out if she *really did* hear Mr. Rochester call her name, "Jane," from across the moors; and, having published her book, Charlotte Brontë has lost all right authoritatively to settle these matters for us. But what literature exhibits "purely," exemplarily, as it were, is true in varying ways and degrees of every other discourse. No one ever gets privileged access to the Secret that sits smiling behind all language and interpretation waiting for us but to knock; we are all in the same textual boat together, forced to do the best we can with such signs and traces as we can piece together. (p. 80)

We, not having access to the "secret" correct interpretation of Derrida's words, can say only that we have a supposition of accurate reception (SOAR) in connection with Caputo's reading.

On the other hand, Weiss's (2000) interpretation seems off the mark to us. Weiss used the Derrida quotation to demonstrate that postmodernism views the world as "largely illusory." We have two problems with Weiss's usage of Derrida: (1) Weiss dealt with the quote out of context, making no mention of Derrida's point that one cannot get outside of a linguistic system to discover the "transcendental" meaning of the text; and (2) Weiss's wording of the quote differed from that of the Spivak translation he cited.

The Spivak translation read, "There is nothing outside of the text [there is no outside-text; *il niy a pas de hors-texte*]." Instead of following Spivak exactly, Weiss quoted Derrida as claiming, "all the world is a text," which apparently meant to Weiss that the world was "largely illusory" (p. 716). However, "all the world is a text" seemed to originate with Weiss rather than Spivak or Derrida.[1]

Weiss's reading and others of a similar ilk are noteworthy in view of the fact that Derrida explicitly railed against them. Sixteen years before Weiss's article, Derrida said in an interview, "I never cease to be surprised by critics who see my work as a declaration that there is nothing beyond language.... Every week I receive critical commentaries and studies on deconstruction, which operate on the assumption that what they call 'post-structuralism' amounts to saying that there is nothing beyond language, that we are submerged in words—and other stupidities of that sort" (p. 123) (Kearney, 1984).

We must be cautious here to not overweight this particular statement by Derrida about his own intent. We agree with Derrida (as explicated by Caputo) that even an author cannot be an absolute authority on his or her own earlier intended meaning. On the other hand, we also agree with Derrida (1976) that "a reading cannot legitimately transgress the text toward something other than it" (p. 158). Our concern is that Weiss seems to have transgressed the text toward something other than itself.

However, communication failures are seldom the responsibility of only one party. Probably Derrida's difficult writing style, especially in conjunction with possible translation difficulties, attributed to the problem. Derrida could be so difficult to understand that his obituary in the *New York Times* (Kandell, 2004) was titled "Jacques Derrida, Abstruse Theorist, Dies at 74."

We do not mean to imply that Weiss and others deliberately oversimplified or misrepresented Derrida. Our point does not depend on any deliberate distortion. Our point is that the debate mentality tends to reinforce behaviors that interfere with good communication rather than to reward the hard work of trying to understand scholars with whom one may not agree.

Those seeking to discredit postmodernism used what we believe is a misreading of Derrida's comment about "no outside text" to caricature that approach; it illustrates why we are so concerned about agonism in the context of the current controversy. However, the dysfunctions of agonism are not confined to critics of postmodernism. Whereas Weiss seemed to champion the orthodox consensus side of the debate, our next example is about challengers of that consensus.

Agonism and Positivism Bashing

Hunt (1994) chastised many critics of the orthodox science view for employing a positivism-bashing rhetoric that advanced an inaccurate view of positivism.

Although Hunt acknowledged the beneficial contributions of qualitative methods to management inquiry, he was concerned that many proponents of these methods misrepresented their approach as an alternative to "positivist research." They misrepresented positivism through inaccurate attributions to positivist research in management, such as it "(a) is the same thing as using quantitative methods but also (b) is deterministic, (c) involves the search for real causes, (d) adopts a realist ontology, (e) engages in reification, (f) is functionalist, or (g) is objectivist" (Hunt, 1994, p. 222). Based on his study of the history of positivism, Hunt concluded that while positivists were objectivists many of the other attributions noted above were incorrect. He wrote:

> Although research guided by positivism would believe in the ideal of objectivity and in science's ability to achieve that ideal through the use of empirical testing, such research (a) would not necessarily be either quantitative or deterministic, (b) would avoid metaphysical concepts such as "cause," (c) would reject the scientific realist ontology, (d) would be leery of functionalist explanations, and (e) could not possibly engage in reification. To the extent that advocates of qualitative methods are *right*, they are *wrong*; that is, if they are right that contemporary management research searches for causes, adopts a realist ontology, reifies unobservables, and is necessarily quantitative, deterministic, and functionalist, then they are wrong that management research is positivist. (p. 231)

Hunt was concerned that "positivism" in the management literature had become "a convenient term of abuse" (p. 231). Because of its technical failures, positivism was discredited in philosophy. Consequently, attacking contemporary management research by labeling it positivist would likely be a successful rhetorical ploy for gaining converts to qualitative methods. Hunt observed that if qualitative researchers justified their cause by *knowingly* violating the past, they behaved unethically. He added, "The price paid for historically false rhetoric is the potential destruction of trust" (p. 231). Thus, positivism bashing is unnecessary to justify qualitative methods. Moreover, it endangers the integrity of our field. Hunt concluded that it is time for a rhetorical ceasefire and historically informed discourse. We strongly agree.

Hunt flagged two terms—*positivism* and *incommensurability*—that contributed to the harsh debate. We deal with these terms in some depth in the next chapter, where we classify them as "quicksand" terms and suggest they be abandoned or used very carefully.

In sum, Hunt demonstrated how what we see as the agonistic style of communication in organization studies contributed to communication difficulties. Furthermore, we share Hunt's desire for historically informed discourse.

In addition to the problems noted above, we suggest limiting agonism for at least one other reason. After study of the work of a number of contemporary scholars, including Longino (1990) and Sterba (1998), as well as restudy of the work of Francis Bacon, we are persuaded of the merits of viewing inquiry as a cooperative endeavor. Accordingly, we encourage using a communication approach that fosters cooperation. We believe James Sterba's (1998) advice to philosophers to abandon the "warmaking" mode in favor of a "peacemaking" one is on target.

Both of Sterba's (1998) models share the following. They are committed to

1. A fair-mindedness that, among other things, puts the most favorable interpretation on the views of one's philosophical opponents.
2. An openness that reaches out to understand challenging new philosophical views.

3. A self-criticalness that requires modifying or abandoning one's philosophical views should the weight of available evidence require it. (p. 10)

However, there is a big difference. Participants in the warmaking mode are "committed to the pursuit of philosophical victory and the avoidance of defeat as a means of getting at the most justified philosophical views" (p. 10). In such cases, when the pursuit of victory and avoidance of defeat operate at the expense of fair-mindedness, openness, and self-criticism, there is good reason to prefer the peacemaking mode.

In our view, the peacemaking mode seems likely to stimulate actions that promote cooperative scholarship.

Sterba's own experiences support this view. Sterba reported marked differences in how audiences responded to his ideas under the peacemaking model from their responses in the warmaking context. When he used the peacemaking model, he received comments that were friendly and constructive rather than bent on simply attacking central arguments. Even critical points directed at those same arguments "were frequently accompanied by suggestions as to how those criticisms might be met" (p. 13).

CONCLUSION

We believe that some dysfunctions of the knowledge controversy in organization studies stem from the agonistic style of discourse that dominates the Western intellectual scene. Furthermore, we see other ways to reap any benefits often attributed to agonism. Accordingly, one of our suggestions for dealing with the knowledge controversy is to let go of agonism.

Letting go of agonism requires that organization scholars reflect on how they communicate with each other and develop alternative approaches. In Chapter 11, "Toward Postagonistic Communication," we present a proposal for doing better.

ENDNOTE

1. A possible source of confusion was a definition of writing that Weiss quoted from an earlier chapter in *Of Grammatology*. Derrida stated, "To affirm in this way that the concept of writing exceeds and comprehends that of language, *presupposes* of course a certain definition of language and of writing … one says 'language' for action, movement, thought, reflection, consciousness, unconsciousness, experience, affectivity, etc. Now we tend to say 'writing' for all that and more.… And thus we say 'writing' for all that gives use to an inscription in general, whether it is literal or not and even if what it distributes in space is alien to the order

of the voice: cinematography, choreography, of course, but also pictorial, musical, sculptural 'writing'" (pp. 8, 9). The above statement strikes us as purely definitional. It does not imply to us in any way that the world is "largely illusory."

REFERENCES

Aquinas, T. (1952). The *Summa Theologica* Volume II of Saint Thomas Aquinas (Fathers of the English Dominican Province, Trans., Daniel J. Sullivan, Rev.). In R. M. Hutchins (Ed.), *Great books of the Western world 20*. Chicago, IL: William Benton. (Original work published 1265–1274)

Caputo, J. D. (1997). *Deconstruction in a nutshell: A conversation with Jacques Derrida*. New York, NY: Fordham University Press.

Derrida, J. (1976). *Of grammatology* (G. C. Spivak, Trans.). Baltimore, MD: Johns Hopkins University Press.

Gouldner, A. W. (1965). *Enter Plato: Classical Greece and the origins of social theory*. New York, NY: Basic Books.

Hunt, S. D. (1994). On the rhetoric of qualitative methods: Toward historically informed argumentation in management inquiry. *Journal of Management Inquiry, 3*, 221–234.

Kandell, J. (2004 October 10). Jacques Derrida, abstruse theorist, dies at 74 [Obituary]. *The New York Times*, p. N1.

Kearney, R. (1984) Dialogue with Jaques Derrida. In R. Kearney (Ed.), *Dialogues with contemporary continental thinkers* (pp. 105–126). Manchester, UK: Manchester University Press.

Longino, H. E. (1990). *Science as social knowledge*. Princeton, NJ: Princeton University Press.

Madison, G. B. (1993). Introduction. In G. B. Madison (Ed.), *Working through Derrida* (pp. 1-4). Evanston, IL: Northwestern University Press.

Moulton, J. (1983). A paradigm of philosophy: The adversary method. In S. Harding & M. B. Hintikka (Eds.), *Discovering reality* (pp. 149–164). Dordrecht, The Netherlands: Reidel.

Norris, C. (1987). *Derrida*. Cambridge, MA: Harvard University Press.

Ong, W. J. (1981). *Fighting for life: Contest, sexuality, and consciousness*. Ithaca, NY: Cornell University Press.

Sterba, J. P. (1998). *Justice for here and now*. New York, NY: Cambridge University Press.

Tannen, D. (2000). Agonism in the academy: Surviving higher learning's argument culture. *The Chronicle of Higher Education, 46*(30), B7–B8.

Tannen, D. (2002). Agonism in academic discourse. *Journal of Pragmatics, 34*, 1651–1659.

Weiss, R. M. (2000). Taking science out of organization: How would postmodernism reconstruct the analysis of organizations? *Organization Science, 11*, 709–731.

Willard, D. (1993). Predication as originary violence: A phenomenological critique of Derrida's view of intentionality. In G. B. Madison (Ed.), *Working through Derrida* (pp. 120–136). Evanston, IL: Northwestern University Press.

CHAPTER

11

Toward Postagonistic Communication

Conversation in Organization Studies

In Chapter 10, "Letting Go of Agonism," we demonstrated how poor communication helped to intensify debates in organization studies. We are now ready to recommend some ways consistent with our generative uncertainty perspective to improve communication in organization studies.

First, we consider scholars who addressed the role of communication in recent debates in organization studies. These scholars took diverse paths. Members of one group, which we call the antidialogue group, regarded communication as a threat to diversity. They promoted the idea of incommensurable paradigms as a way of protecting less powerful voices in organization studies from assimilation by the more powerful. The other group, the one to which we belong, sought ways to improve dialogue.

We begin by presenting the ideas of these two groups and then go on to make recommendations for improving dialogue. The paradigm incommensurability thesis was a major source of controversy. Members of the antidialogue group advanced the paradigm incommensurability thesis. Analysis of that thesis revealed how values helped shape the incommensurability controversy and how two quicksand terms, *paradigm* and *incommensurable,* complicated matters.

THE PARADIGM INCOMMENSURABILITY THESIS

The paradigm incommensurability thesis was rooted in Feyerabend's (1962) and Kuhn's (1962/1970) use of both words. These two scholars used *incommensurability* to deal with problems they encountered in interpreting scientific texts (Kuhn, 1983).

Kuhn's work attracted special attention from social scientists in part because they found his term *paradigm* in the *Structure of Scientific Revolutions* (1962/1970) very attractive. Unfortunately, he used both *paradigm* and *incommensurability* ambiguously.

Kuhn's Use of Paradigm and Incommensurability

In the postscript to the second edition of *Structure,* Kuhn himself pointed to his ambiguous use of *paradigm*. He acknowledged using the term in 22 different ways in the first edition. Problems related to Kuhn's ambiguous use of *paradigms* were heightened by parallel ambiguity in his use of *incommensurability.*

Kuhn wrote that both he and Feyerabend borrowed *incommensurability* from mathematics. In mathematics, commensurable refers to situations in which two numbers are divisible by the same factor an integral number of times. For example, 6 and 9 are commensurable because they are both divisible by 3.

Kuhn said that he and Feyerabend both adopted *incommensurability* to show that the meaning of at least some scientific terms (e.g., *force* and *mass*) varied according to the theory in which they were used. Some of the problems with incommensurability resulted in part from Kuhn's inconsistent use of the term.

Sankey (1993) suggested Kuhn's use of the word changed over time. Sankey divided Kuhn's thinking about incommensurability into three stages. Sankey argued that in the first stage Kuhn maintained that proponents of incommensurable theories could not communicate with each other. In Sankey's words, there was "no recourse to neutral experience or objective standards to adjudicate the theories" (p. 760). In the second stage, according to Sankey, Kuhn restricted incommensurability to semantic differences resembling those in translations. In the third stage, he treated incommensurability as a translation failure between localized clusters of interdefined terms within the language of theories.

In spite of what seems to us to be clear changes in his position, Sankey (1993) observed that Kuhn downplayed any alteration. On the one hand, in his later work Kuhn (1983) stated that the claims made by incommensurability are more modest than most critics of the term supposed. At this point he wrote:

> The claim that two theories are incommensurable is the claim that there is no language, neutral or otherwise, into which both theories, conceived

> as sets of sentences, can be translated without residue or loss. No more in its metaphorical than its literal form does incommensurability imply incomparability, and for much the same reason. Most of the terms common to the two theories function the same way in both; their meanings, whatever they may be, are preserved; their translation is simply homophonic. Only for a small subgroup of (usually interdefined) terms and for sentences containing them do problems of translatability arise. The claim that two theories are incommensurable is more modest than many of its critics have supposed. (pp. 670–671)

Despite Kuhn's denial of change, it appears to us that this unassuming claim differed greatly from the far less modest claim he made in 1970. Kuhn (1962/1970) wrote that scientists using different paradigms resembled people who function in "different worlds":

> In a sense ... the proponents of competing paradigms practice their trades in different worlds.... Practicing in different worlds, the two groups of scientists see different things when they look from the same point in the same direction. Both are looking at the world, and what they look at has not changed. But in some areas they see different things, and they see them in different relations one to the other. That is why a law that cannot even be demonstrated to one group of scientists may occasionally seem intuitively obvious to another. Equally, it is why, before they can hope to communicate fully, one group or the other must experience the conversion we have been calling a paradigm shift. Just because it is a transition between incommensurables, the transition between competing paradigms cannot be made a step at a time, forced by logic and neutral experience. Like the gestalt switch, it must occur all at once (though not necessarily in an instant) or not at all. (p. 150)

Placing theorists in different worlds and postulating a need for conversion appeared to introduce almost insurmountable barriers to communication and represents a far less modest claim than Kuhn's (1983) statement.

In short, there is good reason to concur with Sankey (1993) that Kuhn's treatment of incommensurability changed over the years. We suggest that this variation contributed to *incommensurable* becoming a quicksand term and to unnecessary controversy in organization studies.

In organization studies, a variety of understandings of incommensurability and its possible implications resulted. Consider two of them:

1. Burrell and Morgan (1979) rejected the idea that a paradigm can be evaluated by an outsider.
2. Hassard (1988) noted that Kuhn seemed "to deny any possibility of communication between paradigm [*sic*]" (p. 249). This implied that since the social sciences were polyparadigmatic, communication and debate among social scientists was not possible.

Burrell and Morgan on Paradigm Incommensurability

Burrell and Morgan (1979) helped make the paradigm/incommensurability debate central in organization studies when, in *Sociological Paradigms and Organisational Analysis*, they argued that the paradigms they developed were incommensurable. They muddied the waters further by using *paradigm* and *incommensurable* differently than Kuhn.

For one thing, Burrell and Morgan defined *paradigm* more broadly than Kuhn did. Although they warned readers of this difference, unfortunately they relegated the warning to an endnote, so many readers may have overlooked it.

The difference was such that Jackson and Carter (1991) suggested there was "no basis for a comparison between paradigms of Kuhn and those of Burrell and Morgan" (p. 111). However, in at least one respect Burrell and Morgan's use of the term resembled Kuhn's—specifically, like Kuhn, they used the term inconsistently. Sometimes they focused on the experiences of scientists but at other times focused on systems of concepts. For example, they observed that with respect to paradigms, "a synthesis is not possible" (p. 25). However, later in the same paragraph they changed their focus to the experiences of scientists, observing that "one *can* operate in different paradigms sequentially over time" (p. 25).

One of Burrell and Morgan's ideas that seems to have contributed mightily to controversy about incommensurability was their rejection of the idea that a paradigm can be evaluated by an outsider. This view led Scherer and Dowling (1995) to interpret Burrell and Morgan as implying that a paradigm could be understood only from the inside and therefore that paradigms are isolated from one another.

Reflecting on Kuhn's and Burrell and Morgan's ideas about paradigm incommensurability, it is easy to understand the ensuing confusion among organization scholars. Scholars interpreted incommensurability in a variety of ways. Some interpreted it in what Weaver and Gioia (1994) called the "strong sense"—"implying the impossibility of meaningful communication across paradigms" (p. 572). Hassard (1988) observed, "In organization theory, few concepts have been employed as inconsistently as that of *paradigm*" (p. 248).

The problems introduced by the inconsistent usage were amplified as scholars used *paradigm* and *incommensurability* to promote their own values and interests.

Values and Interests in the Incommensurability Debate

Values and interests (i.e., concerns and aspirations[1] for social science) played a key role almost from the start of the debate in organization studies about incommensurability. Burrell and Morgan, and later Jackson and Carter (1991), emphasized paradigm incommensurability hoping to keep weaker paradigms from being subsumed by more powerful ones. Burrell (1996) captured this sentiment tersely: "Dialogue is a weapon of the powerful" (p. 650). Incommensurability of theories would preserve the legitimacy of alternative perspectives by reducing the chances that dominant perspectives would subsume or drive out less widely accepted ones. Likewise, Jackson and Carter (1991) promoted incommensurability to protect the "plurality of modes of scientific inquiry from the imperialistic aspirations of an orthodoxy whose interests are rooted in performance and control" (p. 111). This objective had provocative implications. It challenged the orthodox view of science, which maintained that a body of scientific universal knowledge existed or at least was possible. Jackson and Carter noted that the pluralist view implied that "there is no single homogeneous body of scientific knowledge" (p. 112).

This position challenged the ultimate authority of science. Bernstein (1991) noted that many scholars saw this perspective as a great threat. In organization studies, some perceived a position on paradigm incommensurability such as Jackson and Carter's as potentially opening the door for many perspectives they objected to, such as subjectivism, irrationalism, and nihilism. Leading champions of the orthodox view challenged the incommensurability position. McKelvey (2002) and Donaldson (1985, 1998), among others, voiced strong challenges.

Reflections on Incommensurability Debate

Much of the incommensurability debate boiled down to disagreement about the possibility of communication among proponents of different perspectives. The debate was divisive; its tone was often agonistic—so much so that many used the term *paradigm war* to describe it.

The debate about incommensurability demonstrated many of the dysfunctional features of the agonistic mode (e.g., misunderstanding, misattributions concerning the positions of those on the other side of an issue, use of quicksand terms, and failure to explicitly address differences in values).

Poorly articulated concepts and political agendas spawned heated debate. Along the way, some scholars drew implications from the incommensurability thesis. These included: (1) In order to fully understand a perspective, a person must assent to it (reminiscent of Augustine's famous precept, "Seek not to understand that you may believe, but believe that you may understand"); and (2) meaningful communication among advocates of different paradigms is not possible.

Reframing the Debate

Eventually, some scholars, including Weaver and Gioia (1994), Jackson and Carter (1991), and Scherer and Downing (1995), began to treat the debate in terms of language and dialogue.

We believe this turn to language reframed incommensurability in a productive way. For example, it helped Weaver and Gioia (1994) gain insights about communication across paradigms. They wrote that maintaining that people cannot communicate across paradigms "runs counter to what all of us routinely manage to do in one fashion or another every day, i.e., understand each other in a way which, although fallible, does not seem subject to constant, systematic, and necessary failure. Cross-cultural communication may be difficult for both anthropologists and ordinary persons, but it is nonetheless" (p. 572) possible. They added:

> It is not at all clear that our attempts to fathom competing "paradigms" must be any more subject to error—much less systematic failure—than our attempts to fathom other people, in the fashion of translators, cultural anthropologists, etc.... Although there are many complex difficulties in such tasks (questions of rationality, issues of charity in interpretation, etc.), we seem to persist in the effort anyway. Why should inter-paradigmatic translation be any more impossible than cross-cultural translation? (p. 575)

This linguistic turn is highly relevant to the current chapter because it helps to frame incommensurability as a communication issue. Scherer and Dowling's (1995) work was especially useful in this regard. They noted that in a concrete situation, participants' experience of incommensurability should stimulate them to begin a discussion. They observed that even Gareth Morgan (1983), in his book *Beyond Method*, changed his position to write less about incommensurability and more about conversation and engagement.

Reflections on Paradigm Incommensurability

The incommensurability debate grew from the use of equivocal terms in a setting charged with conflicting values and interests. Although we oppose using incommensurability as a political tool in intellectual discussions (we see doing so as distorting scholarship for political ends), we support the efforts of Burrell and Morgan and Jackson and Carter to keep the study of organizations open to diverse voices. Since what Foucault (1980) called the "regime of truth" is always waiting to solidify around conventional wisdoms, we want to reserve space for challengers to these wisdoms. Although we share many of the emancipatory concerns of the scholars who advanced the incommensurability thesis for political reasons, we nevertheless consider the tactic ill-advised for the same reason we object to Hunt's (2005) advocacy of adopting philosophical realism because it engenders client trust. We question the integrity of adopting intellectual ideas for political purposes and fear that in the long run doing so might erode the trust outsiders have in our discipline and interfere with scholarship within the discipline.

Incidentally, there is evidence that political use of incommensurability can actually inhibit diversity. Recall that many champions of the incommensurability thesis supported it because they saw it as aiding diversity. However, Weaver and Gioia (1994) found it also acted as a repressive force. They described how the incommensurability thesis itself is "sometimes unreflectively invoked, or institutionally entrenched, in organizational inquiry" (p. 576). They reported that at one point in the review process of one of their manuscripts Gioia and Petré were given to understand that the paper they submitted for publication would not be accepted if it contained a direct rejection of the incommensurability thesis. Ironically, this thesis, once advanced as an antidote to limits that values and interests might place on intellectual openness, came to develop its own regime of truth.

Aside from pointing to its potential for misuse as a political tool, our primary concern about the incommensurability thesis involves its implications for meaningful dialogue among scholars from opposing perspectives. Sometimes, users of *incommensurable* imply that understanding is impossible unless a person agrees with the perspective under discussion. If we agreed with this position—and we do not—inquiry as a social process would be severely limited.

To treat this topic further, we reintroduce the supposition of accurate reception (SOAR), the criterion (however fallible) we believe people use to assess communication as being successful. As we explained, SOAR can occur on the part of a speaker, a listener, or one or more observers. Achieving SOAR in discussing different perspectives does not depend on people agreeing with any of the perspectives. We experienced all three types of SOAR in connection with communication among opposing theorists. We felt understood by scholars who disagreed with us and also felt that we understood them. We also supposed that two scholars who appeared to disagree with each other understood each other's positions.

For an example of our observation of SOAR for a complex communication involving disagreement, we refer you to Feyerabend's (1987) explication of Putnam's (1981) view of incommensurability. Let us explain.

Feyerabend (1987) disagreed with Putnam's (1981) claim that Putnam refuted incommensurability. Feyerabend began by quoting three central tenets of Putnam's position. He then introduced assumptions he believed these tenets rested on. He addressed these assumptions fully, although concluding they were invalid. He then turned to definitions of the term and suggested he and Putnam did not mean the same thing when they used *incommensurable*. We experienced third-person SOAR when we read Feyerabend's paper. His discussion led us to believe that he received Putnam's message accurately without assenting to it.

The question of whether or not assent is necessary for experiencing SOAR could, of course, be tested empirically. If, as we suggest, understanding is possible in the absence of agreement, then scholars should be able to experience SOAR about opposing perspectives. If they can do that, even if they advocate different paradigms, they should be able to engage in meaningful dialogue—something we maintain many organization scholars have done all along.

Our rejection of the antidialogue position aligns us with a number of recent attempts to improve communication among organization scholars.

PARADIGM INCOMMENSURABILITY AND THE PRO-DIALOGUE POSITION

Recently, a number of organization scholars expressed concern that issues related to the paradigm incommensurability debate were disrupting communication in organization studies.

Many of these proposals, some of which we already mentioned, sought to reduce the argumentative tone. They included Moldoveanu and Baum's (2002) idea of responsiveness, Calás and Smircich's (1999) proposal to write in friendship, Weick's (1999) approving commentary on Calás and Smircich's ideas, and Lewis and Grimes's (1999) notion of meta-triangulation. The same spirit appeared to move Czarniawska (1998) to emphasize understanding and humbly call for abandoning "self-centered rhetoric" (p. 274) and working to gain "from time to time … an illusion of understanding what the Other is saying" (p. 274). Gergen (2001) advanced related proposals.

Moldoveanu and Baum

Moldoveanu and Baum (2002) asserted that responsiveness is vital for good communication. By *responsiveness* they meant that individuals, who hold different epistemological commitments than others, respond directly to the others' arguments. This demands that "claims of that argument (including the evidence statements on which the argument is based) be specifically addressed in reply" (p. 747). For example, in a conversation between a realist and a constructionist, commitment to responsiveness would require "both constructionist and realist researchers to abandon the self-justification practice of citing only the works in the philosophy and epistemology of science that substantiate their position, and that they specifically engage the counter-arguments that have been advanced to these positions" (p. 747).

Further, Moldoveanu and Baum argued that lack of philosophical sophistication in organization studies limited responsiveness, thereby contributing to the turmoil, by impeding communication. They recommended two general steps to improve dialogue. The first called for scholars to make informed choices about their epistemological assumptions rather than relying on philosophers as authorities. Toward this end, they recommended including the study of epistemology in research methods courses.

In addition, they called for scholars to develop interactive reasoning skills by recognizing the foundations and assumptions underlying other scholars' perspectives. Such awareness, they argued, could reduce misunderstandings of the type involved in the paradigm war.

Calás and Smircich

Calás and Smircich (1999) implicitly recognized agonism's inhibiting effects on organizational theorizing when they called upon their colleagues to write in friendship. In their words:

> Our modest hope is that ... we will be able to sustain a conversation through a ... kind of engagement that does not require arguing for the superiority of our views in relation to those of others ... some of what this entails is for authors to specify the aspects of the world with which they are trying to engage and why; to situate knowledge and so de-reify it; to speak in a way that takes ownership of their arguments; and to be accountable for the choices made. "It posits a different basis of engagement, one which is reciprocal not hierarchical. It is a call for writing in friendship" (Townley, 1994b: 28). (p. 650)

Weick

In support and refinement of Calás and Smircich's position, Weick (1999) wrote:

> The image of paradigm "wars" has the unfortunate connotation that it suggests the path to victory and truth lies in monologues that overwhelm rather than in dialogues that reconcile.... But there is hope. There are invitations to conversation densely seeded throughout the articles in this special issue. ... Calás and Smircich invite us to "drop our tools" in the interest of refashioning our identities as theorists. By this they mean that we should drop things like writing styles, definitions of what constitutes research, and pretensions to expertise. Those are dramatic shifts, but shifts happen.
>
> I want to fine tune and reframe their recommendation. Wildland firefighters, the blue collar professionals with whom the image of tool dropping originated (Weick, 1996), have refined the admonition so that now it reads, "drop your *heavy* tools." ... Theorists should heed this differentiation of tools. If theorists drop their heavy tools of paradigms and monologues, they still retain the equivalents of survival gear.... Most of all, they still have their capacity for attentive listening. Once these resources are in place, *then* theorists can converse about what tools they should drop. (p. 804)

Lewis and Grimes

Lewis and Grimes (1999) presented three approaches for dealing with the paradigm debate: (1) multiparadigm reviews; (2) multiparadigm research; and (3) meta-paradigm theory building.

1. Multiparadigm reviews are literature reviews that use paradigm bracketing to help reveal different sets of assumptions that are embedded in alternative perspectives.

2. Multiparadigm research calls for using competing paradigms empirically as alternative lenses.
3. Multiparadigm theory building entails comprehending "paradigmatic differences, similarities, and interrelationships" (p. 675) to develop a richer, more holistic, and contextualized perspective. In doing it, users assume paradigms offer partial truths and juxtapose the various explanations to translate contrasts into theoretical meta-paradigm systems that link contrasting representations.

To guide building such theories, Lewis and Grimes offered traditional meta-triangulation as an analogy. Such a process, they suggested, would stimulate theorists to seek out rather than avoid conflicting interpretations.

Gergen's Call for Improved Dialogue

Kenneth Gergen called for attending to philosophical matters as a step for improving communication among social scientists. To reconcile orthodoxy with postmodernism, Gergen (2001) advised relinquishing "the adversarial/advocacy posture … in favor of searching … for a means of deliberating on the antimony itself" (p. 19)

For what he termed shifting the discursive register, Gergen advocated drawing upon recent developments in family therapy. These techniques can help to reduce angry counterattacks by using such questions as "'Why are we doing this?' 'Is this what we really want?' or 'Is there another way we might handle this?'" (p. 20). He noted that the point of postmodernist critique is "to give all traditions the right to participate within the unfolding dialogues" (p. 808).

Overview of Contributions of Pro-Dialogue Scholars

In one way or another, the writers calling for improving dialogue in organization studies all seemed to recognize the dysfunctions of agonism that we discussed in Chapter 10, "Letting Go of Agonism." In addition, a number of them recognized that awareness of one's philosophical assumptions and efforts to understand positions contrary to one's own would enhance dialogue.

We believe the generative uncertainty perspective we advance in this volume supports these suggestions and contributes to the dialogue position.

GENERATIVE UNCERTAINTY AIDING COMMUNICATION IN ORGANIZATION STUDIES

Our perspective encourages people to accept a degree of uncertainty about the success of any particular communication attempt. It suggests that supposition of accurate reception (SOAR)[2] might well be the most we can expect to achieve from human communication in general or scholarly communication, including that among students of organizations, in particular.

If organization scholars focused on achieving SOAR, they might behave differently than many of them do now. They might reduce the "parallel monologues" that concerned Moldoveanu and Baum and be more likely to write in friendship as Calás and Smircich urged.

The discussion of SOAR in the next section extends our earlier treatment of agonism's contribution to the knowledge controversy and directs attention to how, by seeking SOAR, organization scholars could enhance conversation.

IMPROVING CONVERSATION IN ORGANIZATION STUDIES THROUGH SOAR

The concept of SOAR helps us (Nord and Connell) think and talk about both attempts at understanding and the unavoidable uncertainties that surround interpretation of written and spoken language. We developed the idea from our experiences and observations of what people seem to do.

Please note that working for SOAR is different from seeking intersubjectivity. Since SOAR is only a supposition, it does not imply that a message was received accurately. SOAR's modest aspirations allow one to sidestep concerns about the difficulty in knowing a writer's or speaker's original intent. Even asking an author what he or she had in mind does not fully address this concern. The author might not remember or might never have known his or her original intentions exactly. Moreover, any later explanations he or she provides, like his or her original writing, would require interpretation. With Czarniawska (1998), whom we quoted earlier, we believe in working to gain "from time to time ... an illusion of understanding what the Other is saying" (p. 274), even in the absence of access to what Derrida called a "transcendental signified" (i.e., the one correct meaning) of the message.

Recognizing that people seem to strive for SOAR, we ask what organization scholars might do to achieve more of it. We present a number of specific do's (SOAR winners) and don'ts (SOAR losers) in Table 11.1.

The matrix in Table 11.1 presents our main suggestions for achieving SOAR. The first row lists suggestions for senders of messages and the second row lists suggestions for receivers. The third row presents suggestions for both. The columns contain the suggested do's and don'ts.

SOAR Winners—For Senders (Cell 1)

Cell 1 presents SOAR winners for senders. These include acting to promote iterative exchanges and providing pertinent definitions.

TABLE 11.1 Guides to SOAR

	Actions	
Communicator Role	**SOAR Winners (Do's)**	**SOAR Losers (Don'ts)**
Sender	1. Iterative communication Provision of pertinent definitions	2. Quicksand terms
Receiver	3. Active listening Consulting multiple sources	4. Assumptive listening
Senders and receivers	5. Attention to context Reflexivity	

Iterative Communication in Organization Scholarship

Organization studies has many structures and processes in place that support iterative exchanges. For example, at a formal level, we already have review processes and letters and comments sections in our journals, all of which, with some tweaking, could be used to reduce the prevailing agonistic ethos and increase SOAR. Some journal editors already encourage reviewers to provide more developmental reviews (see Sanders, 2009).

Provision of Pertinent Definitions

Essentialist definitions have a long history in Western intellectual endeavors. Plato (1961/390s–347 B.C., in Hamilton & Cairns, 1961) was concerned that the name of a thing reflect its "true form." In this vein he wrote, "Cratylus is right in saying that things have names by nature" (p. 429). Similarly, for Aristotle in the fourth century B.C., a definition was a phrase signifying a thing's essence.

As this essentialist approach descended into our own time, it brought with it a potential for hindering communication. Recall our discussion with our university colleagues about whether or not taxonomy was part of science. To us, the dispute hinged on members on both sides of the matter holding an essentialist view of the word *science*. It was as if there was an entity out there called *science*, and professors on each side believed they knew its true nature. Since the participants could not agree on the nature of *science*, they could not agree about whether or not it included taxonomy.

Students of organization have similar problems. They can become enmeshed in an essentialist approach to words. For example, consider the 1995 *Administrative Science Quarterly* special forum devoted to theory. Sutton and Staw (1995) wrote, "Lack of consensus on exactly what theory is may explain why it is so difficult to develop strong theory in the behavioral sciences" (p. 372). With Popper (N.D.) we question the value of essentialist definitions and the potential of definitions to eliminate all ambiguities. Furthermore, the quest for essentialist definitions is complicated by a problem that seems to be inherent in definitions themselves. Words, almost always, end up being defined in terms of themselves—there's no way to get out of the circle. Consider Hacking's (1999) description of the game of *Vish*. The game begins with a player looking up a word in the dictionary. Then players look up the words contained in the definition. The first person who gets back to the original word cries *Vish*! (vicious circle).

However, we do not agree with Popper (N.D.) that efforts to define "only increase vagueness and confusion" (p. 27). Rather, we view definitions as imperfect tools that can help to achieve what we call SOAR.

For us, careful definition, although not a panacea, can be tremendously helpful. However, our rationale is a little different from that of some scholars who emphasized the importance of definitions. For example, we differ from Pinder and Bourgeois (1982), who suggested that organization studies should develop an entirely new language, with definitions for every word.

In addition to the circle of meaning, the usages of words change over time and across contexts. A given individual may use the same word to signify quite different patterns in different situations.

Meanings of words depend on context. Even within organization studies, intended meanings and interpretations vary according to context. Our nonessentialist stance denies that there are entities called words that possess their own unique meanings. It suggests that, potentially, any given word can be part of many patterns, depending upon the context in which it is used.

SOAR Losers for Senders—Things to Avoid (Cell 2)

Cell 2 advises senders to avoid "quicksand" terms. Since there are many particular quicksand terms that we believe impede SOAR in organization studies, to make our point clear, after defining *quicksand terms* we describe a number of specific terms that we believe are part of the organization studies knowledge controversy.

Quicksand Terms

We, Connell and Nord (1996), defined *quicksand terms* as terms "that have so many conflicting definitions and connotations that they lead people into … 'conceptual quicksand' instead of to a sense of understanding" (p. 408). Such terms often lead to confusing conversations. A number of words frequently employed in organization studies seem to act like quicksand in that they suck scholars into unnecessary and dysfunctional arguments. Once in the quicksand, the more they struggle, the deeper they sink. Those on different sides of an issue may use the same quicksand term in different ways to mean different things and thus talk past each other, as both sides seek rhetorical advantage. We have already proposed that Hunt's (1994) discussion of how positivism was used in the qualitative versus quantitative debate is a good example. Other examples, discussed earlier in this chapter, are *incommensurability* and *paradigm*.

Frequently, the ambiguity associated with these terms, especially in the context of debate, contributes to misunderstanding as debaters manipulate meanings to serve political objectives.

The problem does not seem to be resolvable simply by insisting that all users define such terms in the same way, even if that were possible. The terms involved now have too much surplus meaning, and perhaps it is best to avoid using them by substituting more careful wording.

In discussions about highly controversial issues, where emotions are strong, use of equivocal terms often elevates associated emotions and misunderstandings simultaneously. When this happens, participants in a communication episode feel misunderstood; SOAR is absent.

The term *quicksand term* itself risks being a quicksand term. To deal with this possibility, we attempt to clarify what we mean by examining a few terms that we believe often function as quicksand terms in contemporary organization studies controversies. We suggest how they might be dealt with; often this involves using alternative expressions that might communicate more effectively.

One caveat before we go further. We view our treatment of quicksand terms and our suggestions for dealing with them as tentative and developmental. It is an early step in consciousness raising about some language problems in the field.

Common Quicksand Terms in the Knowledge Controversy

In addition to *positivism*, *paradigm*, and *commensurable/incommensurable*, treated above, we examine a few other problematic terms that introduced communication difficulties into the knowledge debate.

Many terms might be used as examples. Here we discuss only a few of them: *objectivity, subjectivity, reason*, and *science*. We suggest it is time to rethink how we use these terms and in some cases to avoid them altogether.

Objectivity Objectivity, in large measure because of its implicit tie to commonsense realism, is one of the quicksand words that we advise organization scholars to abandon. We are not the first to suggest dropping this term (see Culbert, 1996).

The meaning of the word is often not clear. Even one of the champions of objectivity, Hunt (1994), noted that terms such as *objectivist* have been used in myriad ways.

Problems with objectivity stem from the unnecessary controversy that the large variety of meanings generates and from the large number of entailments associated with the term.

Literally, *objectivity* means "given by an object." However, in the context of the current knowledge controversy, it often connotes the idea that humans can know objects without being influenced by preconceptions and biases. In other words, it implies commonsense realism's view that humans can have direct access to and can obtain accurate representations of some independent external reality.

If any approach to inquiry could deliver that type of knowledge, it would indeed be viewed as very valuable. Thus, if one simply ignores associated philosophical issues, objectivity offers considerable rhetorical advantages. Perhaps these advantages account for the fact that a number of scholars, including Longino (1990) and Harding (1991), appear committed to retaining the term.

It is noteworthy that these scholars differ in both their view of what constitutes objectivity and the nature of their commitment to the term. Such divergence among advocates of the term is another reason we suggest abandoning it.

After explicitly rejecting the idea of a value-free science, Longino (1990) appeared to want to use objectivity to enable "us to see that the sciences are not … hopelessly subjective" (p. 37). However, because she dealt explicitly with fundamental philosophical matters, her view of objectivity was more nuanced than a number of others'.

Longino (1990) distinguished two different uses of objectivity. One, she observed, "is bound up with truth and referential character of scientific theories, that is, with issues of scientific realism" (p. 62). Describing science as objective in this view entails the claim that it correctly describes the facts of the natural world as they are. In contrast, the second way Longino believed objectivity is used relates to modes of inquiry. The claim here is that the results of inquiry are more achieved by "reliance upon nonarbitrary and nonsubjective criteria for developing, accepting, and rejecting the hypotheses and theories that make up the view" (p. 62). In other words, results derive objective status from use of the scientific method.

> At least two things can be intended by the ascription of objectivity to scientific method. Often scientists speak of the objectivity of data. By this they seem to mean that the information upon which their theories and hypotheses rest has been obtained in such a way as to justify their reliance upon it. This involves the assumption or assurance that experiments have been properly performed and that quantitative data have not been skewed by any faults in the design of survey instruments or by systematic but uncharacteristic eccentricities of behavior of the sample studied. If a given set of data has been objectively obtained in this sense, one is thereby licensed to believe that it provides a reliable view of the world in the first of the two senses of objectivity distinguished above. (Longino, 1990, p. 63)

In contrast to these and several other prominent scholars who recently promoted use of *objectivity*, we are less positive about the treatments of the word. Our major complaint is the failure to sufficiently consider the philosophical underpinnings of the word. In recent decades, several contemporary scholars, including Ghate and Locke (2003), Harding (1991), and Hunt (1994), asserted *objectivity*'s (at least as they defined it) positive value. Among other things, they appeared to believe (as we do) that in our culture the word has substantial political/rhetorical value. We believed this benefit was a major attraction.

In championing objectivity, Hunt (1994) appeared to offer two definitions. On the one hand, he approvingly quoted Hempel's (1970, p. 695) definition: "Science strives for objectivity in the sense that its statements are to be capable of public tests with results that do not vary essentially with the tester" (p. 230). If one accepted this definition without any implicit realist epistemology, it would seem to make objectivity synonymous with repeatable. However, a few paragraphs later, realism seemed to be involved when Hunt observed that "what we see out there is the world," and it can serve as "an objective test of our theories *about* that world" (p. 231).

More evidence of *objectivity*'s definitional ambiguity and scholars' attraction to the term for its rhetorical value appeared in the work of a third champion of the term, Sandra Harding (1991). After labeling the traditional notion of value-neutral objectivity as "weak" objectivity and effectively critiquing this approach, Harding sought to preserve the use of *objectivity* by distinguishing "weak objectivity" from her preferred "strong objectivity," which recognizes that beliefs from the traditional scientific process are historical and socially situated.

Harding recognized some ways that the term was problematic. One possible objection she noted reflected a concern similar to ours—dysfunctional entailments. In her words, "Many would say that the notion of objectivity is so hopelessly tainted by its historical complicity in justifying the service of science to the dominant groups that trying to make it function effectively and progressively in alternative agendas only confuses the matter" (p. 157).

Why not then, one might ask, at least come up with an alternative word? In response, Harding contended, "One cannot afford to 'just say no' to objectivity" (p. 160).

Why? For at least three reasons. First, Harding pointed to the value the term has had in providing standards for distinguishing between how the world is "in empirical fact" (p. 160) and how people want it to be. Second, objectivity is useful in struggles that attempt to hold people and institutions responsible for the fit between the claims they make and their actual behavior. Third, it is helpful in justifying unpopular criticism of entrenched beliefs.

We share Harding's emancipatory goals. However, because of what we see as the dysfunctional role of objectivity in the knowledge and related controversies, we still suggest abandoning it. For the most part, Harding's reasons for keeping the term have more to do with its connotations than with its value for communication.

As part of our call to abandon the term, we invite its advocates to consider substituting more precise alternatives that have less surplus meaning. For example, if by *objective* Hunt means repeatable observations, we suggest he substitute *repeatability* for objectivity. Similarly, if what Ghate and Locke (2003) mean by *objectivity* is based on perceptual data, we ask them to discuss perception, detailing who did the perceiving, under what conditions, and why they trust those particular perceptions. Also, when people mean "free from bias," we would prefer them to say that and support this claim.

We see such steps as very reasonable alternatives to using *objectivity*. However, given how deeply embedded the term is in modern discourse, we are probably fighting a losing battle. Many people may want to continue using the word despite its costs. If so, we urge users to define it carefully.

Doing so would help to avoid many of the problematic connotations that objectivity seems to carry with it. Of course, there are trade-offs. Had Hunt substituted *repeatability* for *objectivity*, he would have lost the latent positive connotations that the word added to his position.

Subjectivity An important use of *subjectivity* in organization studies derives from its contrast with *objectivity*. Since we suggested abandoning the latter, the value of subjectivity approaches zero. Then too, just as it was easy to find a suitable substitute for *objective*, so it is to find a suitable substitute to communicate the patterns that people seem to wish to express by *subjective*. For example, depending on the situation, they might refer to coming to an opinion through some intrapersonal experience such as a dream, fantasy, or intuition. *Idiosyncratic* is a good substitute, which does not imply the possibility of objectivity.

Reason *Reason* refers to patterns that people often want to discuss. We suggest substituting *thinking* for this term. *Reason*, like many quicksand terms, has an implication that we prefer to avoid, namely, that there are absolute correct principles for thinking. However, we know of no evidence to support this implication. Thinking is linked to fewer undesirable assumptions and controversies. We see thinking as treating one of or a combination of the following: deduction, induction, generalization, abduction, model making, category formation, mapping, and sorting. We prefer *thinking* or any of these terms to the word *reason*.

Science *Science* has numerous entailments (many of which, like those associated with *objectivity*, can provide considerable rhetorical benefits for privileging a particular position that one wishes to advance). Consequently, we prefer a less polluted and more descriptive term, such as *inquiry*. Inquiry focuses attention on what we think of as the explicit pattern that science ordinarily denotes, that is, human beings investigating something. Inquiry has less surplus meaning. In contrast to *science*, *inquiry* emphasizes human processes that may or may not imply production of firm knowledge. Moreover, in our opinion, inquiry describes well what people who are currently called scientists do or should be doing. Of course, there are a variety of ways to inquire, and certain descriptors might need to be added to delimit types of inquiry more precisely. Although we prefer to avoid using *science* when we can, sometimes we use it in lieu of a good alternative, especially when it's part of a compound term like *social science.*

Parting Thoughts on Quicksand Terms We began our discussion of quicksand terms with the caveat that at this point we viewed our effort as a preliminary one to encourage you and our other colleagues to watch your language. Doing so could involve organization studies colleagues working together to improve the field's communication. As the process unfolds, it might resemble the gradual modification of gender-related terminology that occurred in our larger culture in recent decades. We suspect that at this point you will not be willing to abandon these terms. However, hopefully we said enough to encourage you to think about how these and similar terms might have contributed to unnecessary controversy and may be continuing to do so.

We now shift our attention from senders of information to receivers. With this we move to Row 2 in Table 11.1 and begin with SOAR winners (actions we recommend) for receivers.

SOAR Winners for Receivers (Cell 3)

We propose three actions for receivers: acknowledge assumptions, active listening, and consulting multiple sources (especially in instances of doubt).

Active Listening

Active listening is a well-known suggestion that students of interpersonal communication proposed for decades. Its objective is consistent with the SOAR winner of fostering iterative communication.

Years ago, the renowned psychologist Carl Rogers (see Rogers and Farson, 1987) advocated a number of useful steps for getting in touch with another person's "felt datum" (p. 215). "Active listening" is perhaps the best known of these actions. By now, it is so well known and so widely believed to be effective that it routinely appears in introductory organization behavior textbooks. However, with the exception of Gergen's (2001) recommendation for applying techniques from family therapy to scholarly interchanges, students of organization studies have given little attention to how they might use it to improve communication with their colleagues.

Consider how students of organization studies might use this approach. Many conversations in organization studies suffer because listening is underdeveloped or absent. Active listening could change this by requiring a receiver to try walking in the sender's shoes and maybe even paraphrase a sent message before responding. Active listening recognizes that effective communication is an interactive process wherein statements need to be rephrased, sometimes repeatedly, based on feedback from an intended receiver, until both the sender and receiver sense that the message was understood, or in our terms, until both attain SOAR.

To gain such an experience, communication experts advise both senders and receivers to take steps that provide additional information, such as repeating, pointing, and introducing examples, demonstrations, measurements, definitions, figures of speech, and provision of context, pictures, and graphs. For example, they have advised receivers to paraphrase, request clarification, empathize, use a dictionary, and study senders' contexts. These techniques contribute to SOAR through providing iterative exchanges that permit people to alter their mindsets to refine their understandings. Such exchanges can help senders to revise their messages in ways that help receivers to understand better.

Our second suggestion in Cell 3 is a specific way to gain additional information. We advise consulting other related messages from the sender.

Consult Multiple Sources

Often SOAR is furthered by attending to more than one document or statement a sender issued. This path calls for encompassing efforts to investigate possible meanings. It is congruent with Derrida's (1976) opinion that a careful reading of the text involves "all the instruments of traditional criticism" (p. 158). Otherwise, as he concluded, "critical production would risk developing in any direction at all and authorize it to say almost anything" (p. 158). Recall our earlier discussion of our lack of SOAR regarding Weiss's reading of Derrida. We believe that more information about Derrida's views would have helped Weiss to grasp Derrida better.

SOAR Losers for Receivers—Actions to Avoid (Cell 4)

Like many of our other suggestions, the advice in Cell 4 for receivers—avoid assumptive listening—is intended to advance attentive iterative interaction.

Assumptive Listening

Assumptive listening occurs when, without checking it out, receivers assume that they understand what a sender is attempting to express. When they make such an assumption, receivers often presume that they share common definitions and frames of reference with the sender. We consider Weiss's (2000) interpretation of Derrida (in the Weiss-Derrida example discussed in Chapter 10 on agonism) a prime example.

One reason we are troubled by the agonistic mode in scholarly communication is that it often leads to assumptive listening as opposed to listening for understanding. We urge listeners to question their understanding. These suggestions are not completely independent of each other. For example, a person who listens actively is less prone to assumptive listening. Similarly, a person who questions his or her own reception is more apt to listen actively.

This brings us to Cell 5, which contains SOAR winners for both senders and receivers.

SOAR Winners for Senders and Receivers (Cell 5)

The first entry in Cell 5, "attention to context," is advice for good scholarship in general as well as improving communication.

Attention to Context

By *context* we mean the collection of other patterns in a person's stream of experience in which a specific pattern appears embedded. Context can refer to a variety of patterns. For example, you might think of a single sentence as the "textual context" of a word. Or you might think of your entire collection of patterns from books, articles, lectures, and discussions about organization studies as a "communal context" or "intellectual context" for the same word or sentence. Then, too, where Person and his or her partner (Other) are standing, or Person's hunch that Other is experiencing some state such as hunger, may be a situational context for a particular word.

In *Anticipating China* Hall and Ames (1995) presented an analogy that helps to clarify our view of context, by relating the Taoist perspective on the relation between individual things and the "totality of things." They wrote:

> Consider the value of a particular note in a symphony. The value of any one note can only be assayed by understanding its place in the entire piece of music and its performance. Any one note thus has implicated within it the entire score. The note thus has a holographic quality, bringing the field of relevant relationships into focus from one particular locus. Important here is that the field of relationships is not circumscribed or holistic, but an unbounded reservoir of particular detail that remains open and available for further inclusion. The field of relevant detail for the particular note can be extended to include a movement in another piece by the same composer, or his entire corpus, or the musical product of a particular era, and so on. (p. 236)

Our view of the relationship between definitions and contexts is analogous. A word may have a different meaning in each context where it appears. Different listeners have different streams of experience. Further, any given listener may respond from different streams of experience at different times. In short, meaning can vary among listeners, and the same listener may give different meaning to the same text at different times.

Our final SOAR winner for senders and receivers is reflexivity.

Reflexivity

Based on what we said so far, it should be clear that we believe that unrecognized assumptions interfere with good scholarship. We propose reflexivity as a tool to help increase awareness of assumptions.

Nightingale and Cromby (1999) defined reflexivity as exploring how "a researcher's involvement with a particular study influences, acts upon and informs such research" (p. 228). Such explanation is important because of the strong effects one's experiences can have on the design and interpretation of research. When being reflexive, one takes this influence on his or her perspective into account. In practice, such looking back directs people to focus on how their own social positions (e.g., cultural contexts, personal opinions, and values) might influence their perceptions and conclusions. Such focus may lead one to realize that his or her intellectual position may be more of a special case than the universal truth it seemed to be prior to reflection. Such realization often increases one's intellectual openness.

Alvesson and Karremon (2007) observed that reflexivity may be gained by asking oneself a question such as "Can I construct/make sense of this material in another way than suggested by some preferred perspective/vocabulary?" (p. 1270). They pointed out that reflexivity can be encouraged by using a variety of theoretical perspectives and metaphors, listening to alternative voices of people in different social locations, considering different political interests and research purposes, and working with colleagues who have different backgrounds or theoretical perspectives.

In addition, we speculate, reflexivity may make one more likely to send messages using a provisional (as opposed to an absolutistic) tone. In our experience, messages having provisional tones are more conducive to SOAR than are ones with more absolutistic tones.

FINAL THOUGHTS ON IMPROVING CONVERSATION IN ORGANIZATION STUDIES

In addition, our approach for improving communication among students of organization studies includes institutionalizing some SOAR winners.

Gaining SOAR is aided by keeping several general points about scholarly communication in mind. Scholarly communication is an interactive process. It is helped by study of multiple types of aid to communication.

With this background, we summarize our own position.

We believe that frequently students of organization studies do not have SOAR when they attempt to communicate with each other. This deficit contributes substantially to the dysfunctional conflicts that currently plague the field.

The norms of agonistic discourse and contest for academic status (see Chapter 10) contribute to the problem, as do difficulties stemming from the fact that, like other humans, students of organizations at both ends of a communication channel are prone to assume, without checking, that a communication was successful. Senders make this assumption even when they have provided little or no context for their position and have not defined key terms. Then, when they fail to experience SOAR with receivers, senders commonly blame the receivers by attributing carelessness or ignorance to them.

Such occurrences generate defensive climates, accelerating communication's downward spiral. Among other things, defensive climates stimulate both parties to be preoccupied with protecting themselves against the possibility that their communication partners will find flaws in what they say. Consequently, the process leads, almost exactly as Aristotle predicted in "Topics," to receivers more or less focusing on flaws in senders' statements. (Of course, we strongly favor critical thinking, but we are troubled when finding flaws takes priority over listening.)

As one final attempt in this chapter to explain the nature of the postagonistic communication we advocate, we present an example from Connell's experiences as a graduate student.

She worked at the Central Institute for the Deaf (CID), which was known for its excellent research on hearing. As a major part of the research process, investigators frequently presented their work to colleagues.

At these sessions, colleagues thoroughly critiqued all aspects of the research. Although the critiques were intense, everyone understood that the purpose was to make the research better, so that nothing but the best work left the halls of CID. As Connell perceived it, the feedback was accepted in the spirit it was given.

This is an example of the way that critical feedback from colleagues can aid inquiry. Among other things, it demonstrates a mode of communication that facilitates the cooperative process we believe makes for productive inquiry.

In this cooperative process, careful listening and critical thinking complement each other. This belief is one reason why, in order to achieve SOAR, we suggest replacing the debate mode with a process that gives higher priority to listening. In short, working for SOAR is an antidote to negative communication spirals. Recall that achieving SOAR requires only that participants and observers judge that communication has occurred.

Moreover, consistent with Derrida and the spirit of generative uncertainty, pursuing SOAR does not entail attributing some absolute meaning to a text and thereby implicitly recognizes that the meaning given to any series of words may change across time and circumstances. The spirit of this perspective is highly consistent with Gergen's (1982) discussion of the multiple meanings of action and his postulate that the identification of any particular action is subject to infinite revision. Further, the anchor point of any particular identification "*relies on a network of interdependent and continuously modifiable interpretations*" (p. 63). Moreover, multiple identifications are possible, "*the relative superiority of which is problematic*" (p. 64).

In some respects, the communication approach we suggest may help to cope with the controversy between the pro-dialogue and antidialogue camps that helped to fuel the incommensurability debate. Recall those members of the antidialogue group, such as Burrell and Morgan, tried to decry the possibility of communication in order to protect the minority positions from extinction.

We, too, are concerned that new and minority positions get a fair hearing. However, we indicated we do not favor using a concept such as incommensurability to make it happen. We believe that socializing members of the field to use the approach to communication we advocate provides a better alternative. If such socialization took place, it is likely that new and competing perspectives would get a hearing.

OVERVIEW

This chapter grew from a combination of our generative uncertainty, our study of the history and dysfunctions of agonism in Western intellectual circles, and the interest that many of our colleagues have expressed concerning the need to improve communication in organization studies.

The chapter built on these calls for improvement by placing them in the context of our overarching framework, generative uncertainty. That perspective heightens awareness of human limitations with respect to the possibility of having indubitably certain knowledge. Advancing SOAR as a criterion for success of communication reflects clear recognition of these limits.

Our interest in SOAR meshes well with ideas of many of our organization studies colleagues seeking to improve communication. For example, it has much in common with Moldoveanu and Baum's advice. Lewis and Grimes's proposed meta-triangulation is also similar to our approach. We view their call for theorists to become more fully aware of their own assumptions, contrast their assumptions with the assumptions of others, engage in self-critical reflection, and attempt to appreciate why their views are different from those of others as very helpful for gaining SOAR.

In addition, we pointed to some helpful techniques for improving conversation in organization studies, including paying attention to context and checking to see if speakers, listeners, and observers appear to experience SOAR.

We also urged members of our field to watch their language. In particular, we asked them to reflect on working to reduce the dysfunctions of quicksand terms and consider abandoning them. We pointed out how several of these have introduced communication problems in the knowledge controversy in organization studies and proposed ways to communicate about some of the important ideas that the problematic terms signify while avoiding the problems use of those terms often entails.

ENDNOTES

1. This use of *interests* follows from Hirschman (1977, p. 32).
2. In our earlier work, SOAR stood for *sense* of accurate reception (Connell & Nord, 1996). We now use it to refer to *supposition* of accurate reception. We made this change to avoid any connotation of accuracy that the word *sense* might convey.

REFERENCES

Alvesson, M., & Karremon, D. (2007). Constructing mystery: Empirical matters in theory development. *Academy of Management Review, 32,* 1265–1281.

Bernstein, R. J. (1991). *Beyond objectivism and relativism: Science, hermeneutics, and praxis*. Philadelphia, PA: University of Pennsylvania Press.

Burrell, G. (1996). Normal science, paradigms, metaphors, discourses and genealogies of analysis. In S. R. Clegg, C. Hardy, & W. R. Nord (Eds.), *Handbook of organization studies* (pp. 642–658). London, UK: Sage.

Burrell, G., & Morgan, G. (1979). *Sociological paradigms and organisational analysis*. London, UK: Heinemann.

Calás, M. B., & Smircich, L. (1999). Past postmodernism? Reflections and tentative directions. *Academy of Management Review, 24*(4), 649–671.

Connell, A. F., & Nord, W. R. (1996). The bloodless coup: The infiltration of organization science by uncertainty and values. *Journal of Applied Behavioral Science, 32*(4), 407–427.

Culbert, S. A. (1996). *Mind-set management: The heart of leadership*. New York, NY: Oxford University Press.

Czarniawska, B. (1998). Who is afraid of incommensurability? *Organization, 5*(2), 273–275.

Derrida, J. (1976). *Of grammatology* (G. C. Spivak, Trans.). Baltimore, MD: Johns Hopkins University Press.

Donaldson, L. (1985). *In defense of organization theory: A reply to the critics*. Cambridge, MA: Cambridge University Press.

Donaldson, L. (1998). The myth of paradigm incommensurability in management studies: Comments by an integrationist. *Organization, 5*(2), 267–272.

Feyerabend, P. K. (1962). explanation, reduction, and empiricism. In H. Feigl & G. Maxwell (Eds.), *Scientific explanation, space, and time: Minnesota studies in the philosophy of science* (Vol. III, pp. 28–97). Minneapolis, MN: University of Minnesota Press.

Feyerabend, P. K. (1987). Putnam on incommensurability. *British Journal for the Philosophy of Science, 38*(1), 75–81.
Foucault, M. (1980). *Power/knowledge: Selected interviews and other writings 1972–1977*. New York, NY: Pantheon Books.
Gergen, K. (1982). *Toward transformation in social knowledge*. New York, NY: Springer-Verlag.
Gergen, K. (2001). *Social construction in context*. London, UK: Sage Publications.
Ghate, O., & Locke, E. A. (2003). Objectivism: The proper alternative to postmodernism. In E. A. Locke (Ed.), *Postmodernism and management: Pros, cons and the alternative* (pp. 249–278). New York, NY: JAI.
Hacking, I. (1999). *The social construction of what?* Cambridge, MA: Harvard University Press.
Hall, D. L., & Ames, R. T. (1995). *Anticipating China: Thinking through the narratives of Chinese and Western culture*. Albany, NY: State University of New York Press.
Hamilton, E., & Cairns, H. (Eds.). (1961). *The collected dialogues of Plato*. New York, NY: Bollingen Foundation.
Harding S. (1991). *Whose science? Whose knowledge?* Ithaca, NY: Cornell University Press.
Hassard, J. (1988). Overcoming Hermeticism in organization theory. *Human Relations, 41*, 247–259.
Hempel, C. G. (1970). On the standard conception of scientific theories. In M. Radner & S. Winokur (Eds.), *Minnesota studies in the philosophy of science, Vol. 4*. Minneapolis, MN: University of Minnesota Press.
Hirschman, A. O. (1977). *The passions and the interests: Political arguments for capitalism before its triumph*. Princeton, NJ: Princeton University Press.
Hunt, S. D. (1994). On the rhetoric of qualitative methods: Toward historically informed argumentation in management inquiry. *Journal of Management Inquiry, 3*, 221–234.
Hunt, S. D. (2005). For truth and realism in management research. *Journal of Management Inquiry, 14*, 120–138.
Jackson, N., & Carter, P. (1991). In defence of paradigm incommensurability. *Organization Studies, 12*(1), 109–127.
Kuhn, T. S. (1970). *The structure of scientific revolutions*. Chicago, IL: University of Chicago Press. (Original work published 1962)
Kuhn, T. S. (1983). Commensurability, comparability, communicability. In P. D. Asquith & T. Nickles (Eds.), *Proceedings of the 1982 Biennial Meeting the Philosophy of Science Association* (pp. 669–688). East Lansing, MI: Philosophy of Science Association.
Lewis, M., & Grimes, A. (1999). Metatriangulation: Building theory from multiple paradigms. *Academy of Management Review, 24*(4), 672–690.
Longino, H. E. (1990). *Science as social knowledge value and objectivity in scientific inquiry*. Princeton, NJ: Princeton University Press.
McKelvey, B. (2002). Model-centered organization science epistemology. In J. A. C. Baum (Ed.), *Companion to organizations* (pp. 752–780). Oxford, UK: Blackwell Business.
Moldoveanu, M. C., & Baum, J. A. C. (2002). Contemporary debates in organizational epistemology. In J. A. C. Baum (Ed.), *Companion to organizations* (pp. 733–751). Oxford, UK: Blackwell Business.

Morgan, G. (1983). *Beyond method.* Newbury Park, CA: Sage Publications.

Nightingale, P. J., & Cromby, J. (1999). *Social constructionist psychology: A critical analysis of theory and practice.* Philadelphia, PA: Open University Press.

Pinder, C. C., & Bourgeois, V. W. (1982). Controlling tropes in administrative science. *Administrative Science Quarterly, 27,* 641–652.

Popper, K. (N.D.). *The problem of induction (1953, 1974).* Retrieved from http://dieoff.org/page126.htm

Putnam, H. (1981). *Reason, truth and history.* New York, NY: Cambridge University Press.

Rogers, C. A., & Farson, R. F. (1987). Active listening. In R. G. Newman, M. A. Danzinger, & M. Cohen (Eds.), *Communicating in business today* (pp. 589–598). Lexington, MA: D.C. Health & Co.

Sanders, W. G. (2009). What it means to be a developmental action editor. *Academy of Management Journal, 52,* 640–642.

Sankey, H. (1993). Kuhn's changing concept of incommensurability. *British Journal for the Philosophy of Science, 44,* 759–774.

Scherer, A. G., & Dowling, M. J. (1995). Towards a reconciliation of the theory-pluralism in strategic management—Incommensurability and the constructivist approach on the Erlangen school. In P. Shrivastava & C. Stubbart (Eds.), *Advances in strategic management* (Vol. 12(A), pp. 195–247). Greenwich, CT: JAI Press.

Sutton, R. I., & Staw, B. M. (1995). What theory is not. *Administrative Science Quarterly, 40,* 371–384.

Weaver, G. R., & Gioia, D. A. (1994). Paradigms lost: Incommensurability vs. structurationist inquiry. *Organization Studies, 15*(4), 565–589.

Weick, K. E. (1995). What theory is *not,* theorizing *is. Administrative Science Quarterly, 40,* 385–390.

Weiss, R. M. (2000). Taking science out of organization: How would postmodernism reconstruct the analysis of organizations? *Organization Science, 11,* 709–731.

SECTION

5

Conclusion

CHAPTER

12

Generative Uncertainty for the Practice of Organization Studies

One of our favorite ideas from one of our favorite scholars, Karl Weick, is: How can I know what I think until I see what I say? A concluding chapter gives us a chance to tell what we think after we said what we said.

We continue to think that in organization studies there are dysfunctional disagreements about what constitutes knowledge. We also think that students of organizations have not dealt with these disagreements as well as they might. We suggest, in the spirit of the Fox-Keller quotation with which we began, that organization studies needs a way of thinking and talking that accounts for the effectiveness of science while allowing for recent developments in the philosophy of science.

Our study of the controversies, informed by generative uncertainty, leads us to believe that dysfunctional disagreements in organization studies stemmed from several interrelated sources: (1) insufficient attention to context; (2) insufficient recognition of the social nature of the inquiry process; (3) treatment of Aristotelian certainty as both necessary and attainable; (4) failure to incorporate philosophical insights; (5) agonism; and (6) poor communication.

INSUFFICIENT ATTENTION TO CONTEXT

We pointed out those participants in the knowledge controversy that failed to note the intellectual contexts of the positions they were either rejecting or advancing. Consequently, the special circumstances that produced the positions were not recognized, and historical relations between the alternative perspectives were not understood. A prime example, we found, was the tendency for scholars to disregard the context of skepticism in which modern science developed. One result was that in the contemporary controversy, participants often understated the degree of uncertainty in the foundation of modern science. Had the related skeptical roots of modern science and the recent postmodern critique of it been more fully appreciated, the nature and intensity of the knowledge controversy might have been quite different.

In addition, disregard of context helped to make room for other difficulties. Of special note is the seeming lack of attention to the process that made appearing scientific so central to the identity of many North American social scientists. Had the institutional processes we reported in Chapter 4 been more fully recognized, the reverence many accorded to scientism might have been tempered.

In addition, greater attention to intellectual contexts might have helped to make the prevalence and dysfunction of agonistic discourse more apparent. Such notice may be aided by study of the origins of that discourse. Recall how awareness of the nature of potential problems with agonism was enhanced by the work of scholars such as Tannen, Gouldner, and Ong, who examined its origins in the Greek contest system.

INSUFFICIENT RECOGNITION OF THE SOCIAL NATURE OF THE INQUIRY PROCESS

We believe the social processes that shape inquiry have been underattended. One consequence was a seemingly underjustified attribution of so-called objectivity to the methods of the natural sciences. Recently, however, scholars in philosophy and in organization studies gave increased attention to the social nature of inquiry. Generative uncertainty promotes this perspective while applauding the valuable patterns human inquiry produced.

Among other things, as advocates of generative uncertainty, we wish to extend Pfeffer's (1993) call to analyze the social process that determines the substance of what is called knowledge in organization studies. We also encourage investigation into the social dynamics that produce conflict within disciplines. In other words we urge study of the social processes affect outcomes from inquiry.

In sum, generative uncertainty draws attention to the social processes of pattern creation and pattern preferences. It helps us recognize that human preferences and values influence what is often called knowledge. We saw the role preferences can play in Giere's (1988) study of the continental drift hypothesis. We think that preferences have such a significant influence that we prefer the term *preferred patterns* to the term *knowledge*.

TREATING CERTAINTY AS NECESSARY AND ATTAINABLE

People in the Western world have been preoccupied for centuries with a requirement that knowledge be certain. Some postulated that certainty was required for moral behavior. (For example, we noted Parker's (1995) concern that postmodernism's rejection of truth and progress threatened the emancipatory project.) Some chose a particular method of inquiry or a particular religion because they saw it as offering certainty. Moreover, some maintained that without certainty, productive inquiry is not possible.

Generative uncertainty calls upon us to take assumptions about certainty as problematic. Doing so heightens our awareness that Western scholars struggled for millennia about the possibilities for certainty. We also see that the issue has yet to be resolved; a fully satisfactory basis for claiming certainty has yet to be found. However, at various points in the quest, some approaches that appeared to offer certainty, such as modern science and Roman Catholicism, became institutionalized. More importantly, we saw that even without a solid foundation for certainty humans accomplished a great deal.

Thus, a major message of generative uncertainty is as follows: Aristotelian certainty might be beyond the reach of humans. At the same time, people can accomplish many things without it.

INADEQUATE PHILOSOPHICAL BASIS

Early in the book we recognized Fox-Keller's call to develop a perspective that dealt with both recent developments in philosophy and the effectiveness of science. To date, students of organization studies have not developed such a perspective. We believe generative uncertainty can help organization studies do so.

The knowledge controversy has featured two major themes. On the one hand, some scholars proceeded without recognition that, to date, philosophers have failed in their attempts to make philosophy foundational. On the other hand, some other scholars (including some self-proclaimed postmodernists) have not attended appropriately to the achievements of modern science.

We believe that generative uncertainty, by emphasizing the absence of a philosophical foundation while simultaneously recognizing the achievements of scientific inquiry, can serve as the needed perspective.

AGONISM

We considered the agonistic nature of contemporary academic discourse in Chapter 10. There, we examined the historical context that contributed to institutionalizing agonism. We traced its origin to the Greek contest system. Then, we saw that more recently scholars pointed to agonism's functions in scholarly communication. We provided some specific examples of how agonism appeared to have added fuel to the knowledge controversy. In this context, we urge consideration of agonism's functions and dysfunctions and letting go of the institutionalized position of debate/argument in modern scholarship.

Because we see inquiry as a social process that depends on the critical thinking of colleagues, we must be careful here. Often, feedback from those with radically different perspectives helps one to become aware of latent assumptions he or she is making. We believe that such feedback is vital for improving inquiry. At the same time, we believe it is more helpful when it is given in the peacekeeping spirit advanced by Sterba (1998) than in an agonistic spirit.

POOR COMMUNICATION

Given the social nature of the inquiry, good communication is vital. However, the agnostic mode inherited from ancient Greece sometimes interfered with good communication among participants in the knowledge controversy. Often, they did not seem to understand the positions of those they were challenging.

CONCLUSION

In this chapter we highlighted six deficiencies of contemporary organization studies derived from viewing the knowledge controversy in the light of generative uncertainty. We believe that if students of organizations rectified these deficiencies, they could address the controversy more productively.

Specifically, we urge them to

1. Pay careful attention to context
2. Recognize the social nature of the inquiry process
3. Recognize that the achievement of certainty may be neither achievable nor necessary
4. Study and incorporate philosophical insights
5. Follow principles of good communication

We suggest that generative uncertainty, as we defined it, can help one take these steps.

REFERENCES

Giere, R. N. (1988). *Explaining science*. Chicago, IL: University of Chicago Press.

Parker, M. (1995). Critique in name of what? Postmodernism and critical approaches to organization. *Organization Studies, 16*, 553–564.
Pfeffer, J. (1993). Barriers to the advance of organizational science: Paradigm development as a dependent variable. *Academy of Management Review, 18*, 599–620.
Sterba, J. P. (1998). *Justice for here and now*. New York, NY: Cambridge University Press.

AUTHOR INDEX

A

B

C

D

E

F

G

H

SUBJECT INDEX

Note *t* indicates tables, *f* indicates figures, and *n* indicates notes.

A

B

C

D

F

G

H

N

Q

T